TOURNAMENT
POKER

TOURNAMENT
POKER

TOM McEVOY

CARDOZA PUBLISHING

Cardoza Publishing is the foremost gaming publisher in the world, with a library of over 100 up-to-date and easy-to-read books and strategies. These authoritative works are written by the top experts in their fields and, with more than 7,000,000 books in print, represent the best-selling and most popular gaming books anywhere.

THIRD EDITION

Copyright © 1995, 2001, 2004 by Tom McEvoy
- All Rights Reserved -

Library of Congress Catalog Card No: 2003114964
ISBN:1-58042-123-7

Visit our new web site (www.cardozapub.com)
or write us for a full list of Cardoza books,
advanced and computer strategies.

CARDOZA PUBLISHING
P.O. Box 1500, Cooper Station, New York, NY 10276
Phone (800)577-WINS
email: cardozapub@aol.com
www.cardozapub.com

CONTENTS

Table of Contents

Dedication

Without the support and encouragement of my family, I could never have risen to the heights of the tournament world. My father, Harry, and my mother, Marie, always encouraged me to do my best. My brothers, Steve and Alan, and my sister, Marcia, have always been true friends as well as siblings. I have also been blessed with three patient and loving children, Melanie, Mike and Patrick. It is with love in my heart and appreciation in my soul that I dedicate this book to the members of my family.

ACKNOWLEDGMENTS

Several special people have inspired, encouraged and assisted me in writing *Tournament Poker.*

Dana Smith, my editor and friend, has worked closely with me throughout the conceptualizing and writing of this book. When we decided to work together on this project, I told her that I wanted to write the "bible" on how to win poker tournaments. *Tournament Poker* is the result of our efforts.

Ron and Teresa McMillan have always been kind and supportive friends. Ron has been generous in giving me his wise counsel over the years, for which I am especially appreciative.

Linda Johnson, former *Card Player* magazine co-owner and coauthor of *Championship Stud*, provided expert advice and editing expertise on several chapters in this book. Linda is a world-class poker player and I am indebted to her for her invaluable assistance. *Card Player* contributor Chuck Thompson allowed me to include his perceptive article on hitting the wall in poker tournaments, for which I am truly appreciative.

Phil Hellmuth stuck by me through the thick and thin (or "the thin and thinner," as he likes to say) of my tournament career. The financial backing and words of encouragement that Phil and his lovely wife, Kathy, faithfully gave me kept me going on the tournament trail when times were tough. And my friends Milt and Phyllis Meyers have always been there with moral support and friendship when I needed them.

Howard Schwartz, marketing director of the Gamblers Book Shop in Las Vegas—and noted gaming authority—encouraged me to write this book for several years running. Happily, I finally followed his advice!

In 1997 I was fortunate enough to recruit my longtime friend and poker guru T.J. Cloutier, probably the world's greatest tournament player, as my writing partner for the *Championship Series* of poker books. T.J.'s insightful analysis of my play (and that of others as well), plus his never-say-die positive attitude have helped me tremendously over the years.

My acknowledgments would not be complete without mentioning Jack Binion, who built the World Series of Poker into the tournament world's premier event. Today he has followed his success in Las Vegas by sponsoring the *Jack Binion World Poker Open* in Mississippi. At his side during the WSOP, you would always find Tournament Coordinator par excellence Jack McClelland, whose excellent management skills and inimitable wit in solving player problems kept the World Series in stride.

And to the legends of the business—Doyle Brunson, Amarillo Slim Preston, Johnny Moss and other famous champions—I doff my Stetson for helping to put tournament poker on the map. Such modern greats as Mike Caro, T.J. Cloutier, Phil Hellmuth, Bob Ciaffone, Vince Burgio, and Mike Sexton are men from whom I have learned valuable tournament lessons and whose contributions to the literature of poker must be deeply appreciated by the thousands of poker players who have benefited from the expert advice in their books and columns.

Finally I thank the many forward thinking casinos across the globe for fostering the growth of tournament poker by sponsoring so many fine tournaments. And I thank each of you, my valued readers, for investing in *Tournament Poker.* I hope that it will become the best poker buy-in you've ever made! ♠

FOREWORD
by Phil Hellmuth,
1989 World Champion of Poker

Tom McEvoy approached me in 1988 while we were on a poker cruise somewhere off the island of Granada and asked me to stake him. I quickly turned him down and laughed about it with some of the other players. The reason I refused his request had nothing to do with trust or honor, nor did it have to do with the way he played. I turned him down because I learned that anyone who would lay the best poker players in the world big, juicy, 80 percent of the field bets on "win and final table" finishes has a peg missing.

Six years later, I now *know* he is missing a peg! Why else would someone who is going to win millions of dollars in tournaments in the future write a book that will help the field catch up with him? Money? No. The most Tom will see from his book is about $25,000, which amounts to fourth place in a decent-sized tournament.

I personally begged Tom not to write this book. In fact, I offered to loan him the $25,000 until he was solid financially if he would *not* write *Tournament Poker*. I mean, here's a guy who won two Best All-Around Player awards in 1994, a man in whom I have invested time and my own poker theory . . . and he wants to give it all away for ego reasons. (I hope these comments sting Tom a little bit, because nobody has edited this foreword!)

I began to notice Tom and his results after his offer to me on the cruise. In January of 1990, he had a great tournament in Lake Tahoe with 4 or 5 top-3 finishes at the *Superstars of Poker*, and I started thinking that maybe someday I would get involved with him. I found out that he has a golden reputation in poker, so I knew that I could trust him. In poker, a good reputation, honor and trust mean everything, although they don't necessarily guarantee success. Here was someone I could trust and who had good results, including "The Big One."

Obviously, the formulation of correct poker tournament strategy has been a key factor in his comeback. The ability to forge great poker theory under pressure is the difference between great players and very good ones. Tom has done this and, unfortunately, has given it to you in *Tournament Poker*.

Having an ego in this business is a necessity. If you don't think you can be the best, why play? One of the reasons why Tom's ego is so big is because of his trophy house. Do you think I meant to say trophy *room*? I didn't! The man has over 100 trophies that spill out all over his home. When one gets damaged, does he repair it? No, he just takes it into the desert and shoots it into small pieces!

I really don't know if Tom likes this foreword very much, but then, I don't like this book very much either! Why write a boring book about theory? In stead, why not write one about real-life occurrences in poker? Why not write a book about people such as Archie, the famous gambler who went from nowhere to $16 million in one year? Or about

Chip Reese or Doyle Brunson or Johnny Chan? I say, "Write a book that has a chance to become a national bestseller and make millions of dollars for you!" But how do you make a guy with one peg missing listen to you?

Chapter 1
INTRODUCTION

Tournament poker is not only fun, but having won millions of dollars in tournaments, I can honestly tell you that it can be profitable as well. In one tournament alone, in 1983 at the World Series of Poker, I outlasted 107 other players, including the legendary Doyle Brunson, to pocket $540,000 in cash and become the World Champion of Poker.

I am going to let you in on the secrets I have used to win tournaments, plus the insights I have learned competing against the best players in the world. Many of the strategies you'll learn here are applicable to all types of poker competitions—and there are hundreds of moneymaking opportunities every year. Whether you are an experienced tournament competitor or a newcomer to this exciting part of the poker world, you'll gain valuable advice on how to win more money, more often, in your regular cash games as well as in tournaments.

This book is packed solid with winning strategies for the 11 major games in the World Series of Poker, with extensive discussions of no-limit and pot-limit hold'em, 7-card stud high and high-low, razz, lowball, plus Omaha high-low, high only and pot-limit. I also include rebuy, half-half, mixed-games tournaments, satellites, super satellites, freeze-outs, low-stakes rebuy events, and strategies for each stage of the tournament. To complete the package and give you the full winning arsenal, you'll also learn about big player profiles, and get expert answers to frequently asked questions about handling difficult tournament situations.

With televised poker tournaments bringing thousands of new players into the exciting world of poker every year, there's never been a better time to try your hand at winning a trophy—and some serious cash—even if you've never played a tournament before.

Online recreational poker player Chris Moneymaker, the 2003 World Champion of Poker, won $2.5 million in the first tournament he ever played in a land-based casino.

It might be your turn next.

The world of tournament poker has changed significantly since I wrote the first edition of this book in 1995. Today more and more tournaments are being held throughout the United States and Europe with new major events cropping up each year while daily rebuy tournaments continue to be held around the clock in cardrooms and casinos everywhere. Poker players seem to love tournaments!

The format of tournaments also has changed since 1995. With the advent of the TEARS tournament software program designed by Tex Morgan, tournaments have additional rounds because of a far more gradual rise in betting increments, with shorter beginning and middle rounds and longer rounds at the final table. The net result is slightly longer tournaments that favor skilled players because of the added levels of play. Also, most major tournaments now complete final-table action on the second day of the event with time added to the clock. This edition takes these changes into account and gives advice on how to adjust to them.

In addition to the change in time limits and the greater number of tournaments, other aspects of tournament poker also have changed. Most notably, the expertise of the typical tournament entrant is much higher today than ever before. In fact, the quality of play in tournaments has risen dramatically over the past five years. With so many more capable players on the tournament trail, tournaments are tougher than ever to win. I have been told, and would like to believe, that *Tournament Poker* is one of the reasons. Of course, with so many more entrants than there used to be, the rewards also are proportionately greater.

Neither extremely tight play nor very loose play will get the money in tournaments. Loose-as-a-goose play is fatal most of the time. The one advantage that it has over tight play in the early rounds is that if you survive, you will probably have enough chips to go all the way. But loose play in the early stages often means an early exit. The style of play that I recommend is *solid aggressive.*

Of course there is a very fine line between loose play and solid aggressive play. Some of the best tournament players have a very aggressive style. They get the chips early and hang onto them or they are out. *Solid aggressive* is a term that you will frequently see in *Tournament Poker.* It is the way that I describe my own style. I throw away a lot of hands but when I'm in a pot, I try to take the lead. Good judgement and knowledge of your opponents' play are also essential for success, and are concepts that I advocate throughout this book.

It is also good to remember that there is more than one winning style of tournament play. Keep in mind that a loose style of play that is successful for you in the early stages of a tournament often has to be tempered in later rounds to hang on to your chip position. Time and time again, I have heard players complain about blowing a superior chip position and finishing out of the money. One of the prime reasons for this is that they *didn't slow down enough*, another point you will frequently read in the strategy sections of this book. Loose aggressive play got them the chips, but they played the same style of poker in the later stages. The result—their alert opponents picked them off.

Instead of discussing slow, medium and fast action tournament play (which is no longer a valuable concept since virtually all major tournaments today are medium-action events), I decided to delineate strategies for winning each of the events in the World Series of Poker. Eleven chapters of *Tournament Poker* discuss how to play specific types of poker tournaments, including the "big four:" limit hold'em, no-limit hold'em, seven-card stud, and Omaha high-low.

No-limit hold'em events have grown significantly in popularity since the first edition of *Tournament Poker* was published. In fact, many players have told me that they credit *Championship No-Limit & Pot-Limit Hold'em* (which T.J. Cloutier and I wrote in 1997) for erasing their fear of no-limit events and encouraging them to give the game a shot in tournament play. If it were not for no-limit hold'em tournaments, I believe that the game itself would be extinct as you seldom find no-limit hold'em cash games being spread anywhere anymore.

In addition to the 11 detailed chapters on freezeout tournament strategy for various poker games, I have included a section on how to win satellites. I asked Shane Smith to add a chapter on low-limit rebuy tournament strategies, which is excerpted from her fine book, *Poker Tournament Tips From The Pros*. (I thank Shane (Dana) Smith for providing the necessary assistance to make *Tournament Poker* a reality. Her efforts are responsible, for good or ill, for the existence of this book.)

In Chapter 16 you will find winning techniques for the increasingly popular combination-game tournaments, the most common being half hold'em and half seven-card stud. And in this revised edition, I have added some advice on how to play the *Tournament of Champions* as well as H.O.R.S.E. games. Also included are some pointers on incremental rebuy events and bounty tournaments.

Chapter 18 on modern trends in tournaments is completely new. It covers most of the latest developments, including some strategies for tournaments that use the TEARS program, the effects of payout schedules that are far flatter than in the past, how to cope with the increasing huge fields in tournaments these days, and some suggestions about how to handle other changes. These chapters make *Tournament Poker* unique in its complete coverage of the myriad aspects of tournament poker.

Following the requests of my many students, I have compiled a list of their most frequent questions about tournament play and have answered them in Chapter 20. I also am often queried about the business aspects of playing on the professional tournament circuit, which I discuss in Chapter 19, which I have updated for this edition. In addition, I have devoted two chapters to beginning and advanced tournament concepts, which you may find useful as either an overview of tournament strategy or as a valuable review before each tournament you enter.

Throughout this book, I have tried to give you the most current and the best advice possible on how to win poker tournaments. There is no high comparable to the thrill of walking away from the tournament table with the winner's trophy in your hands and the lion's share of the money in your pocket.

I know—I've been there many times—and I'd be happy to have you join me at the final table. I truly believe that the strategies outlined in *Tournament Poker* will help you get there faster that you ever dreamed possible. *See you in the winner's circle!* ♠

Chapter 2
TOURNAMENT POKER 101: GENERAL STRATEGIES

A typical $500 buy-in tournament begins with betting limits of $15-$30. The high card in razz, or the low card in stud, brings it in with a forced bet of $5 and the next hand to act must complete the bet to either $15, or call $5, or pass. In Texas hold'em and the Omaha games, the first bet must be at least the size of the big blind.

The limits escalate on a regular basis. In the bigger tourneys ($500-$1,000 buy-in), they increase hourly, and in smaller buy-in tournaments the betting rounds are usually 30-45 minutes long. The play is often affected by the limits, so being aware of these time frames and when they are about to change is important to your tournament strategy.

In freezeout tournaments, if you start out playing $15-$30 with $500 in chips and the limits go up every 45 to 60 minutes, about 20 to 30 percent of the players will usually be eliminated after two rounds of play (after the $30-60 round). After the second round, casualties mount at a much higher rate so that by the end of the third round, about 50 percent of the field is usually out of action.

In limit tournaments, not as many players are eliminated during the first round, but they start dropping out at a rapid pace in the second and third rounds. After about five rounds of play, it is typical for about 80 percent of the field to have been eliminated.

The slower the limits go up, the more important tournament skills become. The faster the limits go up, the more the luck factor dominates. If poker were purely a game of skill, the best players would win all the time, but we all know that doesn't happen. The luck factor is higher in tournaments than in side games because of the escalating limits and the infrequency of getting premium starting hands during the compressed time periods. Players with lesser skills will sometimes win a tournament or have a high money finish. This happens often enough to keep these less-skilled players entering tournaments. However, it doesn't happen so often that it should discourage better players, because skill will dominate over luck in the long run. In fact, the more skill you have, the more chance you will have to get lucky.

I don't want to disillusion anyone, but in tournaments with world class fields of contestants whose skills are fairly equal, the player who catches the best cards that particular day and plays them well, is the contender most likely to win the tournament. Because so many world class players enter the major tourneys, no one has a huge edge over anyone else. In World Series of Poker events, I have sometimes seen a player who may not be of the very highest calibre make it to the final table, but I have never seen a player win it whom you could even remotely label as "weak," no matter how lucky he was. Although luck is a factor, it is tournament *skill* that maximizes your opportunity to win.

General Strategies

There is no magic formula for longevity in a tournament. I can't begin to list the number of players I have talked with about tournament play and what happens when you get to that $150-$300 round, or the $200-$400 round (the fifth or sixth round of the event). We all agree that you just have to catch hands at these betting levels. You can't manufacture a hand that doesn't exist. What you must do instead is play a patient, controlled game to *give yourself a chance to get lucky.* If you play too recklessly on marginal hands and get knocked out early, you cannot make it to the higher levels where, if your hands hold up, you have a good chance of winning.

Payouts are top-heavy for the final three finishers. First place is usually twice the amount of second, and second is often twice the sum of third. With such huge disparities between the top three payouts, you have a lot to shoot for by trying to finish on top. When you hit the bull's-eye and win the tournament, you never need to explain what happened or why or "what if." First place answers all questions.

In tournaments, a lot of the skill is in *surviving* long enough to get lucky. This is where judicious play and good judgment come in. The more correct decisions you make in the earlier rounds, the greater your chances of surviving to the later rounds and getting a good rush of cards. What separates the very best players from the others is knowing how to make the most of the rush when it comes. Tournament experience is also important. One way to get that is by reading and studying; another is by entering a lot of tournaments.

Some players try to win a tournament too early by attempting to accumulate big stacks of chips in the first round or two. Usually, that is simply not going to happen. If you can double up in the first round, you've done a marvelous job, and adding even 50 percent to your stack is a pretty good achievement. But it is unrealistic to believe that you can accumulate three to four times your original stack after only one round of play, unless you catch a tremendous rush of cards. If you do, great . . . but don't count on it.

This means that you have to play a patient, controlled game, steadily increasing your stack with good, solid play . . . and you must maintain strict control of your emotions. If you just don't have a hand, there is nothing you can do about it. So you must patiently wait for your best opportunity.

This doesn't mean you should play like a wimp. Wimps don't push their strong hands boldly enough; they check call a lot; and they play a generally passive game. Their ultra conservative style may help them to last a little longer, but it doesn't win tournaments.

In contrast to the wimp is the tournament wasp, who uses a big stack as the weapon it was designed to be. One famous tournament player claims to be able to win hands on the strength of his chips alone—and he does just that. He forces opponents to play cautiously against him, and yet he also seems to know when to back off.

Actually, excellent tournament players use both styles of play to some degree. They know when to change gears from wasp to wimp and vice-versa. They have the ability to read their opponents and to employ exactly the correct style that will win the most chips with their premium hands, as well as with their marginal ones. These top players are able to get good reads on their opponents because they remain observant even when they are not in a pot.

Lesser players sometimes take the attitude that they want to win as many chips as they can as quickly as possible so they can take a quick shot at the brass ring. If their fast tactics don't work, they figure they can jump ship and slide over to side action games, so they're not totally disappointed if they bomb out of the tournament early.

This is not my attitude. If I'm going to take the time to play in a tourney, there is no other place I would rather be than in that tournament and I want to stay in it as long as possible. I am not unwilling to gamble to build up my chip stack, but I would rather not push some of my marginal hands the way my faster playing colleagues are willing to do because I want to maximize my chances of getting lucky and coming into the money.

If you are not prepared to sit for hours playing a patient, controlled game, you probably should not sign up for a tournament in the first place. Reckless gambling may occasionally get you off to an early lead, but if you don't apply the brakes when you should, you can dig a big losing trench for yourself. Winning requires mental toughness.

I have never led wire-to-wire in a tournament, although I suppose it has happened to someone else. It would be wonderful to have the lead all the way, but the more solid and conservative approach which I advocate will get you to the final table more often than if you use a more liberal style of play. With this attitude, you won't be gambling as often as some of your more reckless opponents. You may not jump off to an early lead or even play very many hands because you won't be staying in pots when you are taking the worst of it. Instead, you will be making the most of the few premium hands you are dealt with selectively aggressive raises and reraises to narrow the field and optimize your winning potential.

Getting married to a hand is one of the biggest mistakes tournament players make. Making proper laydowns is essential to your success because you cannot replenish those precious chips with a rebuy once you lose them. If your hand is beat, it's beat— there's nothing you can do about it except to fold as early as possible. Sometimes, saving only one or two bets with a prudent laydown gives you just enough chips to see one more flop, play one more hand . . . or even turn the whole thing around.

One of the primary reasons people lose tournaments after building up a substantial chip lead is because they don't seem to know when to slow down their action. It seems as though they are trying to win the tournament prematurely when there are five or six tables left. But it doesn't work that way: you can only win the tournament at the final table. It takes good tactics to get there . . . not knowing when to put on the brakes is *not* one of them. Of course, I realize that one of the major reasons why some players are unable to shift out of high gear is because gambling in the early stages may have been the very thing which built up their monster stacks. But luck will take you only so far: you must combine it with skill.

Occasionally, a player will go on a super rush, catching lucky hands one after the other. But what happens more often than not is that the tournament winner has not only gotten what is probably more than his share of good cards, but he has also played them well. He hasn't played recklessly, gambling too frequently with small pairs and suited connectors, relying on luck to take him to the final table. Sooner or later, that type of loose play will catch up with anyone. Winners combine extremely good judgment with some lucky breaks.

There is a real dividing line between tournaments. Unfortunately, there aren't very many people plunking down big buy-ins, such as the minimum buy-in of $1,500 at the World Series of Poker, who are going to be playing weak strategy. Therefore, as a general rule, you won't find nearly as much dead money in the big buy-in tourneys as you sometimes find in lesser events. There will be an occasional tourist or hobby player who just wants to gamble and play with the big boys. But generally, even those players who are not what you would classify as professional poker players have developed much greater skills over the last five years or so, and can play a reasonably competitive game. So you're not going to find yourself in big buy-in tournaments very often against players who are just routinely throwing off their chips on weak to mediocre hands. Mostly, your competition is going to be very solid players.

That is not necessarily the case in some of the other heavily-publicized tournaments in Las Vegas or California that feature smaller buy-ins. Weaker opposition players who are not quite as strong and who don't feel they can (or wish to) compete with the big boys in the major tournaments are often willing to pony up $100 or $200 in the less prestigious and smaller tournaments, such as those at the Gold

Coast in Las Vegas, for example, and take their chances. Although they may possess only average tournament skills, they know that the field will be large, and they will therefore get a great return on their investment if they're lucky enough to win.

You will be facing many of the same players over and over again in tournaments. The tournament trail professionals play against each other all over the country—and it's not unusual for them to try to cut each other's heart out at the poker table and then go play a round of golf or two together. You cannot take things personally when you're playing poker in general, and tournaments in particular. Playing for thousands of dollars is serious business. Though it's exhilarating—even intoxicating—to make the final table, in order to get there you cannot play favorites if you expect to maximize your chances to win.

Many times, deals are cut by the survivors at the final table. The typical tournament pays 40 percent to the winner, 20 percent to the runner-up, 10 percent to third, and maybe 8 percent to fourth. Sometimes, even the second table is paid. Final table action can go fast or slow depending on how many chips are in play and the styles of your opponents, and heads up play can be both grueling and volatile.

Deals are generally struck toward the end, and sometimes drastically alter the play at the final table. The biggest deal I have ever seen made among the most players occurred at a World Series of Poker razz tournament a few years ago. They actually cut a deal with six remaining players, which is highly unusual. More typically, deals are cut among the last two or three (and occasionally, four) players. They are usually made when there are huge differences between the prize money, when the limits are very high, and when the chips are all reasonably close. The players try to avoid a crap shoot by making money *saves* (deals) among themselves . . . and there's nothing unethical about this. It is done routinely.

Quite frequently, they will make a money save, but will still play for some of the prize money, while at other times they will cut up the money entirely. As long as people aren't booking a tournament (betting on certain players to win or lose), cutting a deal is ethical, although this could change if we ever get corporate sponsorship for tournaments. I believe this is going to happen sometime over the next decade. Then, it may have to be understood by the participants that absolutely no deals will be cut which would possibly undermine the integrity of the tournament. That would be fine, but as long as the players are putting up 100 percent of the prize money themselves, as is usually the case, deals are quite reasonable . . . and a lot of times they make good economic sense to the surviving players.

If you survive to the later stages, always be aware of what the chip count is and what the limits are so that you know about where you stand. Any time you can play three or four hands through to the river, at whatever limits you are playing, you're in excellent position. The average stacks can usually play only one-and-a-half hands, one which can go to the river and a second hand which can progress only halfway through the betting. A short stack has only enough to play one hand all the way through, if that. These stacks, of course, are in far more jeopardy than a tall stack. You can always tell what your position is relative to the limits by using this method.

Sometimes, even the big stacks don't have enough chips to play out three or four hands when the limits have become very high. Then, in essence, everyone is short-stacked for that limit. But the more chips you have, naturally, the better off you are to survive it. Any time you're in a tournament situation in which the bigger stacks cannot play more than a couple of hands to the river without going broke, you're in a very fast situation: in what I refer to as "Crap Shoot City," because the luck element is very high at that point. All you can do is go with the best available hand, be aggressive with it, and then hope for the best. Don't second-guess yourself.

You can't maintain the status quo and hope to survive because of the escalating bets. With $1,000 in chips at the $50-$100 round in a tournament, you may be in one of the stronger chip positions, whereas in a ring game, you would not have a lot of money

Don't allow all the distractions that come with final table action to divert your attention away from playing your best poker. Sometimes, a crowd of railbirds has gathered to view the excitement— some are your friends cheering you on, others may be looking for a loan, a few are just curious because it's the best free show in town. Losing your focus becomes easy at this point.

Some tournament players are "home run hitters" They are trying to win as many chips as early as they can; if they fail and consequently lose their stacks, they aren't that concerned and find something else to do for the rest of the day. They're trying to get a decision that will force the action early on—they're going for the long bomb. So, they sometimes attempt to dominate and take control with aggressive raises. Many times it works but just as often, it doesn't. When it doesn't, they suffer either early elimination or crippled stacks. This is not all bad because when they go the distance, they usually get there with a lot of chips. These players have a tremendously successful record once they arrive at the final table, so there is certainly merit to their style of play. One tournament victory is worth more than a half-dozen final table finishes in sixth, seventh or eighth place. It is good to remember that you can win less money with five last-table finishes than a player who has only one finish, but who wins it all.

Although there is merit to the home run hitter's style of tournament play, my own approach is somewhat more conservative. I classify myself as a "solid aggressive" player. In other words I don't play a lot of hands, but when I do, I give action, or the "illusion of action," as I call it. The illusion comes from the impression that observers get when they see a player put in a lot of bets and raises, which leads them to believe he's an action player. Actually, he is just value-betting his hand.

Remember that there are many, many differences between tournament play and side-action play. In side games, you can always replenish the chips in front of you by pulling out more money between hands. You can also do this in a rebuy tournament during the early rebuy rounds. But in a freezeout, you must make do with what is in front of you. This means that since your chips cannot be replaced when you lose them, they are very precious to you.

The fewer chips you have left in tournament play, the more dear they are to you. The more chips you have, the less value they have. This may seem like a contradiction, but it is not. When you have a great many chips, you also have many options, of course. You can play hands you wouldn't normally play against shorter stacks in particular, because you can't get hurt too severely if you lose. You might come in with a rough 9 in razz, for example, and raise against a short stack. If both you and he catch good, of even if you catch bad, you can bet into your short-stacked opponent. But if you are the one with the short stack, you cannot afford to get involved against a big stack. The old adage, "A chip, a chair, and a prayer and you've got a chance" holds true.

Therefore, you are frequently rewarded in tournaments for good survival tactics. You have to last long enough in the tourney to get to the higher limits in order to give yourself a chance to get lucky. This is why the fewer chips you have, the more dear they are: so that you can last long enough to catch that elusive rush of cards which can make you the winner.

If you are fortunate enough to have accumulated a large stack in the late stages of the tournament, use your stack as a weapon, but be selectively aggressive with it. You can bet a marginal hand against a short stack who can't punish you too much. Remember that a short stack that is already crippled by his weakened chip position will often need to play a more marginal hand. But those players in average chip position, who have been playing a patient, controlled game, are more likely to hold a premium hand when they enter a pot.

General Strategies

You need to play the player *and* his stack. Even with a big stack, you must still use judgment and choose your spots. Be aware of which players have loosened up and those who have tightened up to survive to a money spot. Short stacks will sometimes raise with less than premium hands, so you can comfortably call them if you have a big stack.

Never leave a short stack with only one or two remaining chips when you can put him all-in. In the later stages, a chip or two can multiply rapidly because of the high limits, so do not good-naturedly allow a short stack to rebuild himself by not putting him all-in when you have the opportunity. Such a player can come back to haunt you. This is a fundamental mistake players make. Sometimes, you just have to be cruel, even to your poker buddies, your mother or your fiancee. Remember, it is far better for you to break them than for them to break you.

You are always playing your opponents just as much as you are playing the cards. If you're not familiar with their playing styles, you have to get a line on them as early as you can. Pay close attention to what kinds of cards they call with, which hands they raise with, and the calibre of cards they turn over at the showdown. You should always be looking for general tendencies—who you think is playing a little bit conservatively, who's playing loose, who's playing solid (not playing too many hands, but raising when they are in the pot, usually with hands worthy of a raise), as opposed to someone who is gambling with a lot of marginal hands. You might also watch the players who have gained a certain amount of reputation or fame. These players, in particular, are fun to play against and observe in the tournaments, so that you can get an idea of how these supposedly great competitors play.

Sometimes you may wonder how some of the tournament victors ever win, seeing some of the plays they make. But there is usually a method to their madness . . . there is a reason why they're putting in that extra bet or representing a hand they don't have. So be flexible and avoid making a lot of snap judgments at the table until you've been there awhile.

Expert tournament players are quite capable of going from tight play to loose play, or vice versa, depending on their chip position, especially just after the limits have escalated. Some players who were just trying to accrue chips early in the first round or two, begin playing a little bit snug when the limits escalate going into the third round. A player trying to hang onto his existing chip gain, for example, will not jeopardize himself unless he holds a very solid hand, or maybe some players begin to open up their game, playing a little bit looser, taking more chances to try to accumulate chips. Sometimes, a limit change alone will create a lot more action.

You need to continually be aware of the size of your stack in proportion to the size of your opponents' stacks, and what round of the tournament you are in. In the early to middle rounds, chips begin to get redistributed and you need to know who has the bigger stacks and who has the smaller stacks, and where your stack stands in relationship to theirs.

Losing a big hand at the final table can seriously damage your chances of a high money finish and can greatly enhance your opponent's position. This makes it all the more important to remember that the smaller the pot, the less reason there is to continue representing a hand you don't have. When you have only a single bet in the pot, don't give action on fourth street. Get out quickly and cheaply.

But no matter what happens to you, don't recklessly throw off your last few chips. Stay calm, cool and collected, and you will often be rewarded for your patience. Your last few chips are precious. Being mentally tough, especially when you have taken a big loss on a hand, is absolutely essential. I cannot count the number of times I have seen players mentally give up after they took a tough loss. And I *knew* it . . . I knew it was all over for them.

On the flip side, you can come back from a very bad chip position, even at the final table, by not giving up . . . by hanging tough. I've done it myself by being selectively aggressive and using all my tournament skills to get the best possible results. As Winston Churchill is famous for saying, "Never, ever, ever, ever give up!" If you can maintain your mental toughness in the face of what appears to be imminent doom, you will give yourself the best chance to get lucky and win. ♠

Chapter 3
LIMIT HOLD'EM

The standard number of chips you begin with in most limit hold'em tournaments is $500 with $15-$30 betting rounds, which is the game structure I will be discussing in this section. At the World Series of Poker, you will begin with $2,500 in chips in $2,500 buy-in tournaments, and $1,500 in chips in a $1,500 buy-in event. (The number of chips you receive is always the exact amount of the buy-in, excluding the entry fee).

Your strategy in the opening rounds of a $500 buy-in tournament will differ according to the structure of the small blind. In some tournaments, the blinds are $5-$15; in others, they are $10-$15. When the small blind is $10, you can be somewhat more liberal in defending it than you would if it were only $5. It costs you only one-third of a bet to call an unraised pot when the small blind is $10, but the price rises to two-thirds of a bet when the small blind is $5.

When the small blind is $10 and the pot is raised, hands that you would ordinarily pass with a $5 small blind become somewhat more attractive. These include hands that are considered to be marginal in an early position, such as J-10, A-J, K-Q, preferably suited; and suited connectors when there are more than four players in the pot.

Most entrants play more conservatively in the early rounds than they do in their regular ring games, although this is not a universal truth. Some players deliberately play faster than the rest of the table in an effort to capitalize on tight play. The problem with this strategy is that, although the betting limits are still reasonable compared to the number of starting chips in these early rounds, hand values must remain the guiding force of your playing decisions. If you begin raising too often with marginal hands such as K-J, Q-J, or A-10, your opponents will begin to play back at you. When you are playing fast, you have to either out-flop or bluff out your opponents.

In limit poker in general, and in limit hold'em in particular, I believe people try to bluff far too often. If you are trying a bluff, be sure you know who you can run over and who you cannot. Trying to run over the table may work for a while, but don't count on it lasting very long because intelligent players usually put a stop to it quite soon. However, there is more than one acceptable style of tournament play, so if your opponents continue to let you run over them, keep doing it until you lose a pot or two, and then put on the brakes.

Selective, rather than indiscriminate, aggression is probably a better approach for most players. This middle-of-the-road style involves waiting for premium hands and then betting them aggressively to maximize their winning potential.

Most players begin a hold'em tournament by playing their "A" games, but after about an hour, they often get caught up in the heat of battle and begin reverting to their normal styles. Being aware of this tendency can give you an edge if you continue playing your normal, solid game when they start playing their "B" games.

When the second round starts, the chips will begin to get redistributed: a few lucky players will double-up, others will slightly increase their stacks to around $600-$700, a few will become crippled, and some will get broke. At this point, your chip count will begin to affect your strategy.

World Series events are slightly different. The smallest buy-in for any event except the Ladies Seven-Card Stud event is $1,500 with beginning limits of $50-$100. This means that more players are going to get broke during the opening rounds than would normally occur in the $15-$30 or even the $30-$60 structures ($30-$60 is the format in $1,000 buy-in tourneys). If you are planning to play one of these events, keep this important point in mind.

World Series events are far more important in terms of prestige and money than any other tournaments, and they require a different approach. People who play them have a wide variety of playing styles. You never see some of them at any other time of the year, so you need to use keen observation skills to get an accurate read on them, especially during the opening stage. Getting off to a good start in a WSOP tournament can lay the groundwork for all future rounds.

Hand Selection
Playing Small Pairs and Small Suited Connectors

To make them worth the investment, small pairs and small suited connectors such as 7-6 or 8-7 should usually be played in multi-way pots only. Because you cannot always predict how many people will be entering a pot, it is usually inadvisable to play these hands from an early position. Also, you will often be forced to take the worst of it when you try to limp into a pot from an early position and someone raises behind you. (Of course, in a rebuy tournament, you might be more willing to gamble with these types of hands than you would in a freezeout tourney because you can replace your chips with a rebuy. Refer to Chapter 14 on rebuy tournaments.)

Playing a small pair heads-up can also be profitable, especially if you have the advantage of superior position. If it looks as though you will be able to play your small pair against only one player, you might consider reraising an aggressive opponent to limit the field and get heads-up. Of course, two overcards will sometimes fall on the flop and many times you won't flop anything that will help your pocket pair. So you may want to save this play for when you have a very large stack and can't get hurt too severely; for table image purposes; when you just want to show more speed than you usually show; or when you are short-stacked and decide to take a stand, figuring that this hand may be your best shot at winning some survival chips.

The Two-Limper Rule

Once two people have entered the pot, it is more likely to become multi-way action. When there are four people in the pot, including the blinds, you can consider entering with a hand you may have passed in a slightly early position. Small pairs, 7-6 suited, 8-9 suited, J-10 offsuit, K-Q, K-J, and even Q-J, become somewhat more attractive in middle to late position when two or more players have entered the pot in front of you, because you know you will be getting a fair price for them (adequate pot odds to justify a call). You can reasonably assume that if someone raises behind you, the players who have limped into the pot for the opening bet will call a single raise. (They may not call a raise *and* a reraise, however.)

Of course, you don't have *carte blanche* to come in with marginal hands in middle or late position just because someone else has entered the pot. You still should not consider playing such hands as 7-6 offsuit or 10-8 offsuit, although you can shave your standards somewhat in favor of suited hands.

Even suited cards, however, increase the value of a hand by only around 7 percent. Although that small percentage is sometimes enough to warrant a call, many times it is not. Just because you hold a Q♦4♦ with two limpers in front of you does not mean it is correct to call. You must always use good judgment in any of your poker decisions.

With three or four people already in an unraised pot, you can shave your opening requirements slightly if you are in a very late position. However, too many players carry it a "shave" too far: they abuse late position by coming in with extremely weak starting hands, or they come in one seat in front of the button. There is no reason to play a truly bad hand such as an 8-2 or K-5 offsuit, but you might play a few more suited hands when four or five players are already in the pot.

Although middle suited connectors give you both straight and flush potential, it is better to hit the straight than the flush with a hand such as 9♥8♥ or 8♦6♦ because of the danger of being beaten by a higher flush. When you are in late position and have seen the flop with such a hand, you should usually pass your flush draw if the pot has been jammed before it gets to you. But if it has not been raised and you think you still have a good chance, you can take off another card and see what develops with your flush draw.

Playing Middle Position Hands
When No One Has Entered the Pot

The later your position when no one has entered the pot, the more willing you can be to bring it in with a raise. But if even one person has limped into the pot in front of you, be careful about what you raise with because it is unlikely that you can get him to fold.

For example, I may raise from a late middle position with A♦10♦ when no one has yet entered the pot, but would not raise if one other person has called the blind bet. My goal is to pick up the blinds, knowing that if either one of them calls, I still figure to have as good a hand as they have, or maybe even a better one, plus superior position.

What I don't want is for a later-position player to cold-call my raise because he will have better position than I do throughout the hand. In that case, if I have raised with K-J or K-Q, my hand goes down in value and I must proceed cautiously from the flop onward. This is when an accurate evaluation of my opponents becomes vital: are they conservative and can be more easily bluffed? Or are they fairly liberal and are more likely to come over the top of me with a raise if they suspect I didn't hit the flop?

Late Position

In last position with only one or two opponents, your correct play is to try to pick up the pot immediately when the flop is ragged. If you are called, you might be holding overcards or perhaps even the best hand (especially if you have an ace working). However, if you continue to meet with resistance (you are called by both of your two opponents), you must proceed with caution because it is very difficult to bluff two or more players out of a pot. Here again, your judgment and timing are crucial. Would they just flat-call with a pair? Or are they the type of players who will make a play at you? If they are the type of players who won't raise unless they hold at least the top pair, you are better off to pass your hand if they raise you.

But against a super aggressive player who is capable of making a play at you, you must revert to your hand value as a guide to your betting decision. If you don't think he has any of the flop, let your hand determine your next move. Suppose you have raised with Q♠J♠, for example, and the flop comes 9-4-2 with no spades. You bet and your aggressive adversary raises you. Against an action player, you're in a tough spot. If he has called you with A♦6♦, for example, he has the best hand. Unless you are prepared to put in a reraise bluff followed by a bet on fourth street (or even taking the bluff through to the river), you are usually better off passing his raise. In fact, your best option is probably to check on the flop and fold if he bets. Once again, the key is knowing your opponent's style of play.

Raising

Once two or more people have limped into the pot, you should have a very strong hand if you intend to raise: aces, kings, queens, jacks, or A-K suited or unsuited. A hand such as K♣Q♣ or A-Q offsuit, although strong, is probably not strong enough. With a pair of 10s, you should probably just call and wait to see the flop before deciding how to proceed. With two limpers in the pot, a pair of jacks should be your minimum raising hand because the probability of seeing an ace, king or queen on the flop is about even money. You might even just limp in with a pair of jacks and see the flop cheaply, especially if more than two players are in the pot.

Limping in with a pair such as jacks may also offer you the advantage of the element of surprise. If undercards with no straight or flush potential come on the flop, you can sometimes trap players who flop top pair. For example, they enter the pot with A-10 and the flop comes 10-7-4. The A-10 will have a hard time trying not to lose several bets against your unsuspected overpair. Ditto with hands such as A-K and A-Q in unraised pots.

Suppose you are on the button with A-K and six players have entered the pot for the minimum bet. Since you know your raise won't get them out, it is quite correct to see the flop cheaply. If an ace or a king comes on the flop, you again have the element of surprise on your side of the fence. You'll probably get action from players with weaker kickers than yours (unless they have flopped two pair, of course), plus the added edge of your late position.

Although I am not suggesting that you should *never* raise with A-K, who says you have to *always* raise? Even with a hand as strong as two queens,

I would prefer just seeing the flop when six people are in the pot, deferring my gambling to after the flop.

No matter how many people have entered the action, aces and kings are usually worth a raise, even from the big blind. I usually raise or reraise with the big pairs from an early position when only one or two people have entered the pot before me, with the goal of substantially narrowing the field. But if I hold aces or kings in late position with more than two limpers already in the pot, I will seriously consider just calling, to add a touch of deception to my play. Then if the flop doesn't fit my hand, I can quietly fold it, with no one the wiser . . . and I lose only the minimum amount with the same hand that many other players would have lost several bets with.

Of course, if I hit the flop, the element of surprise works to my advantage. I once won a major pot in the late stages of a hold'em tournament when I was holding two queens on the button with six people in the hand. With only an average stack, I decided to smooth call rather than raise and make my strategy decision after the flop. The flop came Q-10-4, with two cards to a flush. Other players had straight and flush draw possibilities, but I flopped top set—a hand which nobody put me on. I got all kinds of action from drawing hands that didn't get there, and even got paid off on the end by a player holding the case queen.

Limping into the Pot

If you have limped in with a hand such as K♥8♥ on the button against several other limpers who are playing hands such as A♣5♣, nothing says that you have to continue playing the hand after the flop, even if you flop top pair. Many players seem to think they are obligated to continue just because they have hit some sort of hand on the flop, but that is not the case at all. Be very cautious about giving too much action if your kicker is weak.

A classic example occurs when you limp in with A-5 suited, for example, and flop top pair. Against a bet and a raise, with no other drawing possibilities, you aren't even close to being able to call: it is a clear pass. If a solid player has bet, be very reluctant to continue playing, even for a single bet.

Or suppose you are playing the K♥8♥ on the button. You flop top pair along with a three-flush. If you don't think anyone sitting between you and the original bettor will raise, you might take off a single card hoping to hit your kicker or pick up another heart for the flush draw. But if you are convinced that the bettor has at least a king with a better kicker than yours, a pass is generally in order.

Playing out of Position

Marginal hands played out of position can become a lot of trouble. That same K♥8♥ you might have played on the button in a multi-way pot can force you to make tricky judgments if you play it from a middle spot. If you make a bet and are then raised, you are almost forced to call, hoping you will hit your kicker. Had you passed the hand in the first place, you would not have placed yourself in jeopardy of losing two or three bets with such a marginal hand. The later your position in a multi-way pot, the more justified you are in calling with such hands; the earlier your position, the less justification you have.

Playing the Blinds

If the small blind is $5 as opposed to $10, with the big blind at $15, you have to be very selective about which hands you defend the small blind with. But when the blinds rise to $15 and $30 in the second round, the value of your hand will determine whether you defend the small blind.

Be very hesitant about raising from the small or big blinds with multiple players in the pot. With five or more players in the pot, a raise must be based strictly on the merits of your hand. Occasionally, you will see players raising with small to medium pairs. Although the raise is a way to build a big pot, you will be forced to flop a set to have your hand stand up against five or more opponents. Therefore, it makes little sense to raise with these hands unless you're in a gambling mood.

A time when you might raise from the big blind with small to medium pairs is when you are almost all-in and several people are already in the pot. With a "What the hell!" attitude, you can fire in your last chips on a raise, knowing that no matter what comes, you will be getting multi-way action on your money, with odds of hitting your set at 7.5-1 on the flop and 5-1 if you go all the way to the river. With an average stack, you are better off just calling from the big blind, hoping to hit your set. If you are in the small blind with only a few chips remaining, you should probably wait for the button.

Raising in the Big Blind

With hands such as A-Q suited, A-K suited or offsuit, or even a pair of queens, be very reluctant to raise from the big blind. It is not a major error to raise with queens, but it may be better to raise with them *only* if you have either a very big stack or a very small stack, to try to extract as much money from your opponents as possible. You won't be in major jeopardy of losing too much if you have a tall stack; and if you have a short stack, you will be giving yourself a chance to win a very big pot by putting in the raise. It is when you have a mediocre stack that you should be most reluctant to raise with your queens.

Although two kings or A-K may be the best starting hand, if there are a lot of people in the pot someone will usually flop something that helps their hand—a good draw, if nothing else. You may be a solid favorite against any *one* of them, but you won't be a favorite against *all* of them. With five or more players in the pot, even two aces will lose about 50 percent of the time. This doesn't mean you have less of a chance than anyone else; but it does mean that you are not a mathematical favorite to win that particular pot against that many opponents.

The reason I advocate not raising in very many instances with these premium hands is simply because the raise will not accomplish its mission: it will not limit the field. It will get more money in the pot, but there's a downside to that, too. Many times, that extra money will only serve as an incentive for other players to enter the pot because the pot odds have become more attractive to them. When they flop a draw or a pair, they will be getting a much better price for their hands and will have even more reason to try to draw out on you.

In addition, the element of surprise you achieve by not raising with a premium hand can work to your advantage when the flop comes your way. You will often get a lot more action than if you had raised.

Also, if a threatening overcard to your pair comes on the flop, it is easy to get away from your hand.

Defending the Small Blind

The starting hand requirements with which you can defend the small blind can be more liberal in unraised pots than in raised pots. In raised pots, you can call from the small blind with small pairs and suited connectors when there are five or more people in the pot, including yourself and the big blind. It will cost you only your original half-bet, plus one extra bet. Suited cards with two gaps and straight potential (such as 8♥5♥, 9♦6♦ or 10♣7♣) are another type of hand you can play for an additional half-bet *only when* there are several people in the pot.

Defending the Big Blind

You can generally defend the big blind with any pocket pair because you will usually be getting the right price. One exception may be when a very solid, tight player has raised from an early position and everyone else has passed. It you know the raiser's minimum raising requirements are either a big pair or A-K or A-Q suited, you are better off just passing with a hand such as two 6s, for example. You can be somewhat more liberal in your defense if one other player calls, in which case you might be willing to see the flop with any pocket pair. With suited connectors, however, you should be less willing to call because they are trickier to play after the flop than pairs are.

When you hold a pair, your decision is more black-and-white: you either flop a set or you release your hand when an overcard comes on the flop and someone bets. Of course, if you are holding two 6s and the flop comes 5-7-8 (giving you an open-end straight draw), you can continue playing. But if you need an inside straight card (such as the 5, if the flop comes 4-7-8), be more reluctant to continue with your hand if there is serious action. You are probably up against a bigger pair, and your chances of drawing the inside straight card are less than they would be if you had the open end straight draw.

Suited connectors require a lot more judgment, especially if you flop a pair along with either an open-end or an inside straight draw. In this case, you will probably have to take off a card. If you flop top pair with a straight draw, you will most likely wind up playing your hand aggressively, or at least going to the river with it. If you are defending from the small or big blind, your judgment must be excellent in deciding whether to continue with the hand because you will be first or second to act throughout the ensuing action.

Although usually a detriment, being out of position can sometimes work to your advantage. If you make a big hand from first position, you are in a perfect position to check raise, if you are about 80 percent certain one of your opponents will bet. Of course, when you flop a big hand, late position is even better, especially if someone raises in front of you. When that happens, you can get a third bet in the pot when you reraise, whereas a check-raise from an early position will usually get only two bets into the pot. Again let me reiterate: *position, position, position!*

The position of the raiser often dictates whether defending your blind (especially the big blind) is correct. The earlier the raise, the more credit for a strong hand you should usually give your opponent. Of course, you can discount the value of a raise which comes from someone who is fast or who puts in more raises than normal. But against a tight player who raises from an early position, you should fold many of the hands you would have called with against a late position raiser.

Defending the blind with a hand such as A-5 offsuit against an early position raiser is usually a mistake. Ask yourself, "What might they be raising with?" Probably either big pairs or big face cards. If they raise with big faces, the only time you will get any action if you flop an ace is when you are outkicked. If you happen to hit two pair or a couple of 5s on the flop and bet them, the raiser will probably fold unless he holds either an overpair or overcards to your trips, and the pot won't be very big. So you are usually better off just passing these types of hands. You might see the flop, however, with two suited cards 10 and above. Your minimum calling hand should probably be J-10 or 10-9 suited because you can make so many straight with them.

You may shave your defense hand requirements somewhat if your hand is suited, depending on how many people have entered the pot: the more, the better. But remember that being suited adds only about 7 percent additional value to your hand. Don't fall into the trap of magnifying that percentage in your mind's eye. Hold'em players in particular often give too much value to suited hands.

Against a loose, aggressive player who raises from a late position, you can defend the big blind with any pocket pair, hoping to flop a set. Sometimes, a small pocket pair will hold up without any improvement, of course, but you have to use good judgment in deciding whether to continue with the hand if one or more overcards come on the flop. Against a known loose player who raises from late position, you can defend with any reasonable hand, such as an ace, any two cards 10 or higher, and most suited connectors. If I am very short-stacked, I prefer defending with a pocket pair, even a pair of deuces, rather than with small suited connectors such as 7-6. If I have to go all-in, I would prefer two cards 10 and above to connectors.

The Importance of Making Correct Decisions in the Blinds

Correct decisions on your blind hands can often spell the difference between success and failure in a tournament. The most expensive hand you will ever play in a hold'em game is the hand you get in for free in the big blind, or the one which costs you only one-half a bet more in the small blind. What often happens is that you catch part of the flop and become involved with a hand you wouldn't have played had you not been in the blind. With a hand such as Q♠8♠, your thinking may go something like this: "This isn't that great a hand, but there are several people in the pot and it's only going to cost me half a bet to call." A fast or unknowledgeable player may then make the mistake of betting the hand aggressively when he flops a queen, when a better option is to just check and see what kind of action happens behind him. If someone raises his bet, he is faced with a quandary: "Should I call the raise or pass?"

More tournament players have crippled themselves by defending a blind they shouldn't have played, or by playing more aggressively than they should when they flop something marginal, than for any other reason. Playing the blinds correctly requires extreme prudence and discretion. The number of opponents in the pot, knowing the styles of the other players, and the nature of the flop are key factors. If one of your opponents is the type who would raise to try to get a free card if the flop offers him a straight or flush draw, you might continue playing when you flop top pair with your Q♠8♠. But if there is no logical draw other than top pair/top kicker or trips on the flop, and if you have no other reasonable outs, you must give serious consideration to just passing his raise.

Troublesome blind hands are even trickier to play when you catch part of the flop in a raised pot. With a hand such as A♥8♥, for example, you must proceed cautiously if you flop an ace. Against any substantial action, you are better off to just give it up. The strongest hand you can hope to flop with your A♥8♥ is top pair with a flush draw. Be willing to go to the river if the flop comes A♦K♥4♥, for example. However, if you are subjected to any type of substantial action, you may be forced to just check-call rather than lead. However, so long as you are not raised, you can continue to take the lead. If your flush fails to materialize on the river, you can just check and decide whether to pay off an opponent who bets.

Against a single opponent who has only called all the way, you may as well bet if you intend to call anyway, unless you believe he may raise you. If you indeed think he may raise, it would be wiser to check to him, thus avoiding being bluffed out of the pot, and giving yourself an opportunity to snap up the pot if your hand is better than his. Checking on the river can sometimes induce a bluff. Your apparent weakness may induce your opponent to bet (when he has actually been on a draw and holds only a lower pair).

Key Concept

A player will often bet a hand he wouldn't call with. Against this type of opponent, a check-call may be more profitable for you because it may induce a bluff. Only against a very tight opponent would you be inclined to pass such a bet.

Blind against Blind

Playing blind against blind is more likely to happen from the middle rounds onward than in the opening stages. Any two cards 10 and above are worth a raise from the small blind against the big blind; or if you are the big blind and the small blind has only called. A-x is worth a raise in a small blind-big blind confrontation, or against a small blind who has limped into the pot. It is usually correct to raise with these hands regardless of chip count.

An important concept in blind against blind is the "bunching factor." If a lot of people have passed, it is likely than none of them is holding big cards. It then becomes more likely that one of the blind hands does have big cards. So be aware that one of the blinds may wake up with a premium hand in these situations (hopefully, it will be you!).

Bluff-Proof Blind Protectors

Some people cannot be bluffed, although this is a less frequent occurrence in tournaments than it is in ring games. If you think a player will defend his blind very liberally, you should base your betting strategy strictly on the merits of your hand rather than trying to run over someone who won't lay down a hand. Trying to bluff a player who is bluff-proof is a costly mistake.

Early Stage

In the second round of play (the $30-$60 level), the action begins to heat up . . . and so do the casualties. At the end of the second round, approximately 30 percent of the field has been eliminated. In WSOP play where you begin with $1,500 in chips and $50-$100 rounds, and the second round is $100-$200, about 40 percent of the field will usually be eliminated by the end of the second round. Therefore, the first two rounds are very important in World Series play. The second round is also crucial in other hold'em tournaments because if you don't survive it, you don't get a chance to compete in the later stages when all the gold and glory is at stake.

To repeat, most players begin a tournament playing their very best games. The average player can play a very good game for about an hour, but after that, he reverts to his normal style of play. So in the second round, some players who have been playing a solid, conservative game will often shift gears when the increments increase.

In general, players bluff far too often in limit hold'em. You will have to show down a hand the majority of the time in these opening stages, because many of the pots are multi-way. Although this doesn't mean you should never bluff, it is very difficult to run over players in multi-way pots with just a marginal holding, so be very selective about when your bluff. Your bets and raises should be based on your hand value more than on their bluffing potential. (One-on-one play is a different story because then you have only person to contend with.)

In select situations, however, a bluff or semi-bluff bet is often correct, even against three or four opponents. For example, suppose the flop comes something like 8-8-4 in different suits: you know you are up against either nothing or the world's fair. In an unraised pot, your opponents could be holding almost anything, but in a raised pot, they are less likely to have either an 8 or 4 in their hands. If the pot has not been raised and you are the last to act, or sometimes when you are first to act, you can bet. However, you must proceed cautiously if you are either called or raised. Unless you have a pocket pair which you think could still the best hand, you will probably have to abandon ship unless you believe someone is just trying to make a play at you.

You are not trying to win or lose a big pot with your bet: you're hoping to pick up a small pot with your bluff when the board looks raggedy or contains a small pair. A tight image often works to your favor in these situations. If you've been playing a solid game, an opponent may not be willing to make a risky call, unless he decides to "keep you honest" by playing the role of sheriff at the table. (We all know what happens to sheriffs: they live fast and die young.) Just be sure the opponents you are trying to bluff are not of the bluff proof variety I discussed earlier. *Never* try to bluff this type of player—not once, not ever.

Drawing Hands

When you are strictly on a draw with no way to win except to complete a straight or flush, it is usually better to have many callers in the pot. One of my favorite plays with a nut flush draw when I am last to act is to raise on an "if come" basis. If I get no improvement on fourth street, I can often take a free card when everyone checks to me and see the river for that half-price third street bet. If you are drawing to the nut straight or have a very powerful straight draw such as K-Q when an unsuited J-10 is on board, you can also play aggressively. In fact, if you believe you may be able to win the pot if either a king or a queen comes on the turn (even though there is always the danger of someone else making a straight), a raise may be in order, and you can even reraise against an aggressive player. Your goal in raising on the flop, of course, is to get more money into the pot, since you know everyone is probably going to continue playing.

Of course, from a middle position with several players yet to act, you might play your draw differently. Say you are playing A♦8♦ and the two-limper rule is in effect: two people have already limped into the pot. You and two players behind you also limp in. The flop comes K♦J♦4♣ and someone bets—you're fairly sure he holds a king. One player calls and one passes. Now it's your turn to act with two players left to act behind you. What is your best move?

Call only. There are two reasons for this: (1) you don't want to drive players out of the pot, because you want to get maximum value for your hand if you make the flush; (2) if you're against an aggressive player, he may reraise you and you will have put in extra bets on a losing hand if you don't make it on fifth street. So many times, just calling is the most appropriate play.

However, if you are last to act with that same A♦8♦, you can put in a raise. In this case, it's not a tragedy if another player reraises because you will still make your hand about one time out of three, and you will still be getting the correct price for it, counting the dead money left in the pot by players who have folded against the raise or reraise. Of course, if they continue to play, you will get a very nice return on your investment if you make your hand.

Sometimes you just have to gamble a little more with your drawing hands in these early rounds to guarantee future action. When your opponents have seen you make a raise on a big draw, they are likely to give you more action than they should when you are *not* on a draw. You frequently have to *make* one of your big draws to win a tournament. Whoever is destined to win the tournament has to run very lucky, as well as play skillfully, on that particular day. As for me, I like to gamble when I know I'm getting the best of it: when there are enough wins in the deck to warrant my aggressive play.

Two factors you can use in deciding whether to raise are how many chips you have and whether the raise will limit the field. If your chip count has deteriorated to the point that you have only two bets left, be more inclined to just call if you believe you are up against top pair, for example. Then, after you make your hand, put in the remainder of your chips. However, if you have only enough left for *one* more bet, you may decide to raise on the flop in an attempt to get as much money into the pot as you can . . . and then hope you get there. With an above-average stack, you can gamble more; but with an average stack, just calling is probably your best move.

What happens when you *don't* get there, that is, when you miss your draw? Suppose you are heads-up and your opponent checks to you. You know you can't win in a showdown. Before you act, take a moment to think over your alternative: can you win with a bet? The majority of the time, the answer is "no," especially when several bets have been placed in the pot. But many players will bet anyway, repeating the old cliché, "Well, betting was the only chance I had to win" In reality, betting was their only chance to lose an extra bet!

I remember a game I once played that illustrates this concept. The pot had not been raised and I was sitting in the big blind with A-7. The flop came A♥Q♣2♥. I bet, another player called and the button raised. I figured him for either a flush draw or an ace with a weak kicker, and thought he may have raised just to find out where he was at. Playing somewhat less aggressively than I perhaps should have, I just flat-called the raise (although, as it turned out, I couldn't have forced the middle player out with a reraise because he was the one with the flush draw).

Another queen came on the turn, making the board A-Q-Q-2. Naturally, I was a little concerned about the queen because I wasn't sure where the middle player was at with his hand. I decided to just give up the hand if anyone bet. So I checked, the middle man with the flush draw checked, and the button also checked. I was pretty sure I had at least one of them beaten, probably even both of them. The last card was the 4♠, a total blank.

I decided it was best to just check, with the intention of calling if one of them bet . . . if the middle man passed and the button bet . . . or if the middle man bet and the button passed. However, the middle man with the busted-out flush draw decided to bluff at the pot and fired in a bet. The player on the button thought about it, agonized over it, and finally called.

That put me in a quandary. I wasn't at all sure that my kicker would hold up against two other players; and so, after much internal debate, I laid down my hand. Low and behold, the button had A♣4♣ so my kicker would have played and I would have won the pot! But whether I played good or bad is not the entire point of this story . . .

The point is that the middle player on the flush draw with 5♥6♥ made a hopeless bluff, a completely futile play. For sure, at least one of us had to hold an ace, and maybe the other even had a queen. Either way, he was going to get called, so he wasted an extra bet. Bluffing in situations such as this can only cost you more money. Bets saved are just as important as bets won.

Making Proper Laydowns

Suppose you begin with a pair. The flop comes with an overcard and no other draw for you. If someone bets into you, you are usually better off to lay down your hand. Against an aggressive player, of course, you don't necessarily have to fold. For example, suppose I have pocket 10s; I raise and an aggressive bettor reraises. The flop comes Q♥9♥4♣. Now he bets into me and we're heads-up. I would be more likely to call him in this circumstance than I would if he were betting into me and three other people, because even an aggressive player must have some sort of hand to bet into so many opponents.

Generally speaking, if overcards to your pair come on the flop, and if you are bet into or check-raised, you should fold. The check-raise comes into play in scenarios such as the following: you are the pre-flop raiser in a late position holding those pocket 10s again; the flop comes with an overcard to your pair; your opponents check to you and you bet; then one of them check-raises your bet. After showing all that strength, now what do you do?

Seriously reconsider how to proceed with your hand because you could be in deep trouble, especially since there has been substantial action before the flop. You need to know your opponent quite well to accurately judge whether he has the strength he advertises or is making a play at you. If he does have the overpair, there are only two cards in the deck which can make trips for you. So generally speaking, it is better to lay down your hand in this situation.

Or suppose you have two jacks in the hole, the flop comes Q-10-4, and an opponent bets into you. You would be better off to be holding A-10 than pocket jacks because with A-10, there are two other 10s and three aces which can help you improve. Obviously if you have five outs instead of two, you can make a somewhat better case for continuing to play heads-up when an overcard falls.

Middle Rounds

During the third and fourth rounds, your chip position becomes increasingly more important. Although you should keep track of your chip status during the entire tournament, these middle rounds are the heart and soul of the tournament—the time when you have an opportunity to accumulate enough chips to go the distance, to survive to the late rounds with good chip status rather than in a state of severe chip depletion, short-stacked and vulnerable.

Jockeying for position begins in earnest during the middle rounds. About half the field has usually been eliminated by the fourth round, so that surviving at this level can put you in position to compete during the "money" rounds. It's like light at the end of the tunnel when you survive the middle stage in decent chip position, because then you know you have a shot at the winner's circle. It isn't extremely important to have the biggest stack going into the late stages because there is still plenty of time to catch the leaders. The important thing is not to push any panic buttons.

Remember instead that if half the players have been eliminated, the average chip count is double what you started with. At the $100-$200 fourth round, if you have $1,500 in chips, you have an above-average amount. Many (maybe even most) of your opponents will be in worse shape than you are. You may be thinking, "Geez, I can only play about three hands to the river . . . I'm in bad shape." But that isn't necessarily true: a lot of your opponents can play only about a hand-and-a-half. So although you may not be in the best of shape, you're not that bad off either.

One troublesome hand to play correctly when you are short-stacked in the middle stages is A-x. This is a hand I do not like very much, because I have frequently busted out of tournaments with it, usually after I have raised from early position because I was afraid I wouldn't get any better hand to play, or even from late position when someone called behind me.

Unless I am within one or two hands of the big blind, which will put me all-in, I will pass with A-x. In other words, if the big blind will take either all of my chips or so many of them that I will have virtually no chance to recover, I will stake a stand with it. If I am dealt A-x in late position and am short-stacked, I am more likely to make an aggressive bet heads-up against the blinds because I have a reasonable chance of holding the best hand. However, if the blinds are very liberal defenders, I may just pass.

Look for many of your opponents to change gears in the middle rounds. They have played a very tight, snug game through the opening stages but now they're firing with both fists. Or, players who may have gambled earlier and have accumulated a nice stack of chips may now begin playing far more solid hands, waiting for premium cards before they risk any of their precious horde. Better players are like fine sports cars: they have multiple gears and can shift from one to the other as needed to maximize their winning potential. So be aware that the best players, rather than reverting to their usual styles of ring game play like so many of their opponents do after an hour or so, will be changing gears, mixing up their styles, during these middle rounds.

Many times, I have been severely crippled going into the middle stages but have survived them with flying colors. A classic example of this occurred at the 1994 *Diamond Jim Brady* limit hold'em tournament at the Bicycle Club in Bell Gardens, California. Against an extremely tough starting field of over 100 players, I "sort of" overplayed a pair of 7s at the end of the $100-$200 level when I tried to represent the ace on board and raised another player. My mistake: he not only had an ace but also a flush draw to go with it! Naturally, he raised me back. I gave him a little too much action because I thought he was making a move on the pot, which he wasn't. I had misjudged him and wound up with only $500 in chips going into the $200-$400 round.

With just four hands to go before I would have to post $200 of my remaining chips in the big blind, did it look like I was in a bad spot or what? But I didn't push any panic buttons, even when I was dealt four straight totally unplayable hands. Zilch—nothing to play with.

Then the big blind hit me. Fortunately, I had not thrown in my last chips as a less-experienced player might have done. Too often, players throw in the towel with hands such as any two suited cards, one random ace, or K-x suited under stressful situations such as this. Although this may sometimes be the best course of action, I prefer waiting as long as possible for a better hand before I put in my last chips.

I was dealt a K-10 offsuit in the big blind. The player next to the button raised. A good player who had been playing somewhat faster than most of his opponents, he didn't need to have too big a hand to make the raise. The person on the button cold-called. He hadn't been playing many hands, so I figured he must have a good hand to call the raise. The small blind also decided to defend. Then it was my turn to either fold or call the raise.

Looking down at my chips, I realized that I would have only the $100 small blind left if I called his raise. I decided that no matter what the flop was, I was almost forced to put in all my chips. So I called the $200 raise and also put in my last $100 chip in order to get the maximum action on it. With four of us in the hand, there was $2,000 in the pot.

A king and a couple of suited cards arrived on the flop, making a flush draw possible. One player held two queens and continued playing, but no one had a king. My hand held up, allowing me to extract the maximum value from it. Of course, a K-10 is a hand with which I would not normally throw in my case chips, but it was a reasonable playing hand and I believed I was getting a good price on it.

The good news is that I took that $2,000 and made it to the last table in second chip position. When we got to three-handed play, I held 22 percent of the chips. I was out-chipped by almost two-to-one by the leader and by around 50 percent by the third player. But fortunately, I was able to make a comeback to win the tournament, which netted me around $25,000.

The key hand, of course, was that K-10. Right after that hand, I went on a short rush and built up my stack. The key attitude was not pushing the panic button, and patiently waiting for the best opportunity to play my remaining chips. Rather than second-guessing myself, I stayed calm, cool and collected. In virtually every tournament I have played, a similar scenario has repeated itself. Therefore, I can highly recommend not becoming discouraged when you suffer a bad beat, you have your aces cracked, or you have to take a stand and go all-in with less than a premium hand.

I emphasize the importance of maintaining a tough mental attitude in the middle rounds because so many players begin to crack under pressure during this stage of the tournament. They lose a few hands, and then both their discipline and their stacks begin to crumble. If you are aware of this tendency, you can capitalize on the deteriorating mental condition of your opponents.

From the middle stages on, it is not unusual to see far more raising than in the earlier rounds. Of course, this naturally implies that there will be far fewer opportunities to limp into pots. Therefore, you won't be seeing as much multi-way action as you probably saw during the early rounds.

Raising with A-K or A-Q

"What if you have raised before the flop with an A-K or A-Q in a heads-up pot and you make nothing on the flop?" one of my students asked during a seminar. Generally speaking, you would judge your play according to the nature of your opponent and the texture of the flop. If you are against a loose, aggressive player who is capable of making a play at you, ask yourself, "Is ace-high good enough to still be the best hand?" If the flop comes 7♦8♦9♠, for example, I would be very hesitant to continue with the hand. But if it comes with total rags such as 8♦5♣3♠, which is less likely to hit my opponent, I might be winning with A-K.

If you believe you have the best hand, but you think your opponent won't give you credit for it and may instead make a play at you, you might induce a bluff by just check-calling. Although this may be a weak play in a ring game, it is sometimes quite correct to check-call in a tournament. Against a loose player, you might check-call on the flop; and if another random card comes on the turn, you may just call him down with A-K or A-Q. Knowing your opponent is the key factor in whether you decide to do that.

With the same 8♦5♣3♠ flop, you might fire a bet into a tighter player if you are first to act. If he raises, your primary concern is not that he hit the flop but that he holds an overpair such as 9s or tens. You might then call his raise to see if you improve on fourth street. If you do improve, you can bet into him or try a check-raise. If you don't improve, you can check and then pass if he bets.

Suppose you have called a tight player's raise before the flop with your A-K. If he bets into you on the flop, be more willing to pass. You might decide to take off one card if you believe that hitting your ace or king will give you the best hand, so long as no flush or straight draws are evident. Then if you don't hit your overpair on the turn, you can simply fold. If a third player is in the pot, be more inclined to fold on the flop to avoid the danger of being whipsawed between the original raiser and a caller who sits behind you.

Late Stage

In $500 buy-in tournaments, the late stage limits will be around $300-$600 to $500-$1,000, and about 85 percent of the field will have been eliminated. One of the most important strategies at this point in the tournament in putting people all-in whenever you can if you have a medium to large stack. If you have a short stack, of course, you are very vulnerable, but I have seen a lot of players rebound from short-stack status because another player did not put them all-in for their last chips when they should have. I have even seen the short stack come back to either knock out the opponent who didn't put him all-in when he could have, or severely cripple him . . . and occasionally go on to win the tournament. So it becomes your "job" with a decent hand and good chip status to put other players all-in at every opportunity.

This is why it is often correct to call even when you are holding a weak hand, especially when you are blind-against-blind or are against a short stack that has raised all-in before the flop. Sometimes, it will only cost you one more bet before the flop. (Remember, any two cards can win in hold'em.)

Key Concept

Take advantage of tight play. Sometimes, an average stack can grow into a large stack by simply taking a few more chances when everyone else is playing super tight. So if you're at a table where everyone is playing tight and jockeying for a money finish, remember this key concept.

For instance, suppose you're down to three tables in a two-table payoff tournament. After each table has lost one or two players, there will be between 22 and 24 players left: the survivors who know they're getting very close to the money round. The only thing many of them are thinking about is lasting long enough for a payday, so they go into their ultra-tight mode (even some of the tallest stacks). Use this to your advantage by taking a few more liberties against them.

Unfortunately, if there are a lot of big stacks at your table, and if they are *not* playing particularly tight but are tending to mix it up a bit instead, you cannot take full advantage of this strategy because, of course, you are *not* up against opponents who are playing tight survival tactics.

At other times, there may be only two big stacks. When you have position on them, especially when they have already folded, you can be somewhat more liberal in your play, knowing that only the shorter stacks will be left to contest the pot. The short stacks are usually waiting for a premium hand before they commit, so they may be less willing to call your raise if they hold a marginal hand, even though it may in fact be slightly better than what you are raising with. Generally, they will be far more likely to raise the pot themselves than to call your raise. Sometimes, all it takes to guarantee a money finish for yourself is picking up a few extra blinds now and then by taking a little extra risk.

Of course, taking that "little risk" can also backfire. No plan is foolproof, and you may either run into a legitimate hand or get one of your premium hands cracked. Those are just the chances you take. These guidelines are designed to maximize your chances to finish in the money. Sometimes squeaking into the money at the second table is fine . . . at least it's a start and an assured payoff. But the payoff is often barely more than your buy-in, whereas the top prize may be a hundred times more. So naturally, you want to maximize your chances of winning the top spot. As I mentioned earlier, you can't "win" the tournament too soon: you can try to dominate your table, but you cannot win the tournament until you are at the last table (and hopefully, with a monster stack).

At this point, there is a minuscule line between selectively aggressive play and wild loose play. Players who have a wild, loose image can sometimes be very intimidating in these late rounds. This is one reason why some players who are not considered to be good ring game players can successfully get away with their more aggressive tactics in a tournament. In fact, these tactics are far more correct and effective in tourneys than they are in side games.

Playing a Short Stack

If you are short-stacked in this late stage, you will be looking for the right time to take your stand. When that time comes, it if far better to be the aggressor than the caller, although that isn't always possible. A situation when you might need to gamble with the worst of it in order to give yourself a chance to win the tournament is this: the pot is multi-way . . . you have only two bets left . . . and you hold a hand such as 10♠9♠, J♦10♦, Q♥J♥, A♣10♣, or a small pocket pair. You will be getting five-to-one for your money so that if you win, you will be right back in contention. If you lose, you would probably have been ground out of the tournament in another few hands anyway, because you were short-stacked to begin with.

Be less inclined to gamble, however, if you are only one or two spots out of the money, because you want to ensure a money finish for yourself, if at all possible. What so often happens is that contenders are playing ultra tight *until* they squeak into the money. The short stacks are then far more willing to mix it up and gamble. Sometimes, even the big stacks will become involved with less than a premium hand, but they are more likely to get involved *after* they have locked up some type of money payoff.

When I decide to gamble, I usually wait for a multi-way pot, after I have already assured myself of a payoff slot. The next payoff might be only slightly more than what I have already locked up, and I want to give myself a chance to win the tournament. So when I am short-stacked and a multi-way pot is developing, I will seize the opportunity to gamble.

If a multi-way pot does not develop for you, the next best thing to do is to raise to try to get the pot heads-up. A good time to take a stand with a short stack is when you have a reasonable hand such as A-J, especially in a middle to late position when no one has yet entered the pot. Your position is your power point, allowing you to play aggressively and get all your money in as early as possible, without second-guessing yourself.

It is always far better to be the aggressor, of course, but I am not advocating being aggressive with weak hands. You wouldn't want to raise and put yourself all-in with a hand such as 10♠9♠ when you can wait four or five hands before you have to post the big blind. These types of hands are just too weak, because the short stacks will get called the vast majority of the time by *someone*. Even a weak blind hand will often have one card higher than a 10 in it, so it is usually prematurely risky to go all-in with a 10-high hand. Of course, if you're certain there will be multi-way action, you can gamble with your 10-9 suited to give yourself a chance to win the tournament. But in the meantime, you are hoping to simply survive and double-up at least once.

Big Stack, Big Blind

"How should you play a large stack late in the tournament when a player raises your big blind?" If the raiser is tight and is also large-stacked, pass all your marginal hands. If he is short-stacked and his raise will only cost you one or two more bets, you may be more willing to gamble because even a tight player has to play some marginal hands in the late stages. Ditto against a late position raise from a loose player who is short-stacked.

Short Stack, Big Blind

With a short stack, I would rather call the raise with a pocket pair than with connectors, because I figure to be taking too much the worst of it with them. Then if I can survive the small blind with enough chips left for a couple of bets, I will be on the button with an entire round to wait for a better hand. With better position, I can be the aggressor rather than simply reacting to someone else's play at the pot.

Taking a chance with a small pair is better than coming in with the 10♠9♠ because you can often win on the merits of the pair alone. But with the 10-high hand, you will usually have to hit something for your hand to hold up. In some cases, you can even reraise with a small pair. With only two bets left, for example, you might reraise with a pair of 6s if you think it will get you heads-up against a single opponent. Although you may be only even-money at best, you are at least giving yourself a chance to win. And being against only one hand is much better than trying to fight off two hands with a low pair.

Mental attitude is vitally important when you have a short stack in these late stages. That "never say die, never give up" stance is essential to giving yourself a chance to win.

Late Stage when Players Are Already in the Money

The action heats up when only two tables are left in a two-table pay-out tourney, or when only the final table is left in a one-table pay-out tournament. This is the time when multi-way pots often occur . . . and this is the time when it is correct to gamble. The important factor now is *timing.* Many times, I will sit back with a large to medium stack because I haven't been getting any fairly strong starting hands. If I can wait until two players have busted out, leaving the table seven-handed, I will need less strength to raise with because there are fewer people to contest the pot. This is a particularly good strategy when several other players are willing to mix it up and go all-in.

Staying calm and collected, and choosing the right time to take your stand, are the keys to success at this point. If you have a big stack and can afford to gamble a little bit, keep putting the pressure on the small stacks, even with bets that would not normally have a positive expectation in a ring game.

Another key ingredient to success is *controlled aggression.* You cannot afford to mindlessly gamble; instead, choose your spots. Look for situations where you can be the aggressor, even with a medium-strength hand if you are the first to enter the pot and can put pressure on the blinds (especially when they are short-stacked).

Be patient. Let other people knock themselves out. If you see players who want to gamble, lay off. Look for reasons *not* to get involved until a few of your opponents have been eliminated.

The Final Table

Sometimes, two or three players will appear to begin engaging in a personal war at the final table—stay out of their battles. If the bigger stacks are willing to keep firing at each other, let them duel against each other with their aggressive raises and reraises. Don't get involved with less than a premium hand, because they may knock each other out. Then you can take on the survivors.

This strategy will help you to inch up the pay scale, which is something you naturally want to do. But while you are making your climb, don't forget that your main goal is to win the tournament. Most tournaments are very top heavy in their payoffs, usually awarding 37 to 40 percent to the winner, 20 percent for second place, and 10 percent for third. Therefore, first place is twice the amount of second and four times the amount of third. Ideally, you want to put yourself in position to take one of these top three spots. Don't take the attitude some of your opponents may have: they are so happy to be at the final table, they lose sight of their ultimate goal. They think their job is done. The exact opposite is true. Their job—*your* job—is just beginning.

Some players, however, try to win the tournament too soon. You cannot win it until you are head-up against one player, and to put yourself in that position, you have to use some survival tactics. This is why "getting full value" from some of your hands is not nearly as important as it is in ring games. If there is a possibility you will be drawn out on, it may not be worth risking the extra bet in a tournament, especially at the final table.

In fact, saving that one bet when the limits are very high can be pivotal to your success. I have often seen a player arrive at the final table in a weak chip status and then go on a little rush, win three hands, and move up from last place to first place in chip position. Because the limits are so high during this final stage, your chip position can change drastically in a very short time span. So you must use good survival tactics to give yourself a chance to go on a rush, to get lucky, and maybe win the whole enchilada. Saving that extra bet is part of survival strategy.

Of course, you don't have to play like a wimp—wimps don't win. What you must do instead is walk the tightrope. Sizing up your opponents and using good judgment are part of your balancing act. Some "instinctual" players who have never read a book on poker tournaments enjoy great success because they have a natural instinct for people, excellent card sense, and an innate feel for what's going on.

"Scientific" players are more oriented toward math than people and sometimes have less of a feel for when to bluff and when not to, whereas the old-line players with fewer math skills but greater people savvy have had very successful poker careers. (Many of them are still holding their own in tournaments against their more-educated, younger, scientific opponents.) You can fine tune your skills by playing in a lot of tournaments, and by practicing in lower limit tourneys until you are ready to move up the ranks.

Playing Short-Handed

Short-handed playing skills when the action is four or five handed are integral to your success at the final table. Small pairs need to be played with caution and the suited connectors go down in value. If every pot is being contested (if you can't just raise it and take it), you must play cautiously with small pairs, being careful not to become overly involved. Small pairs will often hold up against only one player, of course, but even then you must play carefully, especially when an overcard comes on the flop. Players know that the hand values don't have to be as strong short-handed as in a full nine or ten handed game, so they'll get involved with a lot of medium strength hands. Even a hand such as 9-8 suited against two 6s, for example, is fairly close to even money.

Suited connectors have value in multi-way pots, but go down in value short-handed. The majority of the hands you play at the final table will be either heads-up or against only two other contestants. Very seldom do you see five players in a pot at the last table. This means you must do far more raising than calling.

Any two cards 10 and above are usually worth a raise when you can be the first one in the pot, but it's a different story if someone has raised in front of you. For example, say you are on the button with J-10 offsuit and one of your solid, aggressive opponents brings in the pot for a raise. You would be far less likely to want to get involved with your J-10 as a *caller* than you would if you were the raiser.

Now suppose you have the same hand in the big blind with a full bet already invested: you might be inclined to call the raise for a single bet, unless you are against a very conservative, tight player who hasn't been doing much raising. In this case, you should consider passing. Of course, in short-handed final table action, even the most conservative of players have to open up their games a bit. So you could also defend your blind, although not necessarily reraise, with two cards 10 and above or with a small pocket pair. With a small pocket pair, you are hoping to make a set, of course, but many times the flop will come with rags. With no cards higher than your pair on the flop, you have a reasonable chance of having the best hand with your small pair in the big blind.

Playing the small blind is a bit trickier. In a small blind versus big blind confrontation, I will raise with any ace, any two cards 10 and above, and any pocket pair. But if I don't flop anything and am against a liberal opponent who won't allow me to run over him too much, I will have to apply the brakes. If my chip count has become lower than I like when I am in the small blind, I may make an exception to my general rule of playing the hand with a raise before the flop. In this case, I may want to just see the flop with a more marginal holding such as J-10 offsuit, 9-8 suited, a pair of 5s, or 7♥6♥. Although these hands play best multi-way, it is quite correct to call the pot for half-a-bet when the action is short-handed.

Naturally, if you are playing against an aggressive opponent whom you know will raise every single time, you would be better off passing from the small blind with your small or medium suited connectors and with your small pairs. Or you might consider raising if your opponent is capable of making an occasional laydown. If he isn't capable of doing that, then just pass.

Slow-Playing

Slow playing a big pair in short-handed action at the final table is occasionally correct. The times to slow play usually occur when you are in the small blind against only the big blind, or when someone has raised in front of you. When a player has raised before the action gets to you, you may decide to trap him after the flop by just smooth calling with aces or kings. With queens, you should have a tendency to reraise because they are more vulnerable than aces or kings. Usually, you would not slow play with jacks, either, because it is almost even money that an overcard will come on the flop. But when you have a medium stack and are playing against either a big stack or another medium stack, a trap play with your aces or kings may be profitable.

Usually, you should not slow-play an A-K because it is still a drawing hand since you haven't yet made a pair, although it still figures to be better than anything your opponents are likely to be holding before the flop. Against a short stack, be more likely to reraise with any of these hands to get them to commit as many chips as possible before the flop and endanger their status.

Key Concept

Most sophisticated players expect every pot to get raised at the final table when it's four or five handed. Therefore, they will be somewhat suspicious if you just limp in from first position. Because they *expect* the pot to be raised, I will usually accommodate them.

Seldom, if ever, just limp in on the button. The few times you might consider it are when you hold hands such as J-10 suited, Q-10, or Q-J against two players who will defend their blinds 100 percent of the time. In this case, occasionally limp in if you have a medium to large stack and your liberal blind opponents also have medium to large stacks. Your hand is a little too good to pass, but a bit too risky to raise with against an opponent who will never lay down his hand, even when he thinks he may be taking the worst of it.

Sometimes, then, it is better to do your gambling *after* the flop. Personally, I prefer this posture in side games and in most of my tournament play. Of course, I'm not suggesting that you are *gambling* when you hold a big pair—it is with the *marginal* hands that you face a risk when you make an aggressive raise rather than just seeing the flop for a minimum amount. Those marginal situations include holding the 10-9 suited, or J-10 offsuit on the button, or when there is a limper in the pot. If you hold 10-9 suited in a raised pot, for example, your hand is usually too weak to cold-call a raise, whereas you could play it in an unraised pot.

You can occasionally slow play a big hand from the small or big blind by just calling, or by smooth calling an opponent's raise, with the object of setting up a trap play. But generally speaking, your style in short-handed final table action should be *raise or release.*

Ace-x suited is usually worth a raise, unless you are very short-stacked and have decided to wait for something slightly better because you expect to get called. Of course, an ace with a weak kicker can also get you into a lot of trouble. When you are called, it is often by someone who also holds an ace so that even when you flop top pair, you may be outkicked, especially if you hold something like A-2. In most cases, then, be cautious with A-x offsuit after the flop.

The times when you might consider putting on the heat with such a hand are when your opponent is slightly conservative, or when he has a short stack against your big stack. But if you have just lost a series of hands and you know your adversaries are probably going to play with you, your position becomes more vulnerable and you should play cautiously.

Again, let me discuss that fine (almost invisible?) line between being selectively aggressive when you have a good chance for success, and raising too loosely. Of course, if you're getting away with your loose raises, keep at it until things begin to break badly for you. But if things go wrong right away, tighten up immediately and wait for better hands than just a random A-x.

Key Concept

Usually, just checking and calling simply won't get the money—it is too weak and indecisive a strategy. But occasionally, you will have to call down a player even though your hand is only ace-high, especially if you are against an aggressive opponent who plays a lot of drawing hands. Sometimes, he will suspect you don't have a pair and will either raise or check-raise you.

For example, suppose you have raised with A-K before the flop. Your opponent may have called your raise from the big blind with something like Q♥10♥, a reasonable hand with which to defend his blind against one raise and a single opponent. The flop comes J♥4♥3♣. He figures that you don't have any of the flop so he decides to make a play at you. He checks, you bet, he raises, and you call. The turn card is a rag. He bets and you call. On the river, the board again rags off, without either a third suited card, an ace or a king. Your adversary bets into you. Now comes judgment time on your part. Against a more conservative opponent, be more willing to give him credit for at least a pair. But against a more liberal player who is capable of making a bluff raise, tend to give him a little more action. Occasionally, you will just have to call him down with an ace-high hand.

Of course, you can sometimes bluff-raise (with an out) against an aggressive adversary. Here's a good example: I raise with K-J before the flop and my opponent calls. The flop comes Q-10-4 unsuited, giving me an open-end straight draw. My opponent checks, I bet, and then he raises me. If he has a short stack, I may put him in for one more bet because I'll have to call on fourth street anyway. But let's assume that neither he nor I are short-stacked. Now it is just a question of how to proceed in playing out the hand.

If you are check-raised in this situation, you may reasonably assume he holds a queen and has check-raised you for value. Occasionally, you can make him lay down his hand by playing the following strategy: With your open-end straight draw, you have some outs, so the pot warrants calling his raise, which you do. On fourth street, a 10 comes, making the board Q-10-10-4. Since a player will often value bet or call a raise with second pair, if your aggressive opponent again bets, try raising him. If he doesn't have a queen in his hand with a decent kicker, he will have an extremely hard time calling your bluff raise. After all, you have played aggressively all the way . . . and now you have a chance to win the pot without even making your hand.

If he decides to call, you can safely assume he has a queen, but you still have an out. If a king comes on the river, you could win with that; or if a straight card comes, you could also win. It is a great coup if you can get him to lay down his hand. Of course, you have to pick your spot carefully to be successful with this play. You have to be against a player who is capable of making a check-raise on a bluff, or can lay down his hand if he thinks he is beat. Again, you need to "know your man when you get your hand."

Playing Top Pair

When you flop top pair heads-up, you should take an aggressive approach, even if your kicker is weak. It is less likely in heads-up situations that your opponent will also hold top pair with a better kicker than if you were playing in a ring game. For instance, if you raised before the flop with A-5 offsuit, which is reasonable in short-handed play, and make top pair on the flop, you can take an aggressive posture and continue betting until you run into resistance. Sometimes, it is even correct to bet with nothing at all if it is checked to you. Just remain leery of players who check-raise a lot, looking to set up a trap.

Let me reiterate that any hand with an ace is usually worth bringing in with a raise. But if someone has raised in front of you, you may want to fold a hand such as A-6 offsuit, unless chip status comes into consideration. For example, if you are short-stacked and think A-6 may be the best hand you're likely to get, you may decide to take a stand with it. But with an average stack, you would be more likely to pass. If you're up against a very short stack who may be taking a stand because the blinds are creeping up on him, you might raise with A-6 to put him all-in. It becomes a judgment call based on your chip status and your table position.

Again, be willing to put the brakes on your aggressiveness at the final table. Sometimes, you can sense when an opponent is planning to check-raise you. If you suspect a trap play which could make a significant dent in your stack, play more prudently. Many times, your opponent at a short-handed table will be very tricky. His deceptive play may force you to tiptoe through the tournament tulips, utilizing your best judgment of his playing style, and occasionally playing with the utmost of caution.

Limit hold'em is a deceptively simple game. It takes only a short time to learn to play hold'em, but it requires a lifetime to master the nuances of the game. I hope this chapter will speed your personal learning curve. ♠

The Wall

Where the Fox and the Farmer Play Poker
by Chuck Thompson

(This article first appeared in Card Player magazine, November 5, 1993, and is reprinted with permission.)

Long-distance runners will tell you that there's a certain point in a marathon, around the 18th mile, when a participant reaches "the wall." At this critical stage of the 26-mile race, the athletes who can deal with the wall separate themselves from those who fall victims to it. It's a when-the-going-gets-tough-the-tough-get-going sort of thing.

A typical table of players in a limit hold'em tournament will start out playing tight. Halfway through the first limit level, as players become more acclimated, play will loosen up and begin to resemble an ordinary $20-$40 game. As weaker players are eliminated and the tournament moves into the third limit level, the table play will toughen up and become equivalent to a $30-$60 game. In the fifth level, the play will be like that in a very tough $75-$150 game.

It's in the seventh level that you reach *the wall*. Only 15 percent of the field remains in contention. Half the remaining players will finish in the money; the other half will have put in a long exhausting day for nothing. At the wall, the average amount of chips in front of each play is about five and one-half large bets.

About 70 percent of the remaining players are *farmers*, bent on protecting what they have and trying to figure out a way to finish in the money. The other 30 percent are *foxes*, energetic speedsters out to steal from the farmers and the other foxes. The foxes, many of whom have familiar winner-circle names, will *not* be thinking about finishing in the money. They will be thinking about *winning the tournament.*

The limit hold'em tournament started with 90 percent farmers and 10 percent foxes. Those farmers who have managed to reach the wall have had more than their share of good luck. The foxes, with their aggressive style and tournament savvy, tend to make their own luck. They have held only average cards but have stolen their way to the wall.

The pot that the foxes have stolen in getting to the wall are peanuts compared to the pots they will now steal at the wall and beyond. A typical table at the wall will be so snug that three out of four hands dealt will have no flop. The foxes will be in fox heaven picking up blind after blind. Each set of blinds represents three-quarters of a large bet, a significant amount when added to an average holding of only five and one-half large bets.

When the final cut is made (around the ninth limit level) and the remaining players are all in the money, half the field will be foxes. There will be a huge sigh of relief from the farmers who have made the final cut. The foxes will now be slightly more on guard lest some of the farmers, who are now in the comfort zone, begin playing out of character and splashing their chips. This guarded period will be a short-lived one, and soon the foxes will be back to their stealing ways.

When the tournament is down to the final four players, usually there will be three foxes and one very lucky farmer. If the farmer's luck can hold up for another hour or so, he just might win his first tournament.

Back to the wall. If you've reached the wall, either through extraordinary luck or some foxy play combined with good luck, you now have to decide whether you're going to be a farmer or a fox.

It is hoped that you'll be at a table with mostly farmers. Your first job is to notice how many chips are in front of the players who have the blinds. If either of these players is nearly all in, you'll need a fairly decent hand to raise the pot. Also, if either of these players previously has shown a tendency to call in the blinds with a weak holding, then you'll need an even better hand to raise, regardless of how many chips the player has in front of him.

Second, look at your own chips. For you to be a fox, you should not let your chips fall below three and one-half large bets, the amount of chips necessary to raise before the flop and still have a full complement of bets for the remaining streets. It's not that you intend to use all these chips. Your hope is that nobody calls. But you need to have the chips so that you would-be opponent knows he can't run you down cheaply. In other words, if you have just three and one-half bets, you should be willing to make your steal-raise with a weaker hand, simply because you must take the initiative in order to keep your chips up and survive another round of blinds. This is where the theme song from *Damn Yankees* becomes meaningful: "You Gotta Have Heart."

And foxes have heart—lots of it. If you think making an opening raise with a poor hand is not worth the risk, since you are so close to being in the money and you might pick up pocket aces the very next hand and win a monster pot, then you're thinking like a farmer. If your chips get down to just a couple of large bets or less, you no longer can be a fox; you will have to hope that you can pick up a decent hand since a confrontation is likely.

Don't let the early positions scare you. You can be a little more selective, but you simply must make your move if you have borderline fox chips. This is particularly true if you have a fox or two on your right, because these foxes will be stealing in front of you, diminishing your late-position opportunities.

If a farmer raises in an early position—heaven forbid—you need a fantastic hand to confront him. If a fox raises in an early position, you still want to have a very strong hand to take him on. Even if you are certain that you have a better hand than the fox, you may very well be outflopped or outplayed. However, if this fox is stealing so often that you don't get a chance to steal, then you're simply going to have to confront him, even with something as weak as A-9 or K-10. If you do confront him, you must reraise and take the lead. You want to give yourself the best chance of winning the pot if you both have nothing.

When you're doing the stealing, you'd like to have a hand with some showdown quality, such as A-x or 3-3. But when you consider the likelihood that you'll win the blinds without a confrontation, it really doesn't matter much what you hold. The fact that you raised is much more important than what you raised with.

While you're gaining confidence and becoming more and more foxlike, and the field is getting smaller and smaller, you might hear some farmers telling bad-beat stories to each other on the rail.

In most cases, these stories will be about some maniac (fox) who raised the blinds in center field with an 8-5 suited and took out the farmer's pocket kings to eliminate him from the tournament.

Sure the fox "got lucky." But remember: *This is the wall!* The rules are different here. Anybody who sits around waiting for A-A, K-K, or A-K at the wall has very little chance of succeeding.

Funny thing about hold'em. Any two cards can win! ♠

Chapter 4

NO-LIMIT HOLD'EM

Hours of boredom and moments of terror aptly describe no-limit hold'em. Sometimes you will play for several hours without entering a pot when, suddenly, you get a hand and shove your entire stack into the middle.

Doyle Brunson calls it "the Cadillac of poker games." It is also by far the most exciting of all tournament games. In fact, it is tournament poker that has kept no-limit hold'em alive. It is seldom spread anymore in casinos (pot limit is far more popular), but when no-limit side games are spread during tournaments, the lineup is often very strong and the games can become awesome.

No-limit hold'em is similar to both limit and pot-limit hold'em, but it is also quite different from them. In limit games, you must follow fixed betting limits and in pot limit, you are restricted to only pot-size bets. But in no-limit, you can fire in your entire stack any time you want to—before the flop, after the flop, on the nuts, on a bluff, even on a whim.

The fact that no-limit hold'em is the featured main event at every major tournament guarantees its survival. But if this were not true, no-limit hold'em would be following in the footsteps of high draw and lowball as a poker dinosaur. When the World Series of Poker had its genesis in 1970, most of the players were road gamblers from Texas. Their game of choice was no-limit hold'em, and so it became the game that determined the world championship.

However, it is no longer the game that most players choose. Limit hold'em has taken its place. You may wonder, then, why tournament poker hasn't changed to reflect current preferences. So long as most tournaments continue to imitate the format of the World Series of Poker, the main event will remain the granddaddy game of them all, no-limit hold'em.

Unfortunately, many players have few chances to get experience in playing this exciting game unless they play tournament poker. Super satellites at Binion's Horseshoe (and multi-table online tournaments) can be valuable learning experiences for players who want to master the nuances of no-limit hold'em. The fact that you are competing for a $10,000 seat in the WSOP main event is incentive enough to attract many world-class no-limit tournament players to the satellite field. For a nominal buy-in of around $120-$220 (plus rebuys for the first hour), novices and less experienced players can learn invaluable lessons from the expertise of these experts.

Early Stage

In big buy-in no-limit tournaments, the first hour of play progresses very slowly, very conservatively (even more conservatively than pot-limit hold'em). The value of slow-playing is more important in no-limit than it is in pot-limit. I am usually very leery of players who limp into a pot from an early position and then put in a sizable reraise when someone raises behind them, because I suspect they may have limped in with aces or kings (probably aces).

When one or more players have limped into the pot, the first raise is usually around three-to-four times the size of the big blind. Some of the more successful tournament players, however, will consistently violate this rule of thumb. Sometimes, they will make a mini-raise of double the big blind, often with just a medium-strength hand they want to gamble with (J♦10♦, 7♥8♥, or small pairs such as 7s, 6s or 5s). They want to create confusion in their opponents' minds by putting in some extra money, hoping to hit it big on the flop.

When I hold A-K, I will often put in a reraise just to define my hand. If the blinds are $50-$100 and my opponent puts in a small $200 bet, I will call the $200 and raise him $600 more to see what he does against my A-K. Ditto with hands such as pocket 10s or jacks. Then if he puts in a gigantic reraise, I will fold some of my weaker holdings because I suspect he really does have a big pair. A big pair such as queens or jacks will make my A-K a slightly less than even-money proposition.

Another liability in playing A-K against a pocket pair is that, even when you get there with your two overcards, you probably won't win a lot of money because your opponent will correctly put you on the ace or king if it hits on the flop and will fold his pocket pair. So the only time you will get substantial action when you hit the flop is when you are either beaten or tied. This is why A-K usually cannot be played for a substantial raise or reraise before the flop. Against a conservative opponent who is willing to jeopardize most or all of his stack by putting in a big raise or reraise after the flop with an ace or king showing, you will often have to get away from your hand.

Small pairs and suited connectors also have a lot of value if they can be played cheaply before the flop. Putting in three to five percent of your stack when you hold a small pair or suited connectors is probably reasonable, especially if you hit a big flop. The problem with suited connectors is that they don't play quite as easily after the flop as does a pocket pair, which is an either-or type of hand. You need excellent judgment when you play suited connectors in no limit. Of course, it is always best to play them in position: the earlier your position, of course, the more vulnerable you are.

Suppose you play the 7♦6♦ and the flop comes 7-5-4, giving you an open-end straight draw and top pair. You could still be in jeopardy because players will often limp in with hands such as 8s, 9s, or 10s. Even though you have lot of potential—a reasonable drawing hand with top pair—if you have to put in too many chips with it, you are almost certainly beaten when someone raises you. It then becomes debatable whether you have enough outs to justify calling the raise.

You may be forced to put in all your chips in an early round when you have to call either a raise or a reraise with a hand such as the one above Though continuing to play may not necessarily put you all-in, it may jeopardize a substantial portion of your stack. Then you will have to decide whether you want to gamble with the hand or just give it up instead. Most of the time, you will need to improve your hand to win the pot. With only about a 45 percent chance of doing that, you will be an underdog against your opponent's most likely hand, so it is usually incorrect to continue.

Of course, if you were able to rebuy, you might be more willing to gamble with it, but it is questionable whether you should do that in a freezeout tournament when your opponent puts a lot of heat on you. Just calling is usually out of the question, because it is such a weak play to put in, for example, 25 percent of your chips on the flop and then fold on the turn. You will usually either move in all your chips, or give up the hand.

In a $5,000 buy-in event, you receive $5,000 in chips with opening round blinds of $25-$50. That is a lot of chips in relation to the size of the blinds. For this reason, players are often willing to mix it up on the flop, even in small pots, if they think they have the best hand. Therefore, the betting sometimes gets out of proportion to the size of the pot, so you will occasionally get a big flop with a medium-strength hand and will have to be prepared to put in your entire stack, especially during the first round of play.

Many times, players will fold strong starting hands because they don't want to risk getting broke in the first round of the tournament. I've even heard of players (not the top professionals) mucking pocket aces against heavy action, because they don't want to risk going out of the tournament first with a hand that is an underdog in a multi-way pot. Sounds absurd, doesn't it?

Unless I thought I was being cheated or cold-decked by the dealer (and I say this in jest!), I just could not lay down two aces before the flop. I would be much more likely to raise or reraise to limit the field, and to shove in my entire stack if I had to.

The fear of getting raced out of the tournament first never enters my mind. In fact, it has happened to me several times. Some of the greatest tournament players are frequently early casualties because they are willing to gamble more in the opening rounds, and they don't care if they are the first player to be eliminated.

Stu Ungar is a classic example of this. He usually tries to double up in the first round and if he doesn't, he's often out of the tourney. After he won back-to-back WSOP titles in 1980-81, he was out of the tournament fairly early in 1982. A lot of times, players like Stu will bomb out when they are trying to bluff or semi-bluff with a drawing hand, and then get picked off when they don't make their draw. Jack Keller is another example of a world class player who frequently goes out early, unless he's playing in a rebuy event. In that case, he often rebuys 'til the cows come home. John Bonetti is also willing to risk his entire tournament fortune as soon as the first hand is dealt and think nothing of it, particularly in a rebuy event.

But even faster players will use their best judgment in a freezeout, and won't just randomly throw money into a pot. However, they are far more willing than some of the "tourist" types of players to jeopardize themselves. These tourist types often play only one or two major tournaments a year, where they like to mix it up with the professionals. Their mind-set is different: they don't want to be the first one eliminated, because of their notion that an early-out carries a stigma with it. I don't think that way at all. If I'm the first one out, so be it. So long as I believe that my decision is correct, I will go with it, no matter what the consequences.

Of course, there is no defense against being drawn out on. Sometimes, when a player is up against an opponent whom he believes he cannot outplay, he will try to outdraw him instead. Say you flop top set and your opponent has a flush draw. Knowing you are a highly-skilled player, your adversary may not want to have to deal with you over an entire series of hands: he would prefer gambling right now with his flush draw, when he has about a one-third chance of making his hand. Since you will find it virtually impossible to lay down your top set, you will have to put in your money if he moves in on you. And he will outdraw you a fair percentage of times. Therefore, this strategy is not totally unreasonable for a player who knows he is not as strong as the competition. He may even win the pot outright if his more skilled, perhaps famous, opponent doesn't have a hand as strong as top set, for example. And if he does get called, at least he has about a one-in-three chance of drawing out on him. He may even break him in the process and wind up with a great story to take home to his friends.

More skillful players, of course, will not usually jeopardize their entire stacks on a draw. But if they think they can run over a player with a reasonable chance of drawing out if they are called, they will go ahead and make an aggressive play. As usual, it takes a lot of judgment.

In most cases, I am not willing to risk most or all of my chips unless I hold a premium pair. But even a pair of kings can be a vulnerable hand because a lot of players will slow-play a pair of aces. For example, suppose you are playing the $5,000 main event at the Four Queens Classic. You start with

$5,000 in chips and the blinds begin at $25-$50, which makes them very small in relation to the number of chips you start with. This means that you have more incentive to try to trap your opponents for extra bets with a hand such as pocket aces. Of course, you also take the chance of getting yourself eliminated with your slow-play tactics by a player who comes in with a hand he wouldn't have played against a big raise, and then gets a lucky flop. But tricky players are often willing to take that risk.

If you hold pocket kings and are up against one of these deception artists who has limped in from an early position, you have to be very careful if he raises or reraises. You will have to make a delicate judgment in deciding what to do with your hand. If you think you're beat, you'll have to lay down your kings.

I witnessed a champion player do just that at the 1992 WSOP final event. Six players advance to the final day's action and at this point in the tournament, seven players remained with Hamid Dastmalchi as the clear chip leader. Mike Alsaadi, a very solid player who had previously announced that he intended to make it to the final day's play, made a gigantic move-in reraise against Hamid, who had raised the pot before the flop with two kings.

Hamid just stared silently at Alsaadi. Mike asked him, "What do you think I've got?" Hamid answered, "I know you've got aces." Although Mike's statement could have been misleading, I believed he had pocket aces. I knew how much he wanted to get to the final day and figured he wanted to win the pot right then and there.

Even if Hamid called the reraise and subsequently lost the pot, he would come out in about third chip position. He also realized that Mike would not have jeopardized his chance of getting to the final day against an opponent who could easily call without damaging himself too badly. So Hamid took those two kings and threw them in the muck. (Mike wasn't lying about his pocket aces: he flashed them to the audience.) I think Hamid made a class fold. Dastmalchi went on to win the championship the next day and Alsaadi finished fourth.

This example points out the vulnerability of two kings in a trap play. Even in the middle rounds, the same may be true because there are still a lot of chips in play in relation to the size of the blinds.

Middle Stage

From the middle rounds on, raising is usually more prevalent than limping. However, if a lot of players are limping into pots, you might as well limp in also if you hold small pairs or suited connectors. But if limping is not the general mode, consider varying your play by bringing in your small pairs and medium connectors with a raise. Don't try this too often, just once in a while when if you are in a middle to late position and no one has yet entered the pot. In a front position, raising with these hands becomes far more risky because if someone comes over the top of you with a raise, you will almost certainly have to fold your hand.

In no limit hold'em, you don't want to play in a totally predictable pattern. Avoid the A-B-C style of play. Don't always play only A-A, K-K, Q-Q or A-K from early position—or 9-9, 10-10, J-J, A-Q, K-Q suited from the middle spots. You may also want to keep your standard raise about three to four times the size of the big blind, no matter what the strength of your hand. If you hold K♥J♥ in middle position, for instance, make the same raise you would if you held pocket aces. This way, you won't be giving too much information to your opponents.

Remember that players will sometimes be deceptive in the amount of their raises. With the big blind at $100, they may make a raise of only $100, which can be a very misleading play. They may be hoping to get played with so that they can play back.

At other times, they may make a small bet just to keep someone else from making a bigger bet. This usually occurs when they have a drawing hand with which they don't want to invest too many chips. They're afraid an opponent with superior position will make a substantial bet if they check, so they make a smaller bet to try to fend off a mega raise. If you think a player is trying this maneuver, consider what your optimum strategy might be. If you believe that a reraise will cause him to lay down his hand, then reraise him. But if you're against a tricky opponent who may be willing to call a pot-sized raise, for example, reconsider your best move. Sometimes, a player will call your reraise in the blind with a decent holding, or with a short stack if he thinks it may be the best hand he's going to get, or even if he thinks you might be making a move at the pot.

The Value of Deception
Deception is important in all stages of a no-limit hold'em tournament. In the early rounds, it is

important because the pots are smaller in relation to the number of chips in play. In the middle rounds when the action begins to escalate, you can't just sit there with a short to medium stack without making an occasional play.

A tight image will help you to take a few more liberties in picking up a few blinds here and there. A loose image and a tall stack can also be a frightening combination, because your opponents may not be able to figure out where you're at. With enough chips in your possession to break them, your opponents may become very fearful of you. Whatever your table image is, capitalize on it. Just be ready to put on the brakes when you come in with a marginal hand and get played with.

Throughout all stages of the tournament, you will be rewarded more for aggressive play than for passive, timid play. Checking and calling will absolutely not take down the money in no-limit poker. You must also remain on the alert for a player who is willing to call with a medium-strength hand in the hope of snapping off a bluff. So be far less willing to try to bluff him than you would a more reasonable, solid opponent. Sophisticated, solid players are usually far easier to bluff because they will make an intelligent laydown. Too often I have seen players literally throw their chips at a much weaker opponent whom they are trying to run over. Time and again, the weaker player ends up with the chips because he is practically bluff-proof. Against this type of unpredictable player, you can value bet but be very reluctant to throw in a lot of money on a stone cold steal. Some players just like to sleep well at night and are willing to become a sheriff to do it. But sooner or later, of course, their more sophisticated adversaries will trap them with legitimate hands by deceiving the sheriffs into thinking they are bluffing when they are not.

Key Concept

The bluff is an important weapon in no-limit hold'em. The larger your stack, the more intimidating your bluff. Sometimes you will see a big stack vastly over-bet the pot, and sometimes they will do it with a legitimate hand. For instance, in the middle stages, with an ante of $50 and blinds of $200-$400, a reasonable bring-in raise would be $1,200-$1,600. Instead, a player with a tall stack, or someone with a medium to short stack who has decided to take a stand, brings it in for $4,000.

What happens when a player makes such a huge over-bet? Often times, they have been bullying the table with medium-strength hands and getting away with it, so they are simply continuing their tactics. This type of player is often willing to go further with his over-bet than a more conservative player. He won't necessarily back off if you decide to play with him. Sometimes, of course, he has a strong hand and hopes you will believe he is weaker than he is. A caller holding A-Q, for example, may decide to take a stand (thinking that the aggressor can't always possess the hands he's been advertising) and unknowingly find himself looking down the barrel of two kings or two aces. When this happens, the aggressive player has a chance of winning a gigantic pot.

It's never easy to make a close judgment decision against an aggressive player. For that reason, aggression can reap a big harvest of chips. Sometimes, however, the aggressor will make what

I believe is a strategic mistake: move in a lot of chips with a big over-bet before the flop, get reraised, and then lay down his hand. Of course, sometimes you do have to fold. For example, suppose you have put in an oversized bet with K♥Q♥. The only other player at the table who could possibly bust your big stack then moves in with a mountainous raise. In this case, you'll simply have to fold.

But what if someone with only a medium stack of around $8,000 decides to take a stand and throw in all his chips when you raise the pot by $4,000. In this case, you would not be quite as likely to give up your K♥Q♥, although you know you are probably taking the worst of it. The pot will be laying you a big enough price (in fact, you have forced it to do just that) to warrant the gamble. Of course, you could have avoided this situation by not overbetting the pot in the first place.

On the other hand, overbetting the pot against short stacks is often correct. You will be forcing your opponents to jeopardize their whole stack, not necessarily before the flop, but after flop when they will have to put in the rest of their chips to continue. This can be a very effective betting tool. Again, the line between mindless aggression and bold, solid play waxes thin.

I have been giving a general description of the different types of situations and styles you may run into in no-limit hold'em. Most of the time, however, you will be playing at a "normal" table, at which there isn't a lot of pre-flop raising. Usually, one player puts in a raise, nobody contests it, and that's the end of it. Nobody is trying to dominate the action or run over the table. In the middle stages, in fact, you can play for a long time without ever seeing a flop.

Occasionally, in a big tournament where you have a lot of chips in relation to the antes and blinds, you will see more limping and more multi-way pots. The more chips you have in these middle rounds, the less willing you should be to play a drawing hand because you don't want to jeopardize your stack.

From the fifth round forward, the action usually consists of one player raising, with either one or no callers. "Raise and take it" is the general rule of the day, which is why I call no-limit hold'em "hours of boredom and moments of terror." It can be exhilarating to have all your chips in the middle with more cards to come when you have either the best hand or the best draw.

It may sometimes be quite correct to just smooth call with big hands such as aces, kings, queens, or A-K, rather than tip off your opponents to the strength of your hand, especially when you are hoping to trap an aggressive opponent who has been involved in a lot of pots. Sometimes, this ploy will backfire when he reraises and the flop comes with an overcard to your pair, especially if you're holding queens, which are more vulnerable than aces or kings. This can be a tricky scenario to play. He may bet into you when the overcard to your queens hits on the flop, in which case you don't know if he bluffing. If you've been able to play the flop cheaply, the less reason you have to continue playing your hand. Again, the smaller the pot, the less cause to get involved after the flop in a marginal situation. You would need an excellent *read* on your opponent to continue.

I once saw Johnny Chan make a class call at the final table of the World Series. He was playing against Irishman Noel Furlong , who won the World

Championship several years later in 1999. Furlong had won many pots by making huge oversized bets. In six-handed play, he was the chip leader. When Furlong made a modest $30,000 pre-flop raise from the big blind with pocket fours, Chan reraised $100,000 more with pocket queens. The flop came K-x-x. On a bluff, Noel decided to move all-in on Chan, but he got a surprise: Johnny called him with his queens, even with the king on board. Chan knew his man and won a gigantic pot by using his innate knowledge of his opponent in making a correct judgment call.

Key Concept

You will have to win with A-K, and you will have to beat A-K to be successful at no-limit hold'em. The action often boils down to players putting in their money with either A-K or a pair, so it often becomes a battle between "big slick" and the pair. The pair is always the slight favorite at around 11.5-10, but with the dead money that is usually in the pot, it becomes a virtual break-even situation. You will see a lot of this coin-toss type of action—and you will have to win more than your fair share of this heads-or-tails combat to be successful in the tournament. Naturally, the more chips you have, the better chance you have to survive these toss-up situations; the fewer your chips, the less your chance.

Against a short stack, you should probably be more willing to gamble in an even-money situation. But with an average-to-medium stack, even-money pots are not to your advantage. With a short stack and the blinds ready to gobble your few remaining chips, the even-money bet is to your advantage with any kind of pair, even two deuces. If you can be the aggressor, you may even win the pot just because of your move-in bet.

In the middle to late rounds of the tournaments (when the blinds and antes are quite high), you will frequently be forced to go all-in, "run the race" as I call it, with a pocket pair. If you can be the aggressor when this happens, you will at least have an even-money chance of winning if you are called by someone playing two overcards such as the A-K. It is important to be the aggressor rather than the caller because you can sometimes win the pot just because you have bet first.

You will be about a 4.5-1 underdog if you're up against an overpair (which is a sad situation to face when you're all in). When you're at the final table and have thus been assured of a payday, you sometimes just have to go all-in in low chip position with almost any pair, because it is usually better to go in with a pair than with suited connectors or two high cards. The trouble with the big cards is that if you don't have precisely A-K or A-Q, and if an opponent calls you, one of your key cards may be tied up in his hand, in which case you could be outkicked. This is why I prefer to take a stand with a pair rather than two high cards.

Late Stage and Final Table

One of the biggest problems of players who have amassed a large stack of chips, especially in the late stages, is not knowing when to apply the brakes. They have often won their big stack with aggressive play, and may have gotten the better end of several of those fifty-fifty decisions

I described earlier. These aggressive players can run into snags if they continue to use the same fast approach they played earlier in the tournament. What happens to them is that they sometimes run into players who are not quite in the money yet have been hanging on, waiting for their shot at a payoff. If they are willing to jeopardize all their chips before the flop, they will usually be doing it with a better hand than they may have played earlier. So the loose raiser who has not adjusted his aggressive style to current game conditions may find himself in danger if someone decides to start playing with him.

Suppose, for example, that the aggressor raises with an A-Q and a shorter stack calls him. Now he is likely to be up against A-K or better, unless his opponent is so short-stacked that he is taking a stand with a lesser hand. (However, even a short stack will usually wait for a hand that is better than A-Q before he goes all in).

I am using A-Q as an example because it can be a very troublesome hand to play in no-limit hold'em. Many, many times, people who go out of a tournament are playing that hand (including myself, I might add!). Doyle Brunson hates A-Q because he says he's lost more money with it than with any other hand in no-limit hold'em. When the ace comes, if you're up against A-K, you're in a world of hurt, usually with a draw to only your kicker. The point is that when a player who has accumulated a large stack in the late stages bombs out of the tournament, it is usually because he has jeopardized himself by not changing gears, by pushing his even-money propositions, and by playing marginal hands he should not have become involved with.

You don't have to become a wimp, of course, but neither do you need to continue being a wasp.

Key Concept

Once you have made the final table, *controlled selective aggression* is of prime importance. But occasionally, you will also see a few "wild cards" make it. This might happen when you have been putting a lot of heat on your opponents and they catch a lucky flop. Even superior starting hands have been cracked by a player who decides to gamble, calls a reraise with Q-9 suited, catches the flop, and snaps off a pair of aces. In fact, that's the best way I know of to win a big pot: play the worst hand and draw out! Of course, this is not exactly a prime tournament strategy, but there is an element of truth to it.

Some of the biggest draw-outs are made by players who don't know where they are at in the pot, or have no idea how few outs they have. Thinking they are in better shape than they are, they sometimes catch their miracle card. *There is no defense against a draw-out.* Even when you flop top set, an opponent with a flush draw will get there one time in three, and you won't be a happy camper when he does. But pouting about it does you no good.

Neither does mumbling about bad beats at the final table. You had to do something right just to get there, so don't expect any sympathy from your opponents . . . they're just hoping you'll suffer another bad beat and become an empty chair. A positive mental attitude becomes especially important when you've had a big draw-out put on you. Maybe you were in a great chip position and now you've become short-stacked . . . but the good news is you're still alive.

Keep in mind that in no-limit hold'em, things can change quickly, for better or for worse. In fact, sometimes you move from the penthouse to the outhouse . . . and sometimes, you go in the other direction! Emotions make bad decisions, so be sure to always make yours with *logic* instead. Of course, if you were playing in a side game, you could get up and take a walk to cool off. Although you have less reason to miss a hand in a tournament, taking a quick stroll when you're emotionally ragged can help you avoid going on tilt. The least you should do is take a deep breath, relax your shoulders, and look for excuses *not* to get involved in the next hand or two.

I defy any player, no matter how skilled, talented and disciplined, who has just taken a bad beat—especially having a one-or-two-outer put on him at the river for a ton of chips—to come back and play the next hand with the same icy calmness he had before the draw-out. We all have emotions: the player who controls his emotions the best, particularly in no limit, has the greatest chance of survival.

Players at the final table are like sharks in a feeding frenzy: They can smell your blood dripping on the table right after you've taken a big beat and lost a lot of chips. They also figure that if you're an aggressive player, you're likely to make a move at the next pot with a mediocre hane, so they are far more likely to get involved. Therefore, if you're lucky enough to get a premium hand such as aces or kings just after a big beat, you have a great opportunity to win a big pot because they may think you're on a steal. I love doing this—making what looks like a steam raise on the very next hand when I have aces or kings in the pocket. But alas, you could get that one cracked, too, and be heading for the door to join your compatriots who have long lists of sad stories to share. Or you can just take it on the chin, shrug it off, and make up your mind to do your best at the next tournament.

At the final table, you will have to wait patiently and then just take a shot with your best hand. Talk about going long stretches without seeing a flop—I've seen the final table at Binion's Horseshoe go as long as 45 minutes without a flop. Then when there finally was a flop, two players were all-in before it hit. So in no-limit play, a lot of the action occurs *before* the flop. In the earlier rounds, of course, there is a lot more play on the flop and the turn card because the pots are usually smaller in relation to the amount of chips in play, and players are less willing to jeopardize themselves with big pre-flop bets. The pots are therefore smaller and there is more action from the flop onward. But as the tournament progresses, there is less and less play from the flop on.

It is often the player with the biggest set of brass balls who has the greatest chance to succeed, but his brass balls can get chopped off if he puts them in the center of the table too often. Again, you must walk the line between *controlled* aggression and *maniacal* speed. This is why players like Bonetti and Keller, who are known to be super fast players, will sometimes crash and burn sooner than they should have at the last table. But they also have a wonderful opportunity to just run over the table, especially when they catch some premium hands while they are playing their loose and aggressive styles of poker. Sometimes, their opponents won't give them any credit for a good hand until they have committed a lot of chips, only to find out a little bit too late that the aggressor has picked the right spot with a legitimate hand. Consequently, the opponent gets crushed.

Your general strategy at the final table should include controlled, selective aggression tempered with a sense for when your opponents are ready to take a stand. Raise just enough to put the heat on your opponent rather than overdoing it, and be willing to put on the brakes when you need to. Even timid players can be bullied only so often before they are willing to take a stand, so you need to time your play so that when they decide to go all-in, they have chosen the wrong time to do it. Timing is very important. It requires a sixth sense, a *feel.* The only way I know to develop a feel for no-limit hold'em is to play it, to let experience be your teacher.

When the action is down to the final three, there is usually a lot of aggressive playing. Hand selection is not quite as strong, of course. Sometimes, you'll have to make an outright play at the pot to pick off an opponent. You might do this on a "resteal," when you think he may be a little weak, and take the lead away from him. Trying to play very conservatively or very tight in shorthanded play when the blinds are huge is not going to work.

Naturally, if your opponents are engaging in raising wars trying to bludgeon each other, you want to avoid them. Even though you may be out-chipped, you still have a good chance of getting heads up with one of them, even if he has three or four times the number of chips you do. Even at a three-to-one chip lead, your opponent is only two hands away from defeat . . . and you are only two hands away from victory. Because the payout usually doubles from third to second, and from second to first, you have every reason to try to survive if you possibly can when you see your two opponents going to war against each other.

A classic example of this occurred at the 1993 WSOP when John Bonetti and the eventual winner, Jim Bechtel, played a gigantic pot when the blinds were $10,000-$20,000. Glenn Cozen was sitting a distant third with less than $100,000 chips out of over $2,200,000 in play, and was only moments away from getting blasted out of the tournament.

With A-K in the hole, Bonetti decided to confront Bechtel, who held pocket 6s. They put in a lot of money before the flop, which came K-6-4. Bonetti made a huge bet and Bechtel called. On the turn, John put himself all-in. Of course, Bechtel won the pot with his set of 6s. This huge heads-up confrontation made a difference of $210,000 in prize money. Cozen took second place for $420,000 and Bonetti won $210,000 for third. Bechtel went home with a million. ♠

Chapter 5

POT-LIMIT HOLD'EM

Pot-limit hold'em tournaments often allow rebuys, with the exception of the World Series of Poker. If a rebuy is allowed, your strategy will need to be modified. (See Chapter 14 on rebuy tournaments.) This chapter assumes that no rebuys are allowed.

In pot-limit hold'em, there are typically three blinds: $5-$5-$10, for example, with one $5 blind on the button, the second $5 blind in the first position to the left of the button, and the biggest blind in the second spot to the left of the button. With this structure, you can bring in the bet for as little as $10 or as much as $40. The biggest bring-in bet in this case is $40, or four times the size of the biggest blind.

Having three blinds is not always the rule, but whether there are two or three blinds should not affect your play very much, except that you can be somewhat more liberal in calling an extra $5 in an unraised pot on the button, because of its added positional incentive. Of course, if you become involved for the extra half-bet and you don't fit the flop, you can always release your hand quickly.

You will be looking for the one correct situation to put in all your chips when you have the best of it to try to double-up. You don't have to win a series of pots like you usually have to do in limit hold'em: you just have to win one double-up pot to be in good chip position.

Contrasts Between Pot-Limit, No-Limit and Limit Hold'em

Comparing big bet poker such as pot-limit and no-limit hold'em to limit hold'em is like comparing apples to oranges. Although they are all in the fruit family, each has a different texture, taste, and feel. Pot limit is more similar to no-limit than it is to limit hold'em. In fact, it is drastically different from limit play.

One difference between pot limit and limit hold'em tournaments is that chip movement occurs at a far more rapid rate in pot limit. Players will frequently double-up early in the first round in pot limit, so that some of the considerations that would not be important until the second, third or fourth rounds of play in limit hold'em become factors much earlier when you're playing pot limit—who has the chips, who doesn't, who may be upset because they have lost some pots, who is doing well, who is doing more gambling.

Players frequently slow-play in pot limit, although not as often as they do in no-limit hold'em. This is because a player who is hoping to trap you with a slow play cannot exert quite as much pressure, especially if you are in the big blind, because he can only raise the pot to $40, for example, when the blinds are $5, $5 and $10. In no-limit play, of course, the raise can be as high as the raiser wants to make it. The first raise in pot limit can be four times the big blind, in contrast to limit hold'em where the first raise can be only double the amount of the big blind.

This means that you have far less reason to defend your blinds in pot limit than you have in limit play. In pot limit, defending with marginal or medium-strength hands in a raised pot can get you into a lot of trouble, so I am usually cautious about defending my blind. But that doesn't mean I will let someone run over me, either. If a player has been raising relentlessly, I will occasionally take a stand with a medium strength hand such as K-J to at least see the flop. With a slightly better hand, A-Q or A-J suited, I may even reraise him to find out exactly how much he likes his hand.

Suited Connectors and Small Pairs

Suited connectors and small pairs increase in value in pot-limit hold'em against even just a couple of opponents, provided you can play the pot cheaply, whereas in limit hold'em, you usually need a volume pot to play them. Their potential to win future bets, especially the big bets that are possible in pot limit, is quite large compared to limit hold'em, where you can raise by only double the amount of the first bet. You can often call a *modest raise* with a small pair or suited connectors in pot limit hold'em, hoping to get a big flop and trap an opponent for all his chips.

The key to this play is "modest raise." You should not ordinarily put in more than 5 percent of your stack on these hands before the flop. Otherwise, the price you pay will be too expensive and the implied odds will decrease. Whereas in limit poker your opponents cannot force you to lay down a draw because they can raise only to a fixed limit, in pot-limit hold'em they can make an out-sized bet which may force you off your draw.

For example, say you flop the nut flush draw in limit hold'em. The bets are $15-$30, the pot was raised before the flop, and a couple of players called the raise. You hold A♦8♦ and flop two diamonds, giving you a 35 percent chance of making your flush with two cards to come. Or suppose you hold K-Q and the flop comes J-10, giving you two overcards and an open-end straight draw. You have a 32 percent chance of making the straight, and with two cards to come, the pot is usually laying good enough odds in limit hold'em for you to continue to the river.

This is not the case in pot limit, where an oversized bet could force you to commit 50 percent or more of your chips on a 2-to-1 draw. Even a nut flush draw usually cannot be played for profit when you have to jeopardize that many of your chips to draw to it. As an example, say you have A♦Q♦ in a late position during the early stage of the tournament when the blinds are $5-$5-$10. An opponent brings it in for $40 with one caller, and you decide to also see the flop. With three people in the pot for $40 each, plus $20 from the blinds who have folded, there is $140 in the center. The flop comes K♠9♦4♦, which gives you the nut flush draw and one overcard. Your overcard may not be that strong, however, since your opponent is likely to have raised with A-K. The raiser brings it in for $140, the size of the pot, and the other player folds. What is your best play?

If you began with $500 in chips and you have already put in $40 before the flop, you will have only $320 left if you call the $140 on the flop. If you don't catch a diamond on the turn, it will cost you the rest of your chips if the raiser again bets the size of the pot. And of course, with only one card to come, your chances of making the flush are substantially less than the 2-1 odds you had with two cards to come. You simply will not be getting the right price in this situation, and so you should fold on the flop.

Key Concept

This example illustrates the concept that once you decide to play a hand in pot-limit hold'em, it is usually incorrect to call a pot-sized bet on the flop if you are not prepared to follow through on the turn. In essence, your opponent is not betting you just the $140 on the flop—he is betting you your entire stack. This is why you want to get in cheap on drawing hands; you usually cannot justify putting in all your chips to draw to them. Therefore, these types of hands go way down in value if you have to wager too much on them.

There are times, of course, when you might prefer to continue in spite of your reduced odds: if your opponent is short-stacked and you hold a tall stack, or if you are short-stacked and he has a lot of chips, for example. Another time you might call is when you decide to gamble by calling on the flop, with the intent of betting on the turn card if your opponent checks to you, whether or not you have made your hand. In this case, you are simply trying to make a play at the pot, rather than attempting to win on the strength of your hand. If that is part of your thinking, you might call the $140.

I am usually glad to take a free card on the flop when I have a drawing hand and my opponent(s) check to me. It often makes more sense than firing in an aggressive bet while the pot is still small. Also, I can avoid falling into a slow-play trap that an opponent may be trying to spring. Although betting my hand to try to pick up the pot when I think no one will call is also a legitimate strategy, I am usually more willing to take the free card on the flop and do my gambling later.

Key Concept

Because you get such large implied odds with small pairs and suited connectors when you get the right flop for them, they have more value against fewer players in pot-limit hold'em than they would have in limit poker. But again, the key is that they must be played as cheaply as possible before the flop, with an investment of no more than about 5 percent of your stack.

Tight Play in Pot-Limit Tournaments

Players sometimes have a phobia against rebuying in pot-limit tournaments and therefore they play excessively tight, often coming in with only aces or kings. This isn't the optimal way to play, of course, but a good case could me made for tight, conservative play when the blinds are small in relation to your starting stack of chips, giving you less reason to gamble. Although this approach won't give you enough opportunities to win a big stack of chips, it will allow you to last longer.

In pot-limit hold'em, you will occasionally be forced to gamble when you don't hold the absolute nuts . . . if you hope to win the tournament. In fact, you will be putting yourself in jeopardy with less than the nuts during all stages of the tourney. To repeat, you can't make an omelette without breaking some eggs. This means that you will sometimes have to play a drawing hand aggressively when you think you can get your opponents to fold.

Traps and Bluffs

Not only are there far more trap plays in pot-limit hold'em, but there are also many more attempts to bluff. A player who might have called the flop for a single bet with less than a premium hand in limit hold'em will often be very reluctant to call a pot-sized bet in pot limit. For example, an aggressive opponent sitting in first position brings in the pot for $40 (when the blinds are $5-$5-$10). You have been dealt pocket nines and decide to call. The flop comes Q♠7♥4♣, so there is one overcard to your pair and no flush possibilities for your opponent. This is a fairly reasonable flop for your hand which you might continue playing against a single opponent in limit hold'em. But when your opponent makes a pot-sized bet, you will have a difficult time calling him with two nines in pot limit.

If you decide to raise him, you will jeopardize your entire stack. If he thinks he has you beaten, he will probably call your bet or reraise. If he doesn't have the queens or a higher pocket pair such as aces or kings, there are only two other possible hands he could have you beaten with: jacks or 10s. Your bluff raise representing queens may throw him off the pot, but how can you be so precise in your ability to read him that you can put him on jacks or 10s? You can't, and so you would be taking quite a risk in bluff-raising him. If he plays back at you, you won't have enough chips left to bet on fourth street and so you have put yourself in a terrible dilemma.

The usual result of such a dilemma is that you must back down against an aggressive player.

The same holds true if you hold an overpair to the flop. Suppose the flop comes 8-7-4 when you are holding those pocket 9s. Your opponent again fires in a pot-sized bet on the flop. A lot of times, he will do that on a bluff, but he may also be betting with a legitimate hand, especially if he is an early-position raiser. Now what do you do? Again, you will be in a dilemma. Remember that when he bets the size of the pot, he is, in essence, betting you your whole stack, because it is not logical to call the flop unless you intend to follow through on the turn. Suppose you call on the flop and another 4 comes on the turn. Again, he bets the size of the pot. You certainly can't put him on trip 4s, so the only hand you can beat is a bluff.

You can see from these examples that the only time you should probably raise an aggressive opponent on the flop is when you believe you have him beaten. Your raise should be made on the strength of your hand.

With small to medium pairs, you are hoping to flop a set and trap an opponent for all his chips. They usually play much better than suited connectors because, with the connectors, you must usually make a draw whereas with low pairs you either flop a set or you don't, in which case you can get away from your hand cheaply. Therefore, I am somewhat more willing to commit slightly more than the standard 5 percent of my chips with low pairs, but not with suited connectors.

Far fewer decisions and much less judgment is required to play the pairs than is needed to play the connectors. For example, if you flop a pair with your connectors, or if you have a flush draw as well as a straight draw, you must count your outs and calculate your odds to make an expert judgment as to whether they are favorable enough to continue to draw, especially when aggressive players are yet to act behind you. So playing suited connectors presents far more problems after the flop than pocket pairs. Even J-10 suited, which is a premium drawing hand, cannot usually be played for more than 5 percent of your stack, although if you are playing in a rebuy event and are prepared to exercise that option, you might increase that percentage somewhat.

Early and Middle Stages

The play during the first and second rounds of pot-limit hold'em tournaments is usually conservative and solid, although this is not a universal rule as some players will be playing faster, so it is important to pay strict attention to the playing styles of the opponents you are facing at your table. Limping into pots is more frequent than it is in later stages.

During the middle stage, players generally raise far more often than they limp in. "Raise or release" becomes the general mode. You may play for long stretches, maybe for 20 to 30 minutes, during the middle and late stages during which you won't even see a flop. Someone raises and that's the end of it: no one contests it.

If raise-and-release becomes the general format at your table, be wary if you are on a steal or a semi-steal and someone calls. For example, suppose you believe that your opponents are playing too conservatively and so you decide to take advantage of their tight play by betting or raising from late position with a medium-strength hand such as K-J suited. An opponent on the button calls. Now you must proceed cautiously on the flop.

Hands like K-Q, for example, can be big trouble makers in raised pots. A-J, and A-Q also go down in value in pot limit. K-J, which most players realize is a trouble hand in limit hold'em, is even more troublesome in pot limit. Whereas A-Q may be a reasonable calling hand against a raiser in limit poker, you are usually better off to give it up in the same situation in pot limit, because it is simply too risky to play. More players are drummed out in pot-limit hold'em with these types of hands than with almost any other kind of holding, with the possible exception of pocket jacks or queens, which also have a nasty tendency to be only 11.5-10 favorites against an A-K.

You will often have to put in a substantial amount of your chips with big pairs like jacks and queens, only to find you're up against an A-K, against which you are only a slight favorite. If the overcard comes on the flop, you will have a difficult time continuing with the hand, particularly if an opponent bets into you. So jacks and queens are very vulnerable . . . and you usually win either a modest pot with them, or you lose a giant pot to overpairs.

I am not advocating that you never play jacks or queens, but that you play them with discretion. Just remember when you hold them that in big-bet poker, players often like to limp in and then just smooth-call with aces and kings in order to set a trap for lesser pairs. Such a trap is often difficult to detect: you have to know your opponents. What I really enjoy is being in a situation where I can trap the trappers by smooth calling with a big hand and then hitting the flop perfectly.

Playing A-K

A-K, which can easily be played for a raise in limit hold'em, is in some jeopardy in pot-limit games. A typical example is when an early position limper and one other limper have entered the pot. Sitting on the button, you decide to raise the pot with your A-K. Now the first limper comes over the top of you for a maximum pot-sized reraise. It's into the muck with your A-K. Why? Because what could he possibly be raising you with? Aces, kings, or possibly A-K? If he has jacks or queens, you are possibly even-money. But if he has kings, you will be in disaster city if a king comes on the flop.

Even worse, what if an ace comes on the flop and he holds pocket rockets? In either situation, you will have a difficult time releasing your A-K after the flop. This example illustrates the point that you should not necessarily be willing to bet all your chips just because you hold an A-K.

Playing with a Short or Medium Stack

When you hold a short to medium stack during the middle stage, you will often have to gamble with less than premium hands. When an aggressive player raises, especially someone who has been playing a lot of hands, you may decide to take a stand with a pair of 10s, for example, by reraising and putting yourself all-in. You hope that you can win the pot before the flop, or at least be even-money against two higher cards. Of course, if you're up against a bigger pair, you're dead unless you flop trips. But because you're short-to-medium stacked, you'll have to win a pot sooner or later anyway, so a pair of pocket 10s is a reasonable hand to take a stand with.

By the middle stage, there are usually several players who have amassed substantial chip accumulations. Also, players tend to get eliminated faster than they do in limit contests. It is not at all unusual for half of the field to have been eliminated by the third round of play if no rebuys are allowed. The result is that the average stack size is double the size of what you began with. In fact, many players will have stacks that are seven to eight times the size of their starting chip count, with around $4,000 already, after having started with $500 in chips. This happens because you cannot withstand very many pot-sized bets without winning one or two hands. Otherwise, your stack will become so eroded you will be in immediate danger of bombing out of the tournament.

Because of this characteristic of pot-limit hold'em tournaments, strategies you would ordinarily wait to employ in the late rounds become important earlier in the middle rounds. Keeping track of your opponents' chip counts, who has tightened up, who has loosened up, and which ones are just playing A-B-C rock-solid poker becomes very important.

Late Stage

The late stage begins at about the sixth round of play, sometimes even the fifth round if the tournament is already down to two tables. 80 to 85 percent of the field has been eliminated and you are now within firing range of the final table and a good payday.

By this late stage, a handful of players usually have massive accumulations of chips, with a much smaller number of contestants possessing survival types of stacks. A lot of players will be jockeying for position, looking to double through once or twice to catch up with the leaders of the pack. You can catch up much more quickly in pot-limit hold'em than you can in limit play, but you can also go down the drain far more rapidly.

You must continue playing a solid game, concentrating to the max. You cannot afford to become discouraged or to give up if you lose a hand or two, and your chip position is suffering from erosion. A lot of heart and the courage of your convictions are requisite to hanging on for a win. If you are positive your opponent is making a move at you and that your hand is better than his, you will simply have to muster the courage to take a stand, even if it puts you all-in.

If you have one of the big stacks, do your job: hammer the smaller stacks into submission as often as you can. Don't play gigantic pots against other big stacks with less than premium hands. Beware of confrontations with bigger stacks, if you can at all avoid them. With a medium-strength hand, you do not want to get involved with a taller stack.

Some players have a "homerun" attitude in these late rounds, and they are willing to risk a strike-out to make the final table. With a big stack in front of them, they are willing to mix it up against another tall stack because they know that if they win, they will have an overwhelming chip position. Then, if they successfully make it to the last table, they will have a commanding stack of chips. But the downside is that the homerun hitter risks getting raced out of the tournament early and may make only a minimum payday when they could have gone on for a much higher payoff.

If homerun playing is part of your philosophy, by all means mix it up with the large stacks. But generally, you may be better advised to inch up the pay scale rather than trying to take by the yard. I don't usually like to get involved for big bets against another large stack with hands like K-J, A-J, K-10 suited, or K-J, K-Q. If I decide to raise before the flop with one of these marginal hands and am called by a big stack, I will proceed cautiously after the flop, even if I flop top pair.

Sometimes, too, you will be trying to avoid another big stack, but he isn't avoiding you: he wants to mix it up with you. If this happens and he begins making some plays against you by raising with marginal hands, you may be forced to battle with him sooner than you anticipated.

Usually, however, you will prefer to wait for a premium hand, A-K or better. Or you might try to trap him with a small to medium pair if you don't have to put a lot of chips in the pot before the flop. Suppose you are playing against a very aggressive player who has a big stack and is constantly trying to run over you and your equally tall stack. You might be willing to put in more than 5 percent of your chips with a medium pocket pair, hoping to hit that set and either bust him or double through him. Of course, you might have to lay down your hand if an overcard comes on the flop and he bets into you. But investing just a few extra chips with your pocket pair may be worth the risk.

The point is to neither encourage a big confrontation with another large stack nor to play like a wimp, either. Sometimes, a player with a big stack will be playing a solid, conservative game rather than a more aggressive one. In this case, you can occasionally raise with a medium-strength hand just to pick up the blinds. If he calls you, he will probably be holding a premium hand, so use your best judgment in deciding how to proceed on the flop.

Playing at the Next-to-Last Table

Suppose you have made it to the third table in a two-table payoff tournament, or to the second table in a one-table payout tourney. Expect the play to be very, very slow and conservative until players are in the money. Once they come into the money or when the blinds double, the contenders seem to hear a bell ring heralding the start of a marathon to the center. The dull, tedious style of play that was putting many of the spectators to sleep suddenly becomes "wham-bam" poker, with players moving into the center so fast you wonder what has happened to their psyches.

Many of the short stacks who have been lagging behind in the race are now gambling with weaker hands than they have previously played. Sometimes, you will have to join them in this faster mode of play, because your opponents are coming in with slightly weaker hands and you don't want to get run over. But if you just have an average stack and will have to commit all your chips with a medium-strength hand, back off. However, if you can be the aggressor and put a short stack all-in with your mediocre hand, be willing to do it.

Once again, your relative chip count is an important factor in how you play, as is an evaluation of your opponent's strategy. With so much happening in the late stage, you have to play double-sharp.

The Final Table

If you have made it to the final table, you are probably there with a decent amount of chips. But even if you don't have a tall stack, you will usually have enough chips in proportion to the size of the blinds to wait patiently for a good hand. Since each rung you can advance on the pay scale will assure you of more money, you might be more willing to inch up the latter with more conservative play.

This conservative style will increase your chances of a better finish, but may jeopardize your opportunity to win the tournament. If you are the homerun hitter type who prefers to mix it up and gamble because you don't mind coming in eighth or ninth so long as you give yourself a maximum chance to win, that's okay, too.

I generally like to take a middle-of-the road approach. I want to slide up the pay scale, but I won't play so ultra-conservatively that I jeopardize my chances of winning the tournament. The majority of the prize money, of course, is in the top three spots and I want to give myself an opportunity to grab one of them. But I don't want to do it at the expense of playing a lot of weak to medium hands, or making inadvisable bluffs and semi-bluffs, and thus risk bombing out when a more diligent approach will at least put more money in my pocket.

Suppose you have made it to the last table with $5,000, so you still have a lot of chips in relation to the blinds, which are $300-$600 with a $100 ante. You are in first position with pocket 7s. Because of the favorable ratio between the size of your stack and the size of the blind, you can afford to wait a while longer for a better hand to play.

You may play differently, of course, if you are sitting either next to or on the button, and no one has entered the pot, in which case you might bet with your 7s or even with a mediocre K-J. But from front position with a short stack, when you have to go through several players, the risk is far too great. Remember, too, that other players are far more willing to gamble against a short stack than they are against a big stack. This means that you can expect to get called most of the time when you are short-stacked.

Now imagine that you are in bad chip status—you have around $2,000—and are looking at that same pair of 7s in first position. In this situation, you can be more willing to jeopardize yourself because your 7s figure to be better than the random blind hand you will get on the next deal. You can still make a pot-sized bet with some expectation of winning the pot before the flop, or if someone with two overcards calls, you will be at least even-money.

Once again, remember that if you have to put in a pot-sized bet, you are actually jeopardizing your entire stack if someone makes a move that would force you to put in the rest of your chips. I prefer a more conservative approach, because it decreases my chances of having that happen.

Playing Shorthanded

In shorthanded play, you will be doing far more raising than calling. In general, calling in pot limit is usually a big mistake unless you are slow-playing a big hand. Therefore, if your hand isn't worth a raise, don't get involved in a pot.

With three or less players, of course, you will frequently be raising with medium strength hands and, depending on your evaluation of your opponents, you may be calling with less than premium hands.

For example, you might call with A-10 to defend your big blind, or even play back at an aggressive opponent who has raised the pot, when you would not have done that in earlier rounds. To repeat, you need less strength three-handed than you do in a full, nine-handed game. Also, be aware of trap plays. Just because the game is shorthanded doesn't mean your opponent doesn't have a legitimate hand.

In conclusion, if you want to go for the jugular and take your chances of bombing out earlier than you could or should have, that's fine. Or if you prefer a more conservative middle-of-the-road approach, then play that way and try to outlast a few more opponents by waiting a little longer for hands that offer better potential for winning. With a short to medium stack in pot-limit hold'em tournaments, you have to walk the tight rope between gambling too soon or waiting too long. A tremendous amount of judgment is necessary to pull off this balancing act.

Again, the fine line is drawn. This is one reason why players so often make deals on the end. When there are such huge differences in prize money between the top three spots, it often makes sense to make a "save." Of course, if you have an enormous bankroll and just don't care, by all means, go for it. Nothing says you have to negotiate. Just remember that players often catch up quickly in pot-limit games.

In my opinion, pot-limit hold'em requires a high degree of skill, though perhaps not quite as much as no-limit. Nevertheless, you need a tremendous amount of judgment to win at it. In fact, you need far more skill and judgment in pot-limit hold'em than you do in limit poker, because you are often jeopardizing your entire stack rather than only a fixed bet or two. To take home the prize, you need to be right most of the time. ♠

18 DOS FOR POT LIMIT HOLD'EM
(This article first appeared in Card Player Magazine on January 26, 1990.)

Following are some hints or "dos" you should find helpful when you play pot limit hold'em.

☞ Do be aggressive with big pairs in early positions.

☞ Do limp in with small pairs and suited connectors in loose games that do not have a lot of pre-flop raising.

☞ Occasionally raise with small pairs and suited connectors just to mix up your play and confuse your opponents.

☞ Limp in once in a while with aces under the gun so that you can reraise any raiser.

☞ Occasionally just call a raise with aces instead of reraising, especially when you are heads-up against an aggressive player.

☞ Usually bet top pairs with good kickers or overpairs on the flop, especially in heads-up play.

☞ Remember to check-raise once in a while. You must not let your opponents think that when you check, they can automatically bet and take it.

☞ Occasionally bet strong drawing hands such as nut flush draws into several players. You want opponents to know that you will bet come hands.

☞ Be prepared to put in all your chips occasionally . . . on a draw only. You need to let your opponents know that you can't always be run off of your strong drawing hands.

☞ Do bluff . . . especially heads-up against timid players.

☞ Do cultivate a loose-aggressive image by being selectively aggressive. Act loose, but play tighter than your loosest opponents.

☞ Do study the opposition when you are not actively involved in the hand. This is often the best time to study them because you can be more objective.

☞ Do be courteous and friendly to opponents— and then bluff them when they least expect it.

☞ Do be prepared to have as many chips on the table as the largest stack. The only exception is when you are trying to hit and run by buying in for the minimum in hopes of doubling through once or twice before quitting.

☞ Do try to be as intimidating as possible at the table so that your opponents will get into the habit of playing passively and checking to you with hands they should be betting.

☞ Remember the object of any poker game is to win money, not pots.

☞ It's okay to enjoy the game, but never forget that your real goal is to make money, not just play a lot of hands so you can stay in perpetual action.

☞ Do play happy or don't play at all. ♠

16 DON'TS FOR POT-LIMIT HOLD'EM

This article first appeared in Card Player Magazine February 2, 1990)

☞ Don't stay married to big pairs when it becomes obvious that your hand is in trouble. Divorce it fast!

☞ Don't feel that you must continue playing a marginal hand after the flop. If you're holding A♦5♦ and you flop an ace, consider laying it down if a solid player bets into you.

☞ Don't routinely fold marginal hands just because you get raised by an aggressive player. Study the board and remember that come hands are often played strongly by aggressive opponents.

☞ Don't be a sore loser when you get drawn out on by a bad player. He will find many other ways to lose back his temporary gain to you . . . *unless* you antagonize him. Then he may start playing tougher against you because he's angry.

☞ Don't forget what has transpired at the table in previous hands. Be aware of who may be on tilt, or who is playing either looser or tighter than normal.

☞ Don't be afraid of getting bluffed. It happens to all good players more often than it does to bad players (that's usually why they are bad players).

☞ Don't play marginal hands such as small pairs and suited connectors in extremely loose games where most pots are raised or reraised before the flop.

☞ Don't be intimidated by either the players or the size of the game. If you are, you shouldn't be playing in the first place.

☞ Don't lose more in one game than you can win. Remember that it's not a good game for you if you are losing.

☞ Don't play in a bad game just because it's the only game in town. There is usually an alternative, even if it is for smaller stakes.

☞ Don't always fold marginal hands such as K-J suited because of a raise from a player on tilt.

☞ Don't succumb to peer pressure in private games if you are not comfortable with what is being suggested, or if you have reason to believe it would work against your chances of winning.

☞ Don't be afraid to quit when you believe it is appropriate, no matter if you are winning or losing. There's always another game.

☞ Don't put a limit on what you want to win, but always limit your losses.

☞ Don't be afraid to put a live straddle on a pot once in a while, whether or not any of your opponents are doing it, to liven up the game.

☞ Don't be afraid to alter your opinion or *read* on an opponent when future betting rounds indicate he can't be holding what you originally put him on. ♠

Continuing**Chapter 6**
ACE-TO-5 LOWBALL
(With the Joker)

Lowball is becoming a poker dinosaur. You seldom find it spread anymore, except in California where it was a mainstay until seven-card stud and hold'em games were legalized. Since then, its popularity has been steadily waning among players new to cardrooms, so that the people who play it in Southern California's card barns are usually an older crowd.

Still, it is a World Series of Poker event which attracts a faithful following, many of whom repeat their visits to the winner's circle, attesting to lowball's stature as a game of skill. Although I don't believe it requires as much skill as seven-card stud or Texas hold'em (nor is it as financially rewarding), lowball does have a certain amount of play to it.

Lowball tournaments are slow-paced compared to hold'em or stud tournaments because lowball has only two betting rounds. As a result, players don't get eliminated as quickly as they do in other games.

What would be considered a mediocre stack in a hold'em tournament is usually a fairly decent stack in lowball. As an example, if you have $1,000 at the $50-$100 limit in lowball, you have a competitive amount of chips because the fluctuations are not as great as they are in hold'em or stud, where a $1,000 stack would be only average.

Therefore, although your chips accumulate at a slower rate in lowball, they also disappear less rapidly. Of course, this doesn't mean you won't get eliminated. But it does mean that after three rounds of play, when around 50-60 percent of the players have been eliminated in a hold'em tournament, only about 35-40 percent have been washed out in lowball.

Typically, lowball is played with three blinds: the smallest one is on the button, with the two larger ones in front of the button. These three blinds are intended to stimulate the action. In a $500 buy-in tournament with $500 in chips, when the opening limits are $15-$30, the blinds will usually be $5 on the button, a $10 small blind, and a $15 big blind.

If you hold a 7-or-better hand, you must bet it after the draw or forfeit any subsequent action, a "California lowball" rule which carries over into World Series play.

However, tournament rules are different from side-game play in one major area: in most ring games, you are not allowed to limp in, referred to as "gypsy in" in lowball. In other words, you cannot simply call the blind—you are forced to come in for a raise. In tournaments, you *can* gypsy in for the minimum bet of $15, for example, or raise it to $30. All subsequent raises must be in $15 increments before the draw, and in $30 increments after the draw.

Hand Selection

The earlier your position, the stronger the hand you need to enter the pot. In the first three spots behind the big blind, most seasoned players will not play anything less than a one-card draw to a seven.

Sometimes, you can win the money with a pat 9 or 10, but you're in jeopardy if you play this type of hand from early position. When I enter the pot with a pat 9, it's usually a 9-7 or better so that if I get a lot of pre-draw action, I can always break up the 9 and take a one-card draw to a 7 or better.

Rough 9s or 10s in very early position are death and destruction in lowball. If there is a lot of pre-draw raising, they should be routinely passed. There are times, however, when you can play them in correct position and under the right circumstances; that is, either on the button, next to it, or two spots away from it.

If a person raises in front of you when you are holding a hand such as 9-7-4-3-joker, you have a good hand to reraise with because of your multiple options: (1) You can force out the other players behind you who have marginal hands; (2) Even if one of them cold-calls for two bets, you can usually safely break the nine and draw one to your 7.

Although you are not a favorite to have your hand hold up against two premium one-card draws, if the first player raps pat, you can discard the 9 and draw one. Very likely, the third player will also draw one, since very few players will cold-call a double bet with a two-card draw. But if the first player draws two, you may rap pat because the player behind you may have either a pat 9 or 10, or need to draw one card.

In general, avoid two-card draws, although there are certain situations when they may be correct. This usually occurs when you have two babies and the joker in the small or big blind against a late position raiser. But if the raise comes from a solid player in first or second position, be more inclined to pass. It is usually better to give your opponent credit rather than give him cash.

Another time you may consider playing a two-card draw is when you are on the button with three wheel cards and nobody has entered the pot . . . especially if you have the joker working for you. In this case, you may even raise because you have several options for playing the hand. If one of the blinds decides to reraise, you are almost forced to call, draw two, and hope for the best. Usually, they will reraise with hands such as rough 9s or even an occasional 10, and then rap pat hoping you are on a two-card draw. But fortunately, since they are often forced to play conservatively after the draw, if they check a pat 9, they will be also be forced to pay you off if you have made your hand. If you are up against a very, very conservative player, you may even try to bluff him, although I wouldn't usually try that because he will often simply grit his teeth and call you.

Some players are so conservative, they won't even draw one card to a rough 7 (such as a 7-6-5-2 or 7-5-4-2) in middle position. But I believe they are playing too tight. Sometimes, when I am in early position, I will decide to play a one-card rough 7 if it seems like the price will be cheap. And occasionally, I will limp in with a one-card draw to an 8 if there have been one or two players who have limped in ahead of me. When two players have limped in, one of them will often have a two-card draw. You need to have a *feel* for these occasions. In lowball, you are always playing your opponent and your position as much as you are playing your cards.

Early Stage

You've probably heard the common jingle, "In lowball, this advice holds true: don't draw to an eight, and don't draw two." Generally, this is fairly good advice, although there are times when you must draw to an 8 or draw two cards.

A very solid approach to the game is necessary throughout a lowball tournament, especially in the early stages. This means premium one-card draws to a 7 in early positions (the first three players to act after the big blind); premium one-card draws to an 8 in middle position; and somewhat more liberal standards in a late position. You can usually play one-card draws to an 8 with the joker working, plus pat 9s if the pot hasn't been jammed.

Occasionally, you'll see players limp into a pot with a fairly strong hand in tournaments. Usually they're just trying to get some extra action. For instance, you gypsy in with a smooth 7 such as a 7-4-3-2-A, a rare pat hand, and hope that someone will raise behind you so that you can open it up yourself with a reraise. But in the majority of cases, players who enter a pot bring it in with a raise.

Therefore, you might be a bit more on your guard when players gypsy in, because it usually means one of two things: either they have a very strong pat hand, or they are a little bit weak (maybe they need to draw one to an 8, or perhaps they have the joker with a couple of wheel cards and are looking for a cheap two-card draw).

Your basic strategy in the opening stages is not very different from the way you would play in a side game. However, that will rapidly begin to change. Once the first round is over with, some players will have increased their stacks by 50 percent while others will have lost half their chips. You must become very aware of the stack status of your opponents and take that into account before you enter a pot.

As is true in all tournament poker, big stacks should attack small stacks whenever possible. You should not tangle with the big stacks unless you have a premium hand—definitely not with a marginal hand or with a marginal drawing hand, which so many of your lowball hands are. The big stacks are the players who can punish you the most severely with their hoards of chips.

Be willing to take slightly the worst of it if you can break a player who doesn't have enough chips to play the hand through to the showdown. You should be willing to gamble more *only* against a medium or short stack, hoping you can eliminate them. Even if you fail to do so, you probably won't get seriously hurt, so you can take more latitude against them.

Many lowball players are very conservative, and they tighten up even more in tournaments. Therefore, the earlier the raise in front of the big blind, the more inclined I am to give them credit for a hand.

Some players are such rocks, there is dust under their chips! So if one of them dusts off one of his prized chips and puts it in the pot, be leery of him. He usually has either a very strong starting hand or a very solid draw. Rocks don't usually get enough quality playing hands to accumulate enough chips to survive in tournaments. Their approach is simply too conservative. It is better to strive for a happy medium between too tight and too loose.

Key Concept

You'll see most of the really fine poker players release a lot of hands, but when they do come into a pot, they bring it in with a raise. This is especially true in lowball tournaments where there is a limited amount of action because it has only two betting rounds. Professional lowball players play aggressively before the draw, trying to force out marginal hands such as rough 9s or 10s, or to prevent them from being too aggressive if they enter the pot. Selective aggressiveness is the key. Too cautious an approach, although it will help you last a little longer, is not going to bear winning fruit.

Middle Stage

Although you may occasionally play a less than premium hand against a short stack, for the most part you should be playing a reasonably solid game. Most of the time, you will be drawing to 7s, and occasionally to a smooth 8 or an 8 with the joker working against a late position raiser who may or may not have a better hand than yours.

If you become too liberal and start raising with pat 9s or 10s in early position, you will run into trouble because you can't bet them with any degree of confidence after the draw. Suppose you are holding a 9-6 and have decided not to break it. A player will often check an 8 to you and pick off your 9-6 when you bet. Or he may bet into you himself. Now what do you do? You're put to the "guess test:" has he made his hand or not? It's a judgment call.

The majority of the time, however, a player who bets into you after you have rapped pat is not bluffing. Your opponent doesn't know how strong your pat hand is, so if he has enough nerve to bet into you, be suspicious. You don't need to fold all the time, of course, because a lot of people know that it is common for a player to reraise before the draw with a 9 and then stand pat. So if they make a hand such as an 8 or a smooth 9, they will sometimes bet into the raiser. Even if they have a slightly worse hand than yours, they won't be fearful of a raise unless you have a pat 7.

Occasionally, you can use this situation to your advantage. Suppose you're up against a player who is capable of drawing one card and then betting an 8 into your pat hand. If you think he's making a play at the pot, you can put in a raise with your 9, a rather tricky and delicate maneuver. Most of the time, of course, you won't raise because if he didn't make his hand, he can't call your raise anyway; and if he has something slightly better than your 9, he may decide to pay you off. What you are really hoping is that your opponent will lay down his hand, thinking that your pat hand probably has his 8 beaten. Obviously, a lot of judgment is necessary to make this type of play—you must know your man, and he must be capable of folding his more marginal betting hands after you raise.

Ace-to-5 Lowball

To win a lowball tournament, you must successfully bluff another player from time to time. This usually occurs when your one-card draw to a 7 has busted and your opponent checks to you. If you've paired or have drawn a king, for example, he may have made an even worse hand and pass; or he may decide you hold the better hand and pass. Some players are liberal about paying-off after the draw, so you have to know your opponents. If a player is bluff-proof, never try to bluff him . . . not once, not ever. Instead of trying to run over them, value bet your marginal hands against these calling stations because they will pay off a lot of your bets.

I am most likely to fire a bluff-bet after the draw when I have made a total bust—I've paired 7s, for example. Even if my opponent has also paired, he probably has me beat so I can't win in a showdown; therefore, I may try a bet instead. But if I'm against a calling station, I will simply give up my hand rather than bet it.

I once made a mistake at the final table of a lowball tournament in which my opponent had been winning a lot of pots. I hadn't played against him until the final table, so I didn't know he was capable of doing what he did. We both drew one card; I paired up; so did he. Because he was first to act, he checked to me. I decided to try to pick up the pot at these very high limits, $2,000-$4,000 with only six players remaining, to put myself in a more competitive position. So I fired a big bet at him. The son-of-a-gun called me with a pair of deuces! He won the pot, and then went on to win the tournament. Crippled, I busted out in sixth place.

I should have known better. If he were capable of calling with a pair, he was virtually bluff-proof. You simply cannot run over players like that. Personally, I thought his play was very poor, but whose play was worse? Mine for trying to bluff a player I didn't know, or his for making the call? I have to place the blame on myself for not reading my opponent better than I did.

Because there are only two betting rounds in lowball, you sometimes have to put a in lot of pressure on the first round of betting to get players out of the pot. If your chip position has eroded, perhaps because you have just been in a holding pattern against the escalating limits, you will sometimes need to commit with less than a premium hand and hope for the best. You may even decide you have to make a stand with a hand such as a pat 9-8. You might raise in middle position, get called, decide not to break your hand to draw to an 8 against an opponent with a probable better draw, and then decide your best play is to simply rap pat.

If your stack is down to only one bet left, you may decide to go ahead and bet if you're planning to call anyway. Or maybe just make a crying call against a bet. You may ask, "If you're going to call, why don't you just bet the hand yourself?" Because, with a pat hand such as 9-8, you will probably lose against a caller. Do you think a player would call a pat hand with a 10? Not too likely, particularly if you both rapped pat before the draw. If he also has a pat 9, his 9 is probably better than your rough 9-8; otherwise, he would have drawn a card. If that's the case, it's too bad for you.

He may try to move you off your hand, however, if he suspects what you have, and if he thinks you may fold. Since many of my usual opponents know I am capable of laying down a hand, I will sometimes just grit my teeth and call them. (Lowball players probably have the smoothest teeth in the cardroom . . . they have to grit them so frequently!)

In another situation, suppose your opponent is a rather liberal player who is playing rough 9s and 10s. He brings in the pot with a raise against your 9-8 and you decide to call rather than reraise. He raps pat. Now what do you do? Try rapping pat behind him. If he has enough nerve to bet into you, which he often will, you may suspect he is a bit weak and decide to call. Some players will take it a step further: they won't reraise with a 7, for example, because they don't want their opponents to know the strength of their hand. They also may not want the other players to break a pat 9 or 8, and possibly beat their 7 on the draw.

A deceptive ploy such as this may also trick the blinds into protecting their weaker hands. One of your opponents may stand pat with a 9 or 8, thinking that because you didn't reraise, you will probably be drawing a card. Your flat call has confused them. When you rap pat, the players after you are in a dilemma: should they draw or not? Sometimes, the player who is first to act will even decide to bet into you after the draw if they think you have an inferior hand. Then you can raise them with your cinch hand. By this time, the pot is probably rather large and they may decide to pay you off. But even if they don't, you still have their money in the pot. This is a standard lowball play.

There are enough opportunities for deception in lowball to give it some intrigue. Unfortunately, since you are not allowed to check-raise, your arsenal of deceptive plays is depleted. Personally, I think lowball would be a much better game if players were not forced to bet a 7, and could check-raise. But those are the dinosaurian California lowball rules that have been around since time began. And since most of the lowball players are dinosaurs themselves, we're stuck with these rules and simply try to make the best of them by being as clever and creative as we can.

Late Stage

When the tournament winds down to two tables with around six players each, you will need to enter the pot with more marginal hands than in the earlier stages. Virtually any one-card draw to a 7 is a raising hand, and you will be playing most one-card draws to an 8 in these late-stage, shorthanded games.

At the last two tables, some of your opponents will be playing more conservatively. If you see that they are just trying to survive to the final table, you can often make great inroads toward victory by taking a slightly more aggressive posture than they do. Although you might be concerned about being picked off by one of them, that's a chance you sometimes have to take.

From my years of tournament experience, I have learned that when players are in their survival modes in the final stages, they are very reluctant to defend their blinds with less than solid starting hands. So you can take a few more liberties against them. For example, you may decide to run a total bluff, which is called a "snow" in lowball parlance.

I try this tactic from time to time, but not so often that my opponents will figure out what I'm doing and be able to stop me by reraising. I usually like to have five cards that are 7-or-better, but maybe I've paired a couple of them leaving me with two 2s, two 5s, and an ace in my hand. With this type of hand, I know I have several key cards other people probably need to draw to improve their hands in the event that they call my raise and decide to draw one or two cards. I don't recommend trying to snow very often—usually, against only one or two opponents when you can rap pat behind them. Then you can bet after the draw when they check to you.

Occasionally, someone will make his hand when you are trying a snow. He may either bet into you, or raise if you are the first to bet. Unless he's a clever player who may be making a devious play, you will have to pass. Your only other alternative is to put in a very dangerous reraise, hoping he's on a total bluff. However, not too many players in this late stage will raise on a total bluff against a pat hand. Therefore, if you're up against players who are capable of making such a play, you probably should not try to snow.

When only a couple of short-handed tables are left, another good opportunity to snow occurs when you are the first to enter the pot. Most players will respect the pat hand and will be very careful about calling. If they improve their hands to only a 9 or 10, they have to make a very tough call, and your snow will work.

The snow also works especially well when your opponent sits in front of you and draws two. In this case, you can rap pat with a variety of hands: K-Q-3-4-6, for example. If one of the blinds calls the opening bet and then draws two, you can rap pat and then bet when he checks to you after the draw. In most cases, the blind will not call your bet, even if he didn't pair but made a 10 or jack, for example. This play also works well in a standard eight-player ring game, but it is particularly powerful in short-handed tournament action.

Key Concept

The final two tables are where you are doing some serious jockeying for position to make it to the last table with a lot of chips. Your play at this stage requires more judgment than you have used in the entire tournament. I have blown tournaments by playing too cautiously or conservatively at the second table. You can't make an omelet without breaking an egg, and you can't win a tournament without taking chances. Sometimes you must play less than premium starting hands, especially in short-handed play. Your opponents, of course, are also less likely to have premium cards, so less strength is required to either defend or attack a blind.

Key Concept

It is far better to be the attacker than the defender, as is true in all tournaments. You have three ways of winning when you are the aggressor: (1) you can win without a contest when your opponents give up; (2) if you are called before the draw, you can win by betting on a bluff after the draw; (3) you can also win by outdrawing your opponent and showing down the best hand. The only negative possibility is losing after the draw when your opponent makes a better hand than you do and calls your bet. With three positive outcomes and only one negative one, it is clearly better to be on the offense than on the defense.

Final Table

Suppose you have played aggressively at the last two short-handed tables, and have had enough of your hands hold up to make it to the final table. Now you must put on the brakes because you are in a full game again, which means there is much more possible strength out against you. Therefore, the quality of the hands you play during the beginning action at the final table will need to be stronger than they were in the previous short-handed action.

Key Concept

More tournaments have been lost by players with big stacks who failed to slow down appropriately than for any other cause. Beware of this trap. In a full game, you cannot recklessly run over your opponents, although you may have been successful with those tactics earlier. Adjusting your play to existing game conditions is what separates the men from the boys (or the women from the girls).

Against homerun hitters such as John Bonetti and Jack Keller—players who try to win all the chips as soon as they can, who try to grab the big pots, and who are reckless in endangering their stacks (even against other big stacks)—I recommend a more conservative approach. Try to slide up the pay scale one rung at a time. Be content to let the big stacks battle it out against each other, hoping one of them will become crippled enough for you to slide past them on the pay scale. Since the money escalates as each player is eliminated at the final table, naturally you are interested in picking up that extra prize money, no matter if it is only a few hundred dollars. So I suggest holding back your aggressive nature just a bit, being less willing to jeopardize your standing with marginal hands.

If you have a premium hand, you don't care who your opponents are. In fact, you prefer to play against a bigger stack because you hope to either double through him and take a commanding lead yourself, or put a serious dent in his stack.

When you're down to the last three or four contenders for the title, you are usually either raising the pot or releasing your hand immediately. Raise or release: these are almost always your only two choices. You will be limping in with very few hands unless you are slow-playing. You can put a dent in your opponents' stacks at these high limits by simply scooping up the large antes and adding them to your stack. So don't be too unhappy when you win without a fight before the draw.

Eventually, you must become more liberal in defending your blind. You can definitely defend with any one-card draw to an 8; or if you hold the joker, you can defend with a two-card draw to a 6-or-better. Other two-card draws are probably too risky to defend with. You can raise on the button with some two-card draws and with any pat 10 or 9 if the other players have passed.

At the final table in the big tournaments, you will be playing a totally different kind of lowball than you would in a normal side game. You have to take a few more risks, mixing up your play and defending your blinds with less than premium hands. Still, there is a fine line between overly aggressive play and solid play. If your opponents know you're playing too aggressively, they will lay in the weeds for you. They won't contest as many pots, but when they do, they'll probably be a favorite over anything you have raised with. So be leery of giving them too much action or trying to bluff them if they do decide to take a stand.

Key Concept

The bottom line is that good play helps you get lucky. What happens on the play of one hand often affects the course of the entire tournament for you. Losing one hand can cause you to lose an entire series of hands which you may not have otherwise played if you had not lost that one key hand. In order to recoup those lost chips, you may find yourself having to gamble more than you want to with less than premium hands because you are short-stacked and in danger of going out if you don't take a few more risks.

Conversely, if you have won a few lucky pots and have substantially increased your chips, you can play the part of the bully more often against the short stacks who are barely hanging on to survive. But even then, you must use good judgment, a trait you cannot learn from books alone. Judgment requires tournament experience and introspection.

Opponents often change their styles of play when the chips positions change, especially at the last table. At these times, you have to tune in to their thinking processes, "get inside their heads." You need to be thinking not only about what your opponent holds, but also what you think *he* thinks you are holding. Then you must act accordingly. Nobody can teach you this skill; you must learn it in the solitude of your own poker mind. ♠

Chapter 7
DEUCE TO SEVEN DRAW, NO-LIMIT

Deuce to seven draw (sometimes called Kansas City lowball) is Southern by tradition and is still played in private games in parts of the deep South. It is always spread in the side games of major tournaments where it is played for huge amounts of money by a strong coterie of world class players who are comfortable playing it against each other. Except for this elite group, however, it is seldom spread.

Only a few tournaments offer a deuce to seven competition each year, the World Series of Poker being the foremost. The buy-in ranges from $1,000 to $5,000 with rebuys for three levels, which puts it in a unique category of its own. Its rather exclusive "clientele" is primarily composed of high rollers who love the game.

Although it is usually played for high stakes, I believe deuce to seven would be far more popular if smaller stakes tournaments were held to give more players a feel for the game. Perhaps tournament directors would be wise to follow the example set by the super satellites of no-limit hold'em, which players are able to enter for a comparatively small buy-in of $120 with $100 rebuys for the first hour. In this structure, less experienced players are able to study the habits of world class no-limit competitors.

Aces are high only in deuce to seven, and straights and flushes count against you, so the best possible hand is 2-3-4-5-7 of mixed suits. It is played with an ante and blinds, which usually escalate every hour. Traditionally, only five players get paid rather than the entire final table because fewer than 50 players usually enter a deuce to seven draw tourney.

Even though deuce to seven draw is played primarily by a rather elite clique of top players, it isn't really a very complicated or mysterious game. There is a lot of play to it, however, and the fact that it is always played no-limit means that it does require additional skills. The pace is much faster than limit ace to five lowball. You also have more betting options, including the check and raise.

Its no-limit format also means that players use slow-play and trapping ploys rather frequently. Sometimes, they flat-call with pat 7s or 8s, which will almost always win the pot. The immortal hand, 2-3-4-5-7, of course, can't be beaten, only tied. Although you don't catch it very often, you do catch other 7s.

Bluffing

The big bluff is king in deuce to seven draw. Although a solid, conservative approach is usually the most productive, you also must add flair to your game plan. You will sometimes have to try to win a pot after you have missed your hand by bluffing your opposition out of the pot.

Value Betting

Value betting is also very important—judging how much to bet to extract calls from your opponents when you think you have the best hand. 8s and 9s will win most of the time, and 10s will also frequently take down the chips. Occasionally, something worse than a 10 will also win. But generally speaking, when a lot of money goes into the pot, particularly after the draw, you need a solid hand to win.

As in ace to five lowball, there is a lot of action after the draw in deuce to seven. But it has a couple of features which are different from its lowball cousin. First of all, you can check and raise, so players will sometimes check what they believe is a cinch hand hoping you will bet so that they can move in a big raise on you. Secondly, you cannot gypsy in: you must come in for at least twice the size of the big blind. If the ante is $10, the small blind is $50, and the big blind is $100, you must come in for a minimum of $200. (The usual bring-in bet is three to four times the big blind.) This stimulates action, but also requires that you take a solid approach to the game.

Sometimes, of course, you'll come in on a total steal. In this case, it doesn't much matter what your starting hand is because you're just trying to make a play at the pot. Generally speaking, though, you'll be doing more value-betting and raising than stealing or semi-bluffing.

Two-card draws are not the greatest strategy in this game. Suppose you're in either a late position or are on the button with a hand such as 10-9-5-3-2. You fire in a raise, hoping to pick up the pot, and get called. Your opponent then raps pat. He may be slow-playing a better hand than yours and is trying to create confusion in your mind, or maybe he actually has a slightly worse hand than you do and is trying to get you to break. Now what do you do? You probably wouldn't want to put in a lot of money with a 10-9 after the draw if both you and your opponent stand pat and he fires a big bet your way. There is a lot of tricky play in deuce to seven draw; it is not a game I recommend for beginners.

Premium draws to one-card 7s or one-card 8s are the types of hands you want to enter the pot with. You can also play pat 9s and 10s in late position when it is less likely that you will be raised. If you play a rough pat 10 in early position for a raise and then someone comes over the top of you, you will usually be caught in a dilemma as to what to do next. So you must be somewhat selective as to the conditions under which you play these types of hand. This doesn't mean you have to routinely pass them, but you will need to be careful with pat 10s in early positions. If it's an extremely rough 10 such as 10-9-8-5-4, be inclined to pass it completely.

A lot of chip movement is characteristic of deuce to seven draw, especially in the first rounds. Therefore, *if you are not prepared to rebuy*, you must be patient and wait for that one good, solid hand that will give you the best chance of winning before you seriously commit yourself. Ideally, you will be more patient than your faster opponents who are willing to gamble more frequently and who are intending to rebuy. Definitely pass rough 10s in a front position and don't fully commit on any kind of drawing hand, even a hand as good as 2-3-4-7-x, in which you are drawing one card to a perfect 7. Certainly you would play it, but you may not want to put in all your money before the draw since you are not going to rebuy.

If rebuying is a part of your strategy, however, you can take a more liberal approach to the game and be willing to take a few more chances. You should include your rebuy policy into your predetermined game plan. If you have decided to rebuy, it makes more sense to rebuy *early* rather than late. The later you are in the rebuy rounds, and the more chips your opponents have captured (especially the better players), the less incentive you have to rebuy. It becomes similar to chasing good money with bad.

For example, suppose you're competing in a $1,000 tournament with $1,000 rebuys. You are in the third round of play (the final time to rebuy) with 20 minutes before the end of the round. Suddenly, you get broke. Looking around, you see that several of your highly skilled opponents have chip counts in the $4,000-$5,000 range. You have less incentive to rebuy for $1,000 in chips because if you make the rebuy, you will probably also want to take the add-on option for another $1,000. So now you're talking about investing another $2,000 in a situation in which you will be out-chipped by two- or three-to-one after the add-on, and five-to-one with only a simple rebuy. That doesn't sound like good mathematics to me; it is sometimes better to just cut your losses, instead.

But if you have a big bankroll, a lot of heart, and you want to gamble, go ahead and indulge yourself. If you make a mistake in tournaments, it is usually better to err on the side of chips . . . it is better to have too many chips than too few . . . if rebuys don't bother you and if you're prepared to make as many of them as you need to stay in the action. If this is your attitude, then go for it. But from a realistic viewpoint, you are probably taking much the worst of it when you continue to rebuy and add on in spite of the fact that your skilled opponents will still have you significantly out-chipped.

Because only the final five players usually receive a payout in deuce to seven draw, instead of the last one or two tables, you will have to take more chances to make it into the money. Whether you rebuy or not, a very solid approach to the game is necessary. So you will have to take a few chances with less than a perfect hand or in order to either win or steal enough chips to survive long enough to give yourself a chance to get lucky and win the tournament.

When you make the final five, you have to do a lot more raising than calling. Pat 10s will usually have added value because there are fewer hands being dealt. It is not unusual to see two contestants go the center for all their chips with pat 10s when it's down to so few players. Naturally, of course, you would prefer a 9 or an 8. In fact, you should have little hesitation in committing most of your chips with a pat 8, and none whatsoever with a pat 7. Of course, even pat 8s can be beaten by running into either a 7 or a slightly better pat 8; or someone who draws and makes a 7 or a better 8 than you do. They are not invincible, but they are usually worth a substantial bet.

It usually takes less time to complete a deuce to seven tournament because of the smaller number of participants, so it is often over in 8 to 10 hours. Clearly, it is a game in which expert judgment and a good evaluation of your opponents are required—

when it is correct to move in with a marginal hand or with a snowing hand, and when to play a little more cautiously are important decision points. Reading about the game's strategy will help you, but only experience and participating in deuce to seven draw tournaments can give you a winning *feel* for the game. ♠

Chapter 8

LIMIT OMAHA

Competing in an Omaha tournament can become one of the most exciting poker adventures you'll ever have. The pots are frequently multi-way, the action is heavy duty, and the drawouts can be devastating. It takes a lot of heart, tons of discipline, and more than your share of luck to be a winner at this highly volatile brand of poker.

In 1992, I won the World Series of Poker championship in limit Omaha. That was the year I came back from a nine-to-one chip deficit to defeat Berry Johnston in heads-up play at the final table. It was also the first time two World Series champions had gone toe-to-toe in another game. *Card Player* magazine featured a photo of me and my dog, Suki, on its cover, which made me very proud. The 1992 WSOP title was my fourth one, as I had previously won at razz, limit hold'em, and no-limit hold'em. I also won the Limit Omaha title at the *World Poker Finals* at Foxwoods Casino in 1994.

Hand Selection

The importance of hand selection in Omaha cannot be overemphasized: all four cards must be working together in some fashion. Occasionally, you may deviate somewhat with a hand such as A-

A-10-4, but even in this hand there is some potential for both a wheel draw and a high straight draw. Virtually any pair of aces is worth playing before the flop, no matter what your sidecards, but trip aces in your hand indicate a clear-cut pass (as do any set you are dealt). Three aces with one suit is marginal at best, although you might consider playing it in late position *in an unraised pot only* and hope to hit your suit or the case ace on the flop.

In the early stages of an Omaha tournament, most people are playing very solid poker. Therefore, three-card hands such as K-Q-J-2 of mixed suits are simply unplayable. You might, however, put in the extra half-bet with such a hand from the small blind just to see the flop, or an extra full bet from the big blind *when* there are a lot of callers in a single-raised pot.

You can see the flop for a minimum bet from a very late position when you are holding a three-card straight such 9-8-7-2 with the deuce suited. You don't *have* to call, but you can call with this type of marginal hand. Anything weaker than this, of course, is unplayable. Again, what you really want for a starting hand in Omaha is four cards working together or big pairs, preferable suited or connected.

Early Stage

There is literally no blind-stealing in the opening rounds of Omaha tournaments. Solid raising only is the norm. Hands that have aces or kings; or two kings with a working ace; or big cards such as A-K-Q-J, K-Q-J-10, A-Q-J-10, are usually worth a raise.

Playable hands also include any four middle connectors such as 10-9-8-7, suited or unsuited, or even with a gap in them (10-9-8-6). I would not want to play them when the pot is jammed before the flop, but even then I might if I figure that the players doing the raising are holding aces and kings, making my hand live because of its middle suited connectors. I usually wouldn't raise with this type of hand, unless I am in late position when no one else has entered the pot and I decide to take a shot with them.

Blind stealing is not a very viable option in Omaha, because four-card hands have so many possibilities that players will find enough playable hands to defend their blinds most of the time. Blind stealing is out: value betting is in.

Other playable starting hands include 9-8-8-7, 6-7-7-8, 10-10-9-8, Q-J-J-10. Sets are frequently flopped because of the number of pocket pairs in players' hands. Therefore, be cautious when you flop a set and there is a lot of action on the flop because you may be against a higher set.

When you have a flush or straight draw, be wary if the board pairs. Usually, it is not a good idea to continue drawing to your straight or flush because if someone has made trips before the board paired, he has you beaten with a full house. Generally speaking, then, don't draw to a straight when the board is suited, and don't draw to either a straight or a flush when the board is paired if there is any substantial action.

In Omaha you will generally have to show down a hand in multi-way pots. It isn't that you can never bluff; once in a while, you can. For example, you can occasionally represent a hand you don't have when there are two suited cards on board, you have two pairs, and your two opponents check to you when the third suited card hits. You can bet, but if you get called you should probably be done with it, because sometimes a player will check and call with a medium flush, fearful that the nut flush is out against him, but nonetheless determined to pay off the hand.

Occasionally, there will be a flush possibility on board when you hold two pairs plus the ace of that suit, so you know that nobody holds the nut flush. In a case like this, you can sometimes fire a bet into your opponents on fifth street if the board doesn't pair, especially when you are last to act and they have all checked to you. Just remember that it is fairly easy for your opponents to call a single bet on the river. Of course, sometimes you will be bluffing with the best hand: your two pairs will hold up.

Sometimes, you will be holding a hand that makes top pair with two three-flushes on the flop. Even though it's about 22-1 that you will make either of your flush draws, the hand may still be playable for a possible profit.

For example, say you are holding A♦K♦Q♠J♠ which you brought in for a raise before the flop. You have two callers. The flop comes K♠9♦7♣. A wraparound straight draw could be out, or maybe two pair with a straight draw (10-9-8-7). You rarely have the best hand on the flop, but with two other players in the pot, you could certainly bet your hand and see what they do.

If you get raised, it is worthwhile to take off a card with your two three-flushes, top pair, and an inside straight draw working for you. If a straight card such as a 5 or 6 comes on the turn, it is probably best to give it up because one of your opponents could have made a low straight, or at least two pair. But if no one bets or raises aggressively, and if the turn card is either a diamond or a spade, the pot size justifies your drawing to the river. Although you probably should not bet the hand, you can either check-call or take the free card.

Middle Stage

Use selective raises against shorter stacks in the middle rounds of Omaha tournaments. If the blinds are short-stacked and no one has entered the pot, you might raise with a hand such as Q-J-10-9, which is a hand you may have just limped in with earlier in the tournament, preferring to do your gambling after the flop instead of before it. But when you have won a good stack of chips and are playing against shorter stacks in the middle stage, if you can be the first one to enter the pot, bring it in for a raise or don't play the hand at all.

If you are short-stacked yourself, your strategy should be to wait for two things: a reasonable hand and a multi-way pot. What is a reasonable hand in these situations? Hands such as 6-6-7-8, 6-7-8-9, 4-5-6-7 or even 3-4-5-5 would qualify. Of course, with a hand like 3-4-5-5 you have to be more careful, especially if a higher straight is possible. With any straight draw, you always want to be sure you are drawing to the nuts. Otherwise, the card which makes your straight may make a higher straight for an opponent and cause problems for you (such as losing your entire stack!). The only exception you might consider is when you are heads-up. In that case, it is less likely that your single opponent will be drawing to a higher straight than you are.

Another play you might make is to either raise or reraise when you are holding big pairs, especially when you have a short stack. You want to either isolate the action against only one other opponent, or drive as many other people out of the pot so that you will have only one or two other players to contest the pot against. Your big pair will hold up much better shorthanded than it would in a multi-way pot.

If your big pair is kings or queens, you will have much greater strength if you hold an ace kicker. When you have the ace in your hand, it is less likely that you will be up against an overpair. Furthermore, if you pair the ace, you may still have the best hand. The same is true if you hold queens with a king kicker.

Big pairs also play better against fewer opponents than they do in multi-way pots. Suppose you hold a big pair and raise before the flop, but your aggressive play still does not drive many other players out of the pot. Now you are at a disadvantage, and you are just hoping to hit your pair and make a set on the flop. Or if your pair is suited to another card, you hope to make a flush or a draw to the flush.

A very strong hand is an overpair to the flop (when there is no obvious straight on board) and a draw to the nut flush. This is a hand you can definitely bet or raise with, and with which you will probably get some action.

In summary, if you have a short to medium stack, you hope to play a big multi-way pot, preferably unraised before the flop. But even if it is raised, you can continue with a reasonable hand such as four connecting cards, or a pair with two connecting cards (particularly if they are also suited). When you can get four or five to one odds for your money, these types of hands can give you a good chance to get back in contention if you make them.

Even when you lose the pot with these hands, if you began with a medium stack you still will not be out of action. At least you will have given yourself the opportunity to win in an optimal situation and return to a competitive position with some chips

You have to win a few multi-way pots in an Omaha game in order to accumulate enough chips to be considered a competitor. Multi-way pots that are contested to the showdown are the rule rather than the exception in high Omaha. You have to give yourself the opportunity to show down the best hand on the river by entering and winning some of them.

However, if you have lost a few of these multi-way battles and have wound up with a short stack, still don't push your panic buttons. You will probably still have enough time left to wait for another round or two before you have to make an all-in commitment. You will usually find some sort of decent hand to play by then, even if it is only one big pair with two random side cards. If you do find such a hand, it is still better—even with a short stack—to play the part of the aggressor to give yourself a chance to be heads-up and to possibly win without any improvement.

Of course, you hope to hold aces, kings or queens in these situations because jacks are too vulnerable, unless you hold J-J-A-K or J-J-K-Q. It is too easy for your opponent to hold two or three overcards to your jacks. But if you are down to your case chips and will have to post the big blind in a couple of hands, you may very well decide to take a stand with jacks, or with four connecting cards such as 10-9-8-7 or 10-9-8-6.

These types of holdings figure to be better starting hands than anything you are likely to be dealt before you are forced to play in the blind. So if you have enough chips to put in a raise, do it in an attempt to limit your opposition with these types of hands. With only one or two players in the pot, it is possible that you can win it with only one or two pairs when you are holding four connectors such as the 10-9-8-7 mentioned above, whereas two pairs usually aren't good enough to hold up against five or six opponents.

Late Stage and Final Table

Your strategy in the late stage is to raise whenever you enter the pot, especially against a short stack. You must also continue to play *solid* starting hands only, even with a big stack. With so many potentially good starting hands, it is easy in high Omaha to get caught up in the late stage action with a big stack and begin playing too many hands. But good judgment dictates that you protect your big stack and try to build it even higher to progress to the final table in a highly competitive chip position. So limit your gambling primarily to those occasions when you can go against a short stack and possibly damage him severely or knock him out of the tournament.

Key Concept

Don't gamble too aggressively with a large stack. Even in the late stage, you still must play solid poker. You cannot try to run over the whole table just because you have a big stack and your opponents don't.

If you have a medium to large stack at the final table, pressure the smaller stacks as much as possible when you enter the pot. When you are playing against an equal or larger stack, base your decisions primarily on the value of your hand. The bigger your hand the more willing you can be to mix it up with equal or higher stacks. With a hand such as a pair of aces double-suited, for example, you don't mind playing against a larger stack because you know you have the best hand before the flop with premium drawing opportunities, even if you don't flop a set of aces.

When you are heads-up or shorthanded, usually play very aggressively. Either raise the pot before the flop or fold. One exception to raising before the flop is when you hold middle connectors, although you can occasionally raise with them, also. With a hand such as 9-8-7-6 you can sometimes limp in just to see the flop when the pot is either three-way or possibly even heads-up. You don't want to get involved with a lot of pre-flop action because if the flop comes with overcards or a higher straight possibility, you will have to release your hand and get away from it early. Still, against a shorter stack, you can be more inclined to raise with your 9-8-7-6 and continue dominating the table because you have a reasonable hand.

Defending the Blind

Playing the blinds correctly can become quite a problem at the final table. Big pairs are definitely worth defending. I may not necessarily reraise from the blind with kings or queens because they are more vulnerable, particularly when I am first to act after flop, although I would probably reraise with aces. I might also defend my blind for one more bet with any four connectors, or three connectors with a pair (7-6-6-5). If I don't like the flop, I fold my hand.

Now, suppose you have defended your blind with J-J-10-8 and the flop comes 7-4-2. Some players would come out swinging with their overpair, but this is usually not the best strategy. Against any type of substantial action, you usually cannot continue playing past the flop. Your opponent could easily hold a higher pair, especially if he raised on the flop, so you usually need some type of drawing hand, in addition to your overpair of jacks. Occasionally, however, you can make a stand with pocket aces.

An exception to taking a stand with your pair of jacks against the same 7-4-2 board occurs when you are short-stacked with only enough chips left for one more bet and so is your opponent; or when he is short-stacked and close to all-in, but you are not. But even against short stacks, some hands are hardly worth defending the blind. Say you have a weak hand such as Q-9-7-4 of mixed suits, which isn't much of an Omaha hand. You don't want to give too much action with such a minimal holding even against the short stacks, because you could be offering them a chance to double-up and get back in contention. Pass also if you have been dealt high trips with a suited connector, such as Q-Q-Q-J.

You might consider giving some action to a short stack from your big blind position if you are holding two pairs which are connected or suited. You may even call a short stack's raise with a hand such as 4-4-3-3, which is a hand you wouldn't otherwise play from any other position *except the big blind.* But it might be worth your while to take a chance on flopping a set or a weak flush draw with such a hand, *if* you can break your opponent. It is also a hand which is very easy to give up once you have seen the flop come with overcards or other damaging draws. ♠

Chapter 9

POT-LIMIT OMAHA

In the mid 1980s when Omaha was at its peak of popularity, many players said it would become "the game of the future." But because of the higher luck factor attendant to games in which you have a nine-card hand as opposed to a seven-card hand, many of the top players began losing to the lesser lights in the poker firmament more frequently than they liked. Of course, in any poker game, the more skilled players will win in the long run. Those people who can best analyze their opponents' hands and react properly based on the accuracy of their reads, will have potentially great rewards.

High Omaha is a complicated game to master and because its popularity has dwindled, the hard-core of players who support the Omaha tournaments are usually very sophisticated. Of course, that is not always true, because Omaha is the type of game that also attracts gamblers. Not as many side games are spread anymore, and when they are offered during the big tournaments, the lineup is frequently very strong with no *live* action in the game (few or no weaker players). So you will usually see a purely professional ring of players in these games, with no one having much equity.

With such equal talent facing off against each other, it is usually the player with the most patience and the biggest bankroll who ends up with the money. Naturally, these are the same players who have the best opportunities in the big Omaha tournaments because they are willing to rebuy enough times to stay in the action until the cards begin breaking their way.

Today, Omaha high-low enjoys far greater popularity than high Omaha; and limit Omaha is more widely spread than pot limit, because pot-limit Omaha usually has very high blinds so that only the deep pockets will usually play it. For this reason, pot-limit tournaments have become tougher and tougher to win, even though the field of opponents you must wade through is much smaller. The strongest of heart, the keenest of mind, and the longest in patience . . . these are the players who usually prevail.

Personally, I think pot-limit Omaha is the most exciting of all tournament games except for the main event, no-limit hold'em. If you like high action, having to make close judgment calls, sweaty palms—and if you have a gambling spirit in your soul, pot-limit Omaha is ready to put you to the test of both character and skill.

My highest finish in a World Series of Poker pot-limit Omaha tournament was third place in 1984. I have won other big tournaments, however, including the 1989 $2,500 buy-in event at Binion's *Hall of Fame*.

Differences Between Pot-Limit and Limit Omaha

Pot-limit Omaha is substantially different from the limit version of the game. The big bluff is king. Premium drawing hands are often favored over sets, so you have be willing to fully commit with big wraparound straight draws that are also accompanied by a four-flush. In the absence of a pair or a flush on board, you will frequently be applying a lot of pressure in pot-limit Omaha because you are trying to win the pot on the flop. Even if you get called, you are probably a favorite, no matter what your opponent holds. In contrast, you would play the hand more slowly in limit Omaha.

Pot-limit Omaha tournaments, including the WSOP, almost always allow rebuys for the first two or three rounds, while limit Omaha events do not. Unless you have entered the tourney cheaply because you have won a seat in a satellite, or have decided to take just one shot at it without rebuying, much of your tournament strategy will be dictated by whether you are willing to rebuy. The more prepared you are to rebuy, the more willing you can be to gamble on straight and flush draws, making moves at the pot, or moving into the center when you have a big draw. If you are not prepared to rebuy, the less commitment you should make on drawing types of hands.

For example, you might decide to gamble before the flop by raising with a hand such as Q-Q-J-10 if you are planning to rebuy, but you would be less willing to gamble if you are not going to rebuy (you would rather see the flop cheaply).

Or suppose you are holding aces and several people have limped into the pot. If you hold something like A♠A♥Q♥9♠, which has two flush and straight possibilities, you might raise before the flop. But suppose you have a hand that is somewhat weaker than that: A♠A♥J♦9♣. In this case, you should be more reluctant to make a huge pre-flop commitment if you are not planning to rebuy. Instead, you should probably just limp in to see if you can hit a big hand on the flop.

Pot-limit Omaha players usually make their pre-flop raises with big pairs, most often with aces. This makes it easy for your opponents to read you and to alter their play accordingly. From the flop onward, they have more knowledge about your hand than you have about theirs. Therefore, occasionally mix up your play by raising with four connecting cards such as Q-J-10-9 or 9-8-7-6, suited or not, to achieve some deception. Frequently, your opponents won't put you on the correct hand after the flop, thus giving you an advantage if you hit it.

The Value of Deception

Deception often plays a major role in pot-limit Omaha, where you have much larger implied odds with the right flop than you have in other types of poker. You may have a chance to either double through or break another player, which is far less likely to happen in limit Omaha. In the limit version, players will have to call only an extra bet or two, but in pot limit, they may have to commit their whole stack just to make a call. They will be far less likely to do this in marginal situations, so if you get a caller when you have made a big pre-flop raise with aces, expect to be up against another premium hand.

Early Stage

There is a lot more chip movement in the early stages of pot-limit Omaha than there is in limit Omaha. This happens because there are so many potential starting hands and because the flop can hit several players who have strong drawing hands or sets. Therefore, players often go to the center early in pot-limit tournaments.

For example, suppose you are holding aces double-suited and bring in the pot for a raise. Two people call, and then a third opponent reraises. What do you do? You're looking at a hand which figures to be better than your opponents, but which won't necessarily stand up against all of them. So you try to blast them out with a massive reraise so you can get heads-up with the original reraiser. You can fully expect to get called by him, unless he (wisely) decides to fold, in which case you will win a sizable pot even before the flop.

Occasionally, one of the middle bettors will stubbornly call your reraise. Although you probably still have the best hand, you would have preferred winning the pot uncontested rather than risking a drawout, or playing it heads-up. If the flop comes with three random cards rather than with a straight or flush possibility, you should usually be willing to put in the rest of the money in an attempt to get your opponent to either fold or fully commit his entire stack if he hopes to draw out.

But if the flop is scary—for instance, it comes J♣10♣8♦, which may give your opponent a flush draw, a straight draw, two pair, or a made straight— you will have to make a close judgment call if you are holding A♦A♠6♦7♠, for example, and are first to act. Your problem is muddied by the fact that a bet will often win the pot for you, but you must have the best hand for that to happen. Your opponent may or may not have hit the flop; you can't be sure. It certainly didn't hit you, and a lot of times, your opponent will have enough of a hand to call your bet. In this situation, if I have half my chips left, I may have to risk being bluffed out of the pot rather than committing the rest of my depleted stack.

From this example, you can see why so much more chip movement often occurs in pot-limit Omaha, even in the very early stages, than it does in limit Omaha tournaments.

Backdoor Draws

Having a backdoor draw such as a three flush or an inside straight draw when you have flopped either two pairs or an overpair will often influence whether you make a call. If you have to make a major chip commitment with a rather weak drawing hand or on top pair with a weak outside draw, or even on an overpair such as aces, it probably won't be worth taking the risk. But sometimes, when you have these extra outs and are against a medium or a short stack, it may be worth your while to bet them all-in or to call your opponent's bet. You should have just enough equity in these circumstances so that you won't get crippled if you lose.

Big Confrontations

Some of the biggest confrontations in the early stages (even in the middle and later stages, too) come when a big draw is playing against a made hand such as a set. Suppose you hold J♥10♠9♠8♣ and the flop comes with K♠8♠7♦. You believe your opponent has made a set of kings. Even if has, you will often be the favorite over him. In this example, you have a pair of 8s, a wraparound straight draw, and a low flush draw. With this strength, you should be prepared to commit your chips and gamble on your draw. If you have a short stack, try to win it outright with either a bet or a raise. If you are against a shorter stack than yours, you can bet to put them all-in. You hope they will pass, but even if they don't, you figure to be the favorite over most hands, including sets.

Much of the betting in Omaha is not so much bluffing as it is semi-bluffing: you're betting on big draws, or you have an overpair to the flop with some kind of flush or straight potential. You are trying to either force your opponents out of the pot, or to force them to make a major commitment if they call. If they do call you, they will usually have you beaten, or they will have a draw of equal value. So you have to make good judgments based on your chip position and theirs, in deciding what to do after they call. Often times in pot-limit Omaha, when two people go to war, they put in all their money on the flop and have no more decisions to make.

Slow Playing

Another factor to be concerned about in Omaha is an opponent who is slow playing a big hand: he has flopped the nut flush or top set, for example, and checks. He is hoping to get some action so he can raise; or he may wait until fourth street or even the river before he raises.

But many times, so many drawing combinations are possible that flopping top set usually requires immediate action in an effort to eliminate players from the pot to ensure that the hand holds up without improvement. Occasionally, a player will make a very big hand on the flop with his top set and go on to make a full house on the turn when the boards pairs. The only hand that could possibly beat it, of course, is four of a kind. If you happen to be caught by quads, it's just too bad for you, as you will probably either go broke against them or double up your opponent.

Of course, if you are the one holding the quads, you are often well-advised to slow play hoping to get some action on a future betting round. You can also value-bet the quads without making a full-sized bet. Say there is $800 in the pot: you could bet $500 and hope for some action. Sometimes by under-betting the pot, but still making a respectable bet, you can lure your opponents into thinking they still have a live hand and they will continue playing. Other times, they will become suspicious of this type of bet, so use your best judgment of your opponents in deciding how much to bet.

You will often have to go to the center with all your chips without having the best hand on the flop. If you have the wraparound straight draw with a flush out, you may be favored over a set, but if you are drawing strictly to a flush, be sure you are drawing to the nuts. The same is true for a straight draw: always be sure the hand you are trying to make will make the nuts.

Middle Stage

By the middle rounds of play in a pot-limit Omaha tournament, there are usually some players with big accumulations of chips . . . far more so than in limit tourneys. For this reason, players do not get eliminated quite as quickly after the rebuy period has lapsed, and the middle stage of the tournament often progresses much more slowly than it does in limit games that do not have the rebuy feature.

This slow movement in the middle rounds gives you all the more reason to play solid starting hands only. Also, be wary of players who will be trying to trap you for all your chips. You will need the ultimate in judgment to distinguish between those times when it is correct to push in all your chips on a drawing hand, and when it is not correct.

If you are on a short stack and have a powerful drawing hand, you should be more willing to commit fully on the flop. You are hoping to force your opponents out of the pot, but even if you get called you know that you at least have a chance to improve to the best hand. You may already have the best hand on the flop because a lot of times, you will be betting with pairs as well as flush and straight draws and your pair(s) could be the best hand at the moment. Other times, it may be quite proper to back off and lay down your hand. This might occur when you flop bottom two pair. For example, the flop comes J-9-5 and you make 9s and 5s against two players. They check to you, you bet, and one of them raises. In this case, you will almost always have to abandon ship.

Betting with the top two pair is a little trickier: what you do depends on the texture of the flop and how many drawing hands may be out against you. If a big stack forces you to commit all your chips when you hold top two pair, you may be better off mucking your hand if there is a flush or straight draw on board and you don't have any part of them. Even if two pairs are the current winners, you could be in serious jeopardy with two more cards to come. Of course, you could also be up against a set and have only a few outs. Concealed sets are quite common in high Omaha because of the four-card hands.

Against a shorter stack, you can be more willing to commit. Or if you are very short yourself with only a few more chips left, and have already committed on the flop, you will probably have to move the rest of your stack into the center with hands like two pairs. With a lot of players contesting the pot, two pairs usually won't hold up well in Omaha, so under ordinary circumstances, they are not worth the investment of a lot of chips.

Late Stage and Final Table

If you are fortunate enough to make the final table in an Omaha tournament, you will find that there are usually a lot of chips on the table compared to the size of the blinds. Therefore, even with a short stack, you will have enough time to patiently wait for the best possible situation before you enter a pot. Many times, I have seen players arrive at the final table with short to medium stacks and go on to win the tournament. How do they overcome the power of the bigger stacks? They use patience as their ally; they have a good feel for when to move chips; and they employ a good sense of timing. But patience is their foremost tool.

Say the blinds are at $800-$1,600 and you have $15,000 in chips. This may seem like a lot, and sometimes it is. You can sit through several rounds without playing a hand, just waiting until the situation looks right, and until you get a decent hand such as aces with two playable sidecards that you can gamble with and commit before the flop, if necessary. The most important mental attitude is not to push any panic buttons when you have a short stack.

Even though the bigger your stack ,the more options you have, you must still continue to play *solid* poker. You cannot allow the short stacks to double through you, so you don't want to be playing weak hands against them. Remember that if the shorter stacks are playing a solid and patient game, they are hoping to make *you* take the worst of it when they finally decide to commit.

Of course, you *can* sometimes take the worst of it, but you can't take *too much* the worst of it and still have a reasonably positive expectation. For instance, say a short stack has been patiently waiting and finally decides to commit himself. You are in the big blind with a big stack and have only the $1,600 blind bet in the pot. The short stack has around $5,000 in chips remaining and decides to commit all his chips before the flop. Everyone else passes. You hold 8-8-5-4. Now what do you do?

Your hand isn't completely terrible, but it isn't very good either. Is this the kind of hand you want to put in your money with? Usually not. If you have a really large stack, you ask yourself if you can afford to put in about triple what you already have in the pot to try to bust the short stack. The answer is "no, you probably should pass." It is almost certain that even if your two 8s are the biggest pair at the moment, your opponent is holding bigger cards. So unless you catch an 8 to make trips or a lucky 7-6 to give you a straight possibility (which may or may not get there), you will surely be taking too much the worst of it to take a stand with this kind of hand. Even with a Q-10-5-3 double-suited, for example, your two high cards with no helpers are too weak to make a call.

Key Concept

The general rule at the final table, particularly shorthanded or heads-up, is "Don't commit on marginal hands and marginal draws against big stacks." When you are heads-up, occasionally slow-play big pairs; just limp in with the idea of reraising.

Suppose you limp in and so does your opponent. The flop comes raggedy, and your adversary fires a big bet at you. He could easily have two small pairs or a set with such a nondescript flop. Now, because you decided to slow play rather than commit a lot of chips before the flop, you can get away from your hand cheaply.

It is a sweet situation when you are playing heads-up and decide to mix up your play by just limping in with a hand such as A-A-K-10. The flop comes with an ace and two random cards with no straight or flush potential. Your opponent flops a small set or even aces-up. Now you can trap him because he won't put you on a set of aces since you didn't raise before the flop. Just remember that you have to be careful when you flop nothing except an overpair and your opponent is ready to mix it up by putting in all of his chips.

Another key concept to recall is that any time you decide to reraise with a hand such as K-K-A-J, for example, having that ace in your hand is a definite plus. Your opponent is less likely to hold aces in this instance, and even if an ace comes on the flop, you figure to either have the best kicker or to at least be tied for it. So having the ace in your hand gives you much more potential strength. Ditto with Q-Q-A-K, because an overpair of aces or kings is less likely to be out since you hold one of each in your hand.

When you are on equal terms with another stack that is willing to fully commit before the flop, you have to be wary even if you are holding pocket kings, because your opponent most likely has pocket aces. I may have raised with my pocket kings, but when that equal stack comes over the top of me, I will probably dump my kings rather than take the risk.

If I am up against a shorter stack with my pocket kings, I still may not like calling his reraise, but I will usually go ahead and play the hand. Ditto if I am the one on the short stack. If someone puts in a big reraise when I already have 40 to 50 percent of my chips in the pot, I will usually commit the rest of my stack—unless the raiser is someone who has been playing very conservatively and virtually never raises with less than two aces in his hand.

But suppose you are on a short stack and have committed only *ten* percent of your chips with your pair of kings. Another player then pushes his entire stack to the center, which would force you to send in a substantial portion of your chips, maybe up to one third of your stack. In this scenario, you will usually have to abandon the kings.

When to commit and when not to commit at the final table often requires a close judgment call, based on your chip position and that of your opponent. There are simply no hard and fast rules. You need to study your opponent, to *know* him, so that you can get as accurate a read on him as you possibly can. When you know him, and when you know how to use optimal tournament strategy against him, you are on your way to victory. ♠

Chapter 10

OMAHA HIGH-LOW
(8 or Better)

Omaha high-low has become an increasingly popular tournament game in the last few years. Currently, the number of Omaha high-low tournament entrants at the World Series of Poker and other major events is frequently second only to hold'em. In popularity, it has caught up with seven-card stud and often surpasses it in player participation.

Although this section discusses higher-limit, freezeout tournaments, you will find many opportunities to play in lower limit Omaha high-low rebuy events in Las Vegas and Southern California. You'll need this type of experience and practice before you move up to the higher limits because there are many tricks to Omaha high-low: it is one of the most complicated of all poker games, with its multitude of different playable-hand combinations and variety of drawing possibilities.

For the first few years Omaha high-low was spread as an official World Series event, the same handful of top players kept making the finals of the tournament (although that has changed somewhat in the past few years). This told me something. The players who kept getting there were competing against each other quite frequently in high-stakes side games at the Mirage in Las Vegas and at tournaments which spread high-action side games. So I said to myself, "Hey, these guys must be onto something."

And they were: they were accustomed to playing against each other and had developed a good feel for the game—when they were counterfeited at the end and when they weren't, for example. They appeared to have a sixth sense, a phenomenon that is hard to describe. (In fact, all poker authors have difficulty explaining it, so some of the concepts we write about may occasionally come across as being somewhat nebulous.) But this sixth sense involves a *feel* for the game, a *read* on your opponents . . . and you can't necessarily get that from this poker book or any other. It's something you learn to develop as you increase your playing skills and card sense.

General Concepts

Omaha high-low has unique characteristics that are totally different from other forms of poker. This game is full of traps! Many times, you'll go from a potential scoop pot with one card to come to getting scooped at the river because the last card—the key card—counterfeits your low. For example, suppose you have A♣2♣K♦Q♥, which is a pretty decent starting hand. The board is K♥6♠5♠ , giving you a working A-2 with a fairly good draw at the high hand, also. The turn card is the Q♦. Now you have top two pair and the nut-low draw. Looks promising, doesn't it?

But Omaha high-low can be a cruel game—the river card is the 2♠. Now your low has been counterfeited; someone may be holding spades for the flush; and if not, a low straight is possible. Suddenly, you've gone from top two pair with the nut-low draw to almost nothing.

So what do you do? I usually just shrug my shoulders when my opponent bets into me, and toss my hand in the muck without paying it off, because it seems all too clear that I am beat. Although my opponent could have made only a low rather than a flush or a straight, I simply can't take the chance of my two pair holding up, especially if there are other players left to act behind me who could raise.

Omaha high-low is also by far the most difficult game for dealers to deal: Inexperienced dealers are notorious for making mistakes at this game, so it is often up to the players to keep an eye on the dealer, including sometimes helping them sort out which are the winning hands. This is especially important because 55-to-60 percent of all hands wind up as split pots. Dealing and controlling the game properly, and splitting the pot accurately, require dealer finesse. For these reasons, whenever you doubt the showdown value of your hand, it is best to turn it up. Although I am not an advocate of always showing your hand on the river, I would rather expose even a weak hand that may or may not win the pot than take the chance of overlooking its potential. Even though I'm ashamed to admit it, I have made more mistakes in reading my hand in Omaha high-low than in any other form of poker, so I have trained myself to habitually expose my hand at the showdown, not only in tournament Omaha high-low, but also in all other poker games.

Another unique facet of Omaha high-low tournaments is that they move at a far slower pace than other tournament games. They often take longer to conclude for three reasons: The pace is slow, the pots are frequently split, and it takes longer to eliminate participants. Fewer hands are dealt in each round because it takes so much time to divide the pots (which often have to be re-split when there are more than two winners). With the limits escalating every forty minutes to an hour in major tourneys, players should try to play in as timely and expedient a manner as possible, although they need not rush so much that they make mistakes. But it is their responsibility to make sure that everything goes along smoothly, that disputes (which are somewhat frequent in Omaha high-low) are ironed out fairly and efficiently to save time.

You also need a good feel for what's going on. You should know when your low is not counterfeited so that you can put in that extra bet or raise, when it will get you half the pot, and when to just call. You have to be able to process all the information that is available to you—what types of hands the players in the current pot have shown down in the past; who are the tighter players; which ones are looser; those who are in-between. You have to put it all together like a poker puzzle and *read* them. And that's not easy to do in a game with as many complexities as Omaha high-low, with both high and low hands to consider. Even experienced players sometimes have difficulty in accurately reading their hands.

Hand Selection

Very powerful starting hands in Omaha high-low are usually Aces double-suited with a deuce-trey working, or an A-2 with perhaps a king or queen.

If you have two aces in your hand, leaving only two remaining in the deck, the less the chance of another player holding one of them with (specifically) a deuce. Therefore, although not guaranteed, the chances of your having to compete with another nut-low draw are substantially reduced.

A hand that is not quite as strong as A-A-2-3 is a hand such as A-A-3-Q, for example. In my opinion, this is definitely a raising hand because it gives you great potential in both directions. As often as possible, you want a hand which can be played for *both* high and low. Although you may prefer to catch an A-A-2-K, of course, A-A-3-Q is still a very strong starting hand.

Any hand containing two aces suited with two small cards (A-A-3-4, A-A-3-5, for example)—even if they are a 4 or 5, instead of 2-3—is still a strong starting hand. However, if there has been a lot of pre-flop action before it gets to me, with a raise and several cold-callers, I don't consider this hand to be strong enough to put in a reraise, because it is highly likely that one or two of the other players is holding an A-2, which means I probably won't flop a set with the aces, and my low won't be as strong as their A-2s.

Key Concept

Generally, anytime a pot is raised with several callers, you can put one or more players on an A-2, giving them an excellent low draw from the flop on. The low hand gets there about 55-60 percent of the time, including the times when only one low card appears on the flop. (Naturally, the low will not get there over half the time when only one low card comes on the flop.)

Other starting hands that have some merit, but which are not great, are hands such as 2-3-4-6, with only one gap. With a flop such as A-2-9, players who hold A-2 will find themselves counterfeited while you have the nut low draw. Sometimes, you can trap them with their two-pair since you have not only the nut low draw, but also a straight possibility, and can win a nice pot if you make it. The key is that you cannot play these speculative starting hands for too many pre-flop bets because more often than not, you will be looking at better low draws. So unless the flop is very favorable for you, you will often have to abandon your hand on the flop. Remember, too, that you should draw only to the nuts to continue playing in multi-way pots.

Key Concept

It doesn't take a rocket scientist to figure out that the middle cards can be quite troublesome to play. You are never drawing to the nut low hand with hands such as 6-7-8-9, and many times your straight draw may not be the nuts, either. These cards must be either avoided altogether, or at least played with utmost caution.

Although hands with two-way potential are the best to play, if I had to favor either an all-high starting hand such as A-K-Q-J, or an all-low starter such as A-2-3-4, I personally prefer the A-K-Q-J (although I realize that many Omaholics disagree with me). First of all, when I make this type of hand, I am more likely to scoop the pot than with A-2-3-4, because I often have to split the pot with another low hand, even if I make a wheel.

Secondly, if the flop comes with all low cards, I can get away from a premium high hand very cheaply by simply abandoning it immediately. Also, if I catch a favorable flop (such as K-Q-2) with my high hand, I can punish players who are trying to backdoor the low by making it very expensive for them to outdraw me. When I flop top two-pair in this situation, I want to put as much heat on as possible, which means I will bet first if there has been no action, or will raise or reraise an opening bet.

Early Stage

Omaha split is so tricky that a good solid approach to the game is essential if you want to be successful at it. Although the most fundamental and important consideration in this game is starting hand selection, your seat position, as well as the action that has occurred before you, are also important factors. Has the pot been raised or reraised? How many people are in the pot, and how many of them have only limped in? Or are you the first one to enter, and so on?

Key Concept

In order to survive, you often need to play more conservatively in tournaments than you would play in side action games. A hand you might raise or reraise in a side game can't always be played that way in tourneys, because you can't reach in your pocket for more chips if you lose your stack. In fact, this conservative strategy is the same even in rebuy tourneys when you're past the add-on stage, (when the tournament *really* begins), because your chips become so precious to you. Remember, too, that the fewer chips you have, the more valuable they become.

The bottom line is this: you need to use a lot of good judgment to reach the final table in an Omaha high-low tournament. The rest of this section is designed to help you develop that judgment.

Because there are so many starting hand variations, being very aggressive before the flop by raising and reraising is often inadvisable. If you put in too much pre-flop action (even with premium starting hands such as A-A-2-3 or A-2-K-Q), you will often find yourself counterfeited for either the high or the low; but more often, the *low* because there will usually be other premium low hands out against you. This is not to say that you should play an ultraconservative game; just be selectively aggressive about when you raise or reraise.

For example, with a hand such as A-2-5-6, I would be very hesitant to reraise if the pot has already been raised before the action gets to me. Certainly, I would call to see the flop. But many times, you will find yourself in trouble with this hand, because it is very likely that you may wind up splitting the low end of the pot with the other holder(s) of A-2.

Key Concept

As a general rule of thumb, if you are certain that you are only going to win a quarter of the pot, don't put in the extra bets and raises, especially in tournaments which do not permit rebuys, since you can't replenish your chips if you lose them. You're not looking to get full value out of every hand: you're hoping to survive. So you don't want to jeopardize your chips in a situation where you may not be getting back more than a quarter of what you're putting in. Tournament chips saved are just as important as chips earned or won.

Generally, I limp in more often than I raise before the flop in Omaha high-low. Any four cards 7 and below are usually worth seeing the flop with if you can play them for the minimum bet from late position. Of course, if I am holding a hand such as 7-7-6-5, I don't particularly want to get involved for even the minimum bet. Hands such as 2-3-4-5 have a lot of potential, even though there is no ace in the hand, because when the ace does come on the flop, you not only have the nut low draw, but you also may flop a possible straight draw.

I don't even mind limping into an unraised pot with hands that have gaps, such as 7-4-3-2, to try to catch the flop. However, if you should limp into a pot with such a hand, and there is a raise and reraise after you, be very hesitant to call a double raise even though you have already put in one bet. Almost certainly, you will be up against at least one high hand jamming the pot, and probably one or more A-2s as well.

Key Concept

In Omaha high-low, you almost have to be drawing for the nuts in one direction or the other. If the pot has been raised in front of you, hands such as A-3-7-9 are virtually unplayable. Too often, you will end up making the second-best low hand, and not a good enough high hand, to warrant playing.

There are occasions, however, when you might play A-3-7-9: in late position in an unraised pot, or from the small blind when the pot has not been raised. Another time you may want to play this type of hand is when you are in the big blind and have been raised by a very loose, aggressive player on the button. When only one or two players have limped into the pot, leading you to believe that there isn't a lot of strength out, you may decide to call the raise and at least see the flop. But from the flop on, you really should be drawing to only the high or the low nuts.

Now suppose you are holding A-2-3-4 in a jammed pot and the flop comes K-Q-8, giving you the best possible backdoor low draw. You are almost forced to take off a single card for one bet, but you should not stay in if the pot is jammed again on the flop, because it becomes too expensive for you to draw to a backdoor low. However, it isn't nearly as difficult to backdoor a low with two running cards as it is to backdoor a flush or other high hands. Therefore, if the pot is large enough, it is often correct to call on the flop and see the turn card.

However, if you saw the flop cheaply with perhaps four callers in an unraised pot, it is clearly not in your best interests to take off a card because the pot size doesn't warrant it. Also, since you are drawing to only half the pot, you want the pot to be larger to justify your draw. Your position will be further jeopardized if other players are holding low cards similar to yours so that, if you take off a card, you may get there with a backdoor nut-low but receive only one-quarter of the pot when it is split between the high hand and two low hands.

Key Concept

The smaller the pot before the flop, the less reason to continue playing from the flop on if you have only three cards to a low draw with no potential for also making a high hand, requiring that you catch two runners to complete your low hand.

Anytime you are drawing to only one-half the pot, you must be careful about how you proceed.

Because there are so many potential starting hands in Omaha high-low, you'll see far more multi-way pots than in other forms of poker. So in the early rounds, you won't find nearly as much tight play as in hold'em or seven-card stud, for example, where tight, solid play in tournaments is usually the norm. Players seem to take off the restraints in Omaha high-low much more quickly to get involved in the action. With so many possible high and low starting hands, this is a game which gives people all too many excuses to get into the action.

So you must be very careful about your seat position and the type of table you're playing at. Sometimes you'll find yourself at a starting table where there is very little pre-flop raising and a lot of pre-flop calling. At this type of table, you can limp in with the types of speculative hands mentioned earlier, preferably as cheaply as possible and in as late a position as possible, because it probably isn't going to cost you too much to see the flop.

You should be drawing for the best possible low or the best possible high in Omaha high-low or, hopefully, both: I cannot emphasize this maxim too strongly. Too often, if you're drawing to second-best, you will wind up losing the entire pot. So be wary of opponents who are doing a lot of betting, calling and raising from the flop on if you are *not* drawing to the nuts. (Sometimes, however, you won't need to be drawing to the nut hand, but those occasions are usually limited to heads-up play.)

It is so easy to get counterfeited in Omaha split that many times, even when you have the absolute nuts for low (with no high hand that can be reasonably expected to contest the top half of the pot), you only have a *calling* hand. This happens because you are frequently up against another player who also holds the nut low (a common problem in this game). There is no substitute for experience in helping you determine when you are likely to be quartered for low—it takes a certain *feel.*

Middle Stage

With the first couple of rounds completed, 80 percent of the field may still be left in action because the pace is slow: fewer hands are dealt and, therefore, fewer players are eliminated during each round. In a typical $500 buy-in tournament, you will be at the $50-$100 betting level at the beginning of round three. Now, players will begin to fall by the wayside.

Far less limping into pots occurs at this stage. Often, the bigger stacks begin to jockey for position with more aggressive play before the flop, attempting to muscle the shorter stacks. It isn't that the tall stacks have doubled-up and have thus become looser: they are simply being selectively aggressive with decent hands, which is a viable strategy.

But I still like to proceed cautiously in this middle stage. If a few players have limped into the pot, I must have a strong hand before I will put in a raise. A hand such as A♠2♠9♥8♥, even though it is double-suited, is still only a mediocre holding because the next lowest card to the deuce is a weak 8, and the suited connectors are the type which often cause you trouble by making either a low straight or a low flush that loses to a higher one. Of course, if it is not suited, it's even worse. This type of hand is a *limping* hand only, so if there is a raise and a reraise in front of me, I will pass without any hesitation whatsoever.

I always ask myself, "What are people raising and reraising with?" Usually, it is with big cards including high pairs, or with premium low hands, probably A-2s. So even if I get there with the low, I will win only a quarter of the pot. In the event that an ace *and* a deuce fall on the board, I would have only an 8 as my next lowest card . . . which will not usually be good enough to win the low end of the pot. Almost invariably, one of my opponents will have a better side-card than my 8, even though they too may have been counterfeited for low. Therefore, this type of hand should be played for a minimum bet only, or not played at all if the pot is jammed.

Key Concept

With small to medium stacks, it is essential that you have a very solid starting hand before you enter a pot in the middle stages. You want to maximize your chances of winning that one key hand that will either double-up your stack or increase it by 50 percent. If you have only $500 in chips left at the $50-$100 level, for example, and the pot is raised, you have barely enough to complete one hand, so you will want that hand to be a strong one. Therefore, you must be more selective in your starting requirements than players with big stacks who have already doubled-up.

With a short stack of $200 at the $50-$100 level, suppose you're looking at a hand such as A-3-7-6. If no one has entered the pot yet, you may want to take a shot with this holding, bringing it in with a raise. If a couple of players have already limped in, however, you may not want to fully commit. In this case, if you can also limp into the pot, you probably should while you still have enough chips left to back off if you catch an unfavorable flop. In fact, a lot of players may be trying to limp into pots with A-2s, which reduces the chances of your A-3 being the nut low.

But if you have a reasonable chance to pick up the blinds—you're in late position and nobody has entered the pot—or if you think you may be able to play the pot heads-up against a random blind hand, you can raise with your A-3-7-6.

Key Concept

Any time you find yourself in a low chip position, you're simply going to have to take a stand. When you do decide to take a stand, however, be prepared to fully commit before the flop and take your chances, especially if you have a decent high hand such as A-A-K-x (if you have one or more suits, all the better).

With hands such as Q-Q-A-K, for example, I will fully commit as many chips as possible before the flop. It's much more likely that I am not up against aces or kings, so that if an ace or a king hits on the flop, I have a good chance of having the best high hand. Even if low cards come, my queens could win the high hand enough of the time to warrant my gambling with them.

The times I am most willing to gamble with these types of hands are when I am short-stacked and need to win a pot; or when I have a very large stack against a smaller stack, and I want to get the short stack to fully commit before the flop.

Key Concept

The bigger your chip stack, the more willing you should be to commit a lot of chips against *short* stacks, but you should be less willing to put in a lot of money against another *big* stack. If possible, see the flop more cheaply and do your gambling afterward.

Late Stage

When it gets down to three tables in a tournament which pays two tables (which many of them do), each table may have fewer than the maximum number of players because so many people have been eliminated. This is when a lot of jockeying for position begins to take place, especially among players who have accumulated some chips. At this point, you will need to be somewhat more aggressive and do some pre-flop raising, especially if you are the first to enter the pot.

However, if players continue to simply limp in (as sometimes happens), you will probably want to put on the brakes. If you don't hold a premium hand, but one which nonetheless seems to be worth seeing the flop with, you may also want to just call when there are a couple of players already in the pot (or even if there is only one other player in) with the blind yet to act. But if you are in middle to late position with a similar holding, you might want to raise with it if no one has yet entered the pot.

If everybody has a big stack and no one seems to be especially afraid of my chip position because they have an equal or even superior one, they are not going to be easily bullied, so I don't want to be doing a lot of raising with marginal hands. There is less reason to try to blind-steal in Omaha high-low because there are so many viable starting hands, which makes it far easier for players to defend their blinds. Therefore, you must be very careful when you try to steal.

Key Concept

A situation when I enjoy playing aggressively at this stage of the tournament is against a short stack that will have to commit a lot chips to play the hand. When I am dealt cards such as A-3-6-7 or A-3-Q-J, where I don't necessarily have the best high or low starting hand, but one with reasonable potential, I'll have a much better chance of scooping (or at least winning one end) against only one player. Even if he has a slightly better starting hand from one direction, I may beat him from the other direction and get a split. And quite possibly, I may be able to break him if the flop goes right, and if the turn and river cards improve my hand.

Sometimes, your opponents may be playing a very tight game, even in the later stages, so you have to be especially wary when they enter a pot. But if you find that a lot of them are not defending their blinds, you have a chance to be more aggressive and occasionally pick up some of their blinds.

I am reminded of a quote which my good friend, Mike Caro, gives at all his poker clinics. He calls it "Caro's First Law of Poker:" *If they're helpless and they can't defend themselves, you're in the right game.* I totally agree with him. If you're up against short stacks who are simply trying to survive to the money round, or opponents who are playing very conservatively with the same thought in mind, you have an excellent chance to substantially increase your chip count by being selectively aggressive against them when you have a large or above-average stack.

This doesn't mean that you have *carte blanche* to raise with any random four cards, but if you can pound on their blinds with marginal hands when no one has entered the pot, do so. Even if your stack is only average, if the bigger stacks have put on the brakes and are playing tighter, you can put yourself in position to survive to the money rounds and increase your chip position substantially by picking up some of the blinds. This is your chance to move: take it.

In another type of scenario, suppose you have made the nuts for high on the river, but a potential low is out, which leads you to believe you are going to split the pot with the low hand. Knowing that you have the best high hand, you will want to be as aggressive as possible to get the most money into the pot.

However, sometimes the best way to get in the most chips when you know you have a cinch for high, and you think you might be able to trap the second-best high and the lows into putting more money into the pot on the river, is to smooth-call the low bettor if he is the first to act. Calling his bet rather than raising it may induce the players left to act behind you to overcall rather than to fold against your raise, thus making your half of the pot that much more lucrative.

Here is an example of this ploy, which can apply to any stage of a tournament. The board is showing

8♦2♦3♦J♣10♥. Holding the A♦K♦10♥9♠, you have made the nut flush. With this board, a straight is also possible, plus a low hand. You are in second position with four of you contesting the pot all the way. You know you have a cinch for high and surmise that the bettor in first position has the nut low. When he bets, should you raise with the nut high?

Usually, no—because you will often win more money by just calling with the nuts, thus encouraging lesser high hands and other low hands to call the last bet. This makes sense when two or more players are left to act after you. If one of them decides to raise, reraise when the action gets back to you, because you now have little reason to disguise your hand. And since they've already put in two bets, they are probably going to call.

Of course, the ideal situation occurs when you are last to act and one of them bets into you with either no callers or only one caller. You can still raise, even though you suspect your opponent is going to split the pot with you, because a player will occasionally misread his hand or he may have a lesser flush with no low possibility. In either case, you have nothing to lose. (Ignore the snickers you sometimes get from other players when you raise with the nut high against the nut low, "when you knew the pot would be split anyway." What they may not understand is that the pot *doesn't* always get split in these situations, making your raise the correct move.)

Although this section assumes that the final two tables will have a payday, the same reasoning applies if only one table is being paid. If the tournament is down to two tables with only 12 or

13 players left, perhaps 6 or 7 at a table, there will be fewer hands with potential out against you, so you can take a few more liberties against very tight opponents. But be wary when your tight opponents are putting chips in the pot, are defending their blinds, and are continuing to play from the flop on. You must give them credit for a hand. Many times, they are calling with hands that are better than the hands you're betting with!

The reason these tight players are not being more aggressive is because they're still trying to survive, or because they don't believe they have the nuts in one direction or the other, or they may be afraid they're going to be quartered. But you cannot reasonably expect them to suddenly give up, particularly if you've raised before flop, have bet on the flop, and have been called by them. Even if the turn card doesn't seem to help either them or you, they are not likely to fold a premium hand.

On the reverse side of the coin, more tournaments have been lost by players who have accumulated chips with aggressive play, but don't know when to put on the brakes, than for any other reason. This especially applies to Omaha high-low where there are more potential starting hands to play.

The Final Table

Suppose you have made it to the final table where you find yourself in top chip position against four adversaries. The prize money is top-heavy for the final three finishers, with the winner usually receiving twice the amount that second place pays and four times what third place pays. Many payoffs are 40 percent for first; 20 percent for second; and 10 percent for third, although sometimes the spread will be closer (40-23-12, for example). Since the most money, the glory and the big trophy all go to the victor, you naturally want to increase your chances of winning.

If you are in top chip position, you have a chance to be the big bully at the table, especially if the prize money to be divided between fifth, fourth, and third places is substantial and some of the shorter stacks are trying to hang on and come in for the next highest payoff spot. If this is the case, take full advantage of their thinking—be even more of a bully, be more aggressive. The only catch is that if you get caught, or if you double-up one of these short stacks, you will put a dent in your own stack. Then you must apply the brakes. But if they're not trying to stop you from bullying, keep running over them until they do.

Key Concept

Good timing wins tournaments. For example, when you have raised before the flop three times in a row, and then you raise a fourth time with a premium hand, an opponent on a shorter stack will sometimes decide to finally take a stand, unaware that this time, you are holding *the* boss hand. It can become a thing of beauty, particularly when the flop is favorable to you and you catch your opponent with the second-best hand. That's good timing. Conversely, bad timing can either lose the tournament for you, or jeopardize your chip position.

If your timing continues to be flawless, make the most of it with aggressive play. But if you're picked off once or twice and some of the lower stacks begin to inch into contention, you're almost forced to tighten up. Whatever happens, don't push any panic buttons. Even if you do lose a couple of hands, stay calm and collected in your actions. Even though we all get emotional at times, the people who perform best are the ones who control their emotions the best. The key is to keep fighting rather than allowing your emotions to get the better of you.

Playing High Pairs and Big Cards

High pairs and big cards go up in value at the final table. The shorter handed the situation, the more valuable they are. Players are less likely to get involved in raised pots at the final table unless they are holding premium hands, because they don't want to jeopardize their chances of sliding up the pay scale. They will generally pass marginal hands that do not contain either premium high cards or excellent low cards.

When you raise with big cards before the flop, you have a good chance of winning the pot uncontested; and even if you are called, you will usually be up against only one (or at the most, two) other opponents. Therefore, your chances of winning with no improvement are increased, particularly when you are playing heads-up. Also, players with low hands often cannot afford to take a draw when only one low card comes on the flop.

The way you evaluate high hands at the final table differs from the way you might think about them in the early stages or in ring games. I previously mentioned that I personally prefer A-K-Q-J to A-2-3-4 because I can win more whole-pots with that type of high hand, and I can easily get away from the hand if low cards flop.

A-2-3-4 is somewhat trickier. Sometimes, you have a low hand with a draw to the wheel and sometimes you don't; so you often wind up splitting the pot. However, in the long run, you will probably make more money with A-2-3-4 starting hands than with A-K-Q-J.

Big pairs and high cards are very vulnerable when the flop comes with low cards only, especially when you know for certain that your opponent already has half the pot locked up with a made low, in addition to having several outs against you that could scoop the whole pot. Therefore, the texture of the flop is very important in evaluating the strength of your hand and in determining how to proceed, particularly at the final table where a mistake in judgment could easily cost you the tournament.

Key Concept

When you are in heads-up play, you need far less strength than you do when you are up against several opponents. However, this doesn't mean you can play truly bad hands with impunity. For example, if your opponent raises and you are holding a hand such as Q-9-7-4 in the big blind, you have no real reason to call unless your adversary will be all-in for one more bet. Even then, I may be somewhat hesitant to put my opponent all-in, because whatever his four cards are, they figure to be better in either one or both directions than mine.

Michael Cappelletti, who writes for *Card Player* magazine, believes there is virtually no match-up in Omaha high-low which favors any player by more than about a 60-40 margin *in heads-up play.* Many hands you would not normally play in a full game or even in a four or five-handed situation will have some value shorthanded. This is particularly true when the limits are very high and losing just a big blind or two can seriously cripple your stack. Therefore, you may have to call with some very marginal hands heads-up that you would not ordinarily play. Keep in mind that almost all of Cappelletti's match-ups are in the 40 percent to 50 percent range, and very few are much more than 60-40, especially with the split-pot nature of the game.

Although you don't necessarily need premium hands to raise in heads-up play, you do need to be somewhat cautious. If you are up against a tight player who begins to make a lot of stands, you will probably want to put on the brakes to avoid doubling-up his stack with hands on which you shouldn't have given him any action. However, more often than not, you're going to be rewarded for aggressive play. Playing a passive, timid game in which you simply call a lot just won't get the chips in heads-up play. Keep in mind that in heads-up situations, you cannot play too conservatively without seriously jeopardizing your chances of winning the whole enchilada.

This concept also applies in satellites where the blinds go up every 15 to 20 minutes. In the fourth or fifth rounds of play, just giving up the blind can undermine your chances of winning. Of course, I am not advocating playing truly hopeless hands, such as starting hands with three-of-a-kind or ones such as 9-9-8-8 (although this type of hand would have some value heads-up). I am suggesting that you remain somewhat flexible and, as usual, exercise your best judgment in choosing which hands to play when you are heads-up.

If you have your opponent on the ropes and you are pounding him into submission, you don't want to let him swing that lucky punch, the upper cut that could change things. So if you have him backed into a corner, go for the jugular, but do it with a reasonable hand, not a truly bad one just to get him to commit all his chips before the flop. If your hand is really weak, his might not be much better, but it usually figures to be if all four of his cards are working. Always use discretion and your key defense: *judgment.*

Concluding Remarks

The future looks very bright for Omaha high-low. A solid Omaha high-low player who knows hand values and has a good feel for the action has a tremendous overlay in lower buy-in tournaments, where I often see some very weak play. Although I still prefer a good hold'em or seven-card stud game for side action play, Omaha split games in which weak players often draw to less than the nuts can become very lucrative opportunities for a sharp player. Even though you will sometimes be outdrawn by a loose opponent who put in money when he shouldn't have and then got lucky, in the long run you will be rewarded for your good decisions. Omaha high-low can be a very profitable game for better players. ♠

I rank seven-card stud and hold'em as the two most difficult poker games to truly master, and the rewards are very great if you do. In 1992 I was the runner-up in the World Series of Poker seven-card stud tournament and placed third in the *Hall of Fame* one year. Although I have yet to win a WSOP title in this demanding game, over the years I have won many other major seven-card stud tournaments.

When I was runner-up in 1992, I lost to Men "The Master" Nguyen. At the final table, we were heads-up with fairly equal chips. I started with pocket aces and a 9 doorcard. Nguyen had a smaller doorcard with pocket tens. For some reason, he didn't believe how strong my hand was and so we put in several bets on fifth street when he somehow picked up a straight draw. On sixth street, I paired my doorcard 9, giving me aces-up and a pair of each of the two cards he needed for his straight. When I bet into him on seventh street, about 80 percent of the chips were in the pot. Nguyen hemmed and hawed and finally called me. He had made his straight! Not only did it break my heart, but it also cost me my fifth World Series title. Although I still had a few chips left, I never fully recovered from that hand and had to settle for second place.

Early Stage

What constitutes reasonable starting hands in the early stages of a seven-card stud tournament, and what strategies should you use in playing them? First of all, drawing hands such as flushes and straights must be played with caution.

Flush Draws

The earlier a player raises, the more credit you should usually give him for having a legitimate hand. The majority of the time when a player raises with a pair, that pair will be the same as his doorcard (his upcard). Beware when an early position player raises with a small card such as a 5 showing. He probably has a hidden pair and, most likely, that pair is big (tens or better).

Therefore, if a player raises from an early position when you are holding a three-flush, it is essential that you have additional factors working in your favor. (1) You need to have a rather large flush draw with no more than one or two of your suit showing in the upcards of other players. (2) It is also to your advantage to have one or two cards higher than the raiser's doorcard.

If you are reasonably sure, then, that you'll be playing against a big pair, you must be drawing to hands that are both *live* and contain one or two *overcards*, to feel safe in calling the raise. (If the pot has not been raised in front of you, of course, you can be somewhat more flexible.)

However, if the raise comes from an aggressive player in a late position, he could be trying to steal the antes. For example, suppose he has a queen showing and five players have passed the forced bring-in bet. He raises. You are next to act with

A♦K♦in the hole and 7♦on top. You can reraise him. If he does in fact have a pair of queens and decides to play back at you, it's not such a terrible situation: you can continue playing the hand, at least through fifth street, even without much improvement. You're trying to resteal from a stealer with your semi-bluff (a hand that has a lot of outs). You may be able to pick up the pot immediately with your reraise because, if the raiser is indeed on a steal, he will have to give it up when you reraise.

This play works even more effectively if either your ace or king is showing. Even if the probable stealer has a pair of queens, he will have a difficult call against your overcard. But if he does decide to call, you still have a live hand to play against him. (Remember, also, that some aggressive players will raise with a three-card flush rather than a pair.)

What if a *tight* player raises in this same situation? Be more likely to give him credit for a hand, even though he is raising in late position. But suppose you know nothing about the raiser, as so often happens in tournaments? Until you get a better *read* on him, assume that he has a hand (probably a pair to his doorcard).

Against these two types of players, I usually flat-call and take off a card rather than make an aggressive reraise. I prefer saving my aggression for opponents who are more likely to be on a steal. So if I figure my adversary for a steal, a reraise is in order; if I'm either uncertain or am against a tight player, I simply call and wait for fourth street to decide how to best play the hand.

Be leery of playing small three-flushes in raised pots. If you can play for the minimum bet and your hand is live—no more than two of your suit are showing, and none or few of your small ranks are showing (giving you pair possibilities)—you can see fourth street. When I am in late position with a small flush draw and have higher cards than the forced bring-in bet, I may raise. But I will only do this when five people (in an eight-handed game) have passed and only one other player, in addition to the forced bring-in bettor, is left to act—and his upcard must be lower than mine, because then he is less likely to raise me.

Key Concept

Generally speaking, players in the early rounds of seven-card stud tournaments play more conservatively than they do in side games, waiting more patiently for a good starting hand. Naturally, this is not 100 percent true, but you can easily recognize players who are not following this policy: they call a lot of opening bets to see fourth street, and they raise more often than their hands seem to warrant.

Against very tight opponents, you can play somewhat more liberally and try a few ante-steals, although not very often. Primarily, you will want to play a very solid game, but just a bit looser than your tighter opponents. Conversely, if your adversaries are playing looser than ordinary, you should play a little tighter than they do.

Again, *solid aggressive* play is your best approach. This is the style I myself use. The hands I limp in with are ones that can improve to big hands: hands such as a small *live* pair; small three-flushes, and extremely live straight draws. I play straight draws with extreme caution—I won't even limp in with them if there are more than two overcards to act behind me because I cannot call a raise.

Flush Draws after Third Street

Keep a close count of how many of your suit cards are out. If you improve by catching another suited card on fourth street, you have close to an even-money chance of completing your flush (depending, of course, on how many cards in your suit are still live: the more of your suit cards showing, the less your chances). Even if three of your suit are out, you still have about a 40 percent chance of completing the flush. Therefore, it is usually correct to continue playing the hand because the pot will often be paying you a good enough price, with the antes and dead money in it from players who have taken off a card and have subsequently folded.

Of course, you don't necessarily have a through-ticket to the river with a four-flush. Other players may also be catching suited cards that are higher than what you are holding. If someone who limped in with a 7♣ catches A♣K♣ on fourth and fifth streets, you are in a very dangerous situation, especially if you don't see many other clubs showing. So use both judgment and caution when you think another player may have already made a flush while you are still drawing to one.

Another time when you must be wary is when someone pairs his doorcard, particularly if he has raised before the turn card. (When that happens, I often say, "That's the strongest play I've ever seen in seven-card stud: you raise and then pair your doorcard!") When someone pairs his doorcard, he has made trips the majority of the time if he started with a pair of that rank. Few things are more devastating than completing your flush only to be beaten by a full house. You will probably lose several bets in the process, too, because it is very difficult for most players to lay down a flush.

I have often seen a player raise with a flush on sixth street only to have someone who has just paired his doorcard come over the top of him with a reraise. The flush then grits his teeth, shakes his head, calls the bet, calls a seventh street bet, and disgustedly throws his hand into the muck when the obvious full house turns up his cards. It seems apparent that when you have already invested two bets on sixth street, and your opponent (who sees your flush-type board) raises you with his paired doorcard, you are beaten. Solid players will make a laydown in this situation, rather than throwing their chips to the wind, unless they have another "super out," such as an open-end straight flush draw (which is very unlikely).

Naturally, before you fold, you should be sure that your opponent is a solid player who is capable of making an accurate judgment of your hand and would not raise with less than a full house. If the aggressor is erratic or a maniac, then you have greater reason to call on sixth street and pay him off on seventh street.

One of my pet plays in side-action games is raising with a four flush to get a free card. I sometimes do this in tournaments also, although it is more risky because I cannot replace my chips if I lose the hand. Suppose you have four cards to a flush on fourth street and your opponent bets into you. Raise, especially if two additional players sitting in front of you have called your opponent's original bet. Good players will probably read you for a flush draw, but that's OK because you still have a 45-50 percent chance of making your hand, depending on how many of your suit are showing.

The object of raising with a four flush is to get a free card on fifth street when your opponent checks into you, which is what you hope he will do. Of course, if you improve to a pair that appears to be higher than his and you also have your four-flush working, you don't need to take a free card: you can value bet instead.

Many times, however, this play won't work unless your opponent has the high card on board and is the first to act. Sometimes it's a toss-up as to who will be the first to act on fifth street. For example, say you start with 9♦ and then catch 8♦, while your opponent started with a 10♠ showing and then catches a 2♣. It won't be clear until fifth street who will have the high hand and have to bet first. Therefore, this play works much better if your opponent has a king or queen showing. Unless you pair-up or spike an ace, he will remain the first to act because he will still have the high board, and your fourth street raise will have a much better chance of working. This is a factor you must consider before deciding whether to raise on fourth street.

Of course, if your opponent is a very aggressive player and is likely to reraise, you aren't going to get the free fifth-street card your raise was intended to receive. In this case, you are better off just calling. The bottom line is that you must have a good *read* on your adversary to determine whether a fourth street raise will work to your advantage.

Another time when you won't want to raise is when two or more players are left to act behind you, because your raise may cause them to fold. In this case, you are better off to just call because you want to have as many people in the pot as possible when you are drawing to four flushes in seven-card stud so that, when you make your flush, you will also make as much money as possible. Therefore, you don't want to drive your "customers" off with a raise in these situations. Even if you don't make the flush, you will be in the pot for only a minimum amount.

However, raising when they are sitting between you and the first bettor, when they have already committed one bet to the pot, is a different story. If the original bettor decides to reraise and they all fold, you have their dead money in the pot with the same chance of making your hand. So you aren't in bad shape, no matter what you do. Furthermore, if you do make your hand, there will often be enough confusion in your opponents' minds for them to pay you off.

The Value of Confusion

Have you ever noticed that when your opponents are not able to put you on a proper hand, they will simply call you with any type of reasonable hand, such as a big pair or two pairs? Therefore, if you are able to disguise the strength of your hand, you will get a lot of calls *just because your opponents are confused* about what you are probably holding.

When you put in a raise with two suited cards against *intelligent* opponents, they will put you on a probable four flush, especially when their doorcards are higher than either of your two upcards. But although your raise may tip them off to your flush draw, they may still be forced to continue playing with a reasonable hand because they are not sure *exactly* what you have. This tiny bit of confusion on their parts can add extra bets to your win when you make your hand.

Playing Defensively

How do you *defense* against an opponent who raises you with what appears to be a four-flush? What I usually do is raise him back if I have already made either two pairs or trips. I won't give him a free card. But if I have only one pair, even though I think I have the best hand, I will just call him. On fifth street, if it doesn't appear that my adversary has improved, I will fire a bet right into him, even if I haven't improved my hand either. He will not get that free card from me.

But if he has shown some improvement, especially if he has caught another suited card, I will have to make a judgment call as to whether he has raised on a four flush. Since many aggressive opponents will do just that, I may have to make a cautious laydown of my one pair. Even if he hasn't improved to a flush (maybe he was raising on a pair and a three-flush, for example, and now has a pair and a four-flush), I am still in just an even-money situation at best against an opponent with a weaker pair and a four-flush working. So if my best scenario is even money, and my worst scenario is that I have one pair against a made flush (in which case I am a huge underdog), I will simply have to pass.

Now suppose that on sixth street, your opponent has not caught another suited card and you still have only one high pair. You can still bet into him. But on seventh street, your best play is probably to just check with the intention of calling, if you think he is capable of bluffing or of betting a worse hand than you have. Frequently, you will have to call with only one pair. I have done this many times, with mixed results. Of course, I never like to call with only one pair, but sometimes it is necessary. You can't routinely get into the habit of laying down your hand on the river after putting in bets on third, fourth, fifth and sixth streets just because you haven't improved your big pair.

Many times, it's an "either-or" situation: either your opponent has improved to a huge hand, or he is betting a complete bust, hoping you will fold. Naturally, you're going to look like a total idiot calling a flush or even a hidden full house with only one pair. (Just ask me—I've done it many times!) But sometimes it is appropriate because an ultraconservative approach just isn't going to get the money in a tournament.

Always remember that in the early stages of a tournament, most of your opponents will be playing in a reasonable fashion, and probably more conservatively than they would in a side game. So you have to give them more credit for a hand when they raise into two or more overcards from an early position, with several players yet to act after them, for example. "It's better to give them credit than cash" so often holds true.

Key Concept

In seven-card stud, you have more opportunities to draw out than you have in a game such as Texas hold'em where everyone must use the same community cards. Even a pair of aces may be only a 65 percent favorite against a pair of deuces in seven-card stud. But the pot sometimes reaches such a size that, although you know you're chasing, you have enough potential for improvement to warrant it . . . especially if you have live overcards to your opponent's doorcard along with your inferior pair.

This also means that the weaker players are sometimes doing the same thing their more skilled opponents are doing. But when the pot odds warrant it, chasing is correct, no matter who is doing it. Of course, you still need a lot of options working for you—live cards, one or more overcards (particularly the ace, which is *the* overcard), and one or more pairs with either straight or flush potential.

Key Concept

Your biggest decisions in seven-card stud occur on third street and fifth street. Of these two key decisions, whether you enter the pot on third street is *by far* the more important. Traditionally, bets double on fifth street, although they occasionally double on fourth street if someone has paired his doorcard and decides to take the double-bet option. Usually, however, the bets on third and fourth street are one-half of what they are on fifth street.

It is far better to fold early than it is to fold late. Therefore, when you are playing a marginal hand and your opponent catches a scary looking card such as an ace or king, or a card which gives him an apparent big draw, you are better off to pass if he bets into you, even if you think he's bluffing or semi-bluffing. If he's semi-bluffing with a come hand such as a straight or flush draw, many times he will get there. And even if you have him beaten at the moment, you may not be a favorite against him. So if you started out playing the hand cheaply, get away from it quickly.

Straight Draws

Straight draws are the most overrated starting hands in seven-card stud—they often create more problems than they are worth. On the rare occasions in a tournament when you are playing in a multiway pot against four or five people, you can reasonably assume that two or three of them are drawing to a flush. Straight draws do not play well against flush draws because, obviously, even if you make the straight, you are likely to be beaten by a flush.

Therefore, if your opponents show any improvement on fourth street with either a suited card or a suited connector (which could enable them to make either a straight or a flush), you must play a straight draw with extreme caution—and it cannot be played at all against a raiser who holds a doorcard higher than any of your three straight cards.

As a general rule, fold your straight draws early and often unless they are very live. For example, if you hold 6-7-8, your key cards are fives and nines. If none are showing, your hand is live. However, you also need to proceed to one more level—how live are the fours and tens? It won't do you much good to catch a five if three fours are out, because then you will be drawing to only one end of your straight.

If you decide to draw to your straight, be very leery of a raiser who may have a high pair. You're better off passing. You can feel somewhat more comfortable, of course, if all three of your straight cards are higher than his doorcard. For example, you hold K-Q-J and the raiser's upcard is an 8.

Suppose you enter an unraised pot with three to a straight, or you have cards higher than the raiser's doorcard in a raised pot. You have improved your hand on fourth street by either pairing, or by catching a fourth card to your straight (with a hand such as J-10-9, for example, you catch a 7 and don't see any 8s on the board). Under these conditions, you can continue playing until fifth street. Of course, if you spot one or two 8s showing on fifth street and an opponent bets into you, you must clearly pass, unless you also have a pair. Even if your pair doesn't appear to be the best one, you probably still have enough outs (even with an inside straight draw) to continue playing the hand. Obviously, you need all four of your straight cards to be live if you continue playing with an inferior pair. Try to play the hand as cheaply as possible; if you can get a free card, take it. On the other hand, if you think your pair has become the best hand on fifth street, value bet based on its strength.

Sometimes, a hand as strong as A-K-Q is playable, even for a raise or possibly a reraise, unless the reraise comes from an ace or king showing. In that case, you simply must pass. Say a 9 has brought in the pot for a raise and a queen has reraised. You hold A-K-Q and suspect the reraiser may have queens. If there are no aces, kings, jacks or tens showing (or one, at the most), you are justified in taking off a card with your two overcards. With three overcards to the raiser's doorcard, and if in fact he has the hand he is representing, you still have a very close hand. The pair is usually a slight favorite, depending on how live the sidecard is and whether it is an overcard to your three straight cards. However, if he holds an overcard which is not live, or if his sidecard is an undercard, you are about even money or maybe a slight favorite, depending on how live your cards are.

But if the raise or reraise comes from a player with an ace or king, and you are reasonably certain he has either aces or kings, you should immediately pass without further involvement, even if no jacks or 10s are showing.

Theoretically, if the deck were neutral, where you didn't know what any of the other cards were (which is never the case in seven-card stud), it is still a close decision as to who will wind up with the best hand at the river in a showdown. But since poker isn't played that way, what usually happens is that on fourth street, when you have a pair but see no visible improvement to your opponent's hand, you can continue value-betting, even if you are reasonably sure your opponent has overcards. So long as you think you have the best pair, even though your opponent has overcards (but has not caught a threatening looking card such as a suited connector), you can continue value betting until you have reason to believe you are beaten.

On the other side of the coin, if you started with three overcards and your hand is live, you can probably justify taking off a card on fourth street if you don't seem to be in danger of being raised by an opponent behind you. But if you are in danger of being raised, you cannot call that first bet on fourth street and will have to pass. Assuming you are heads up, if you have not improved by fifth street, you will have to give it up if your opponent continues betting. But if you have paired, you can either call or try for a check-raise if you're reasonably certain your opponent will bet, and if you think you now have the best hand. (To successfully check raise, you should be about 80 percent sure your opponent will bet.)

A check raise is not advisable if your opponent is conservative and may be fearful of betting when you catch an additional overcard to his pair. In this case, he will probably also check, so you are better off to go ahead and value bet your hand. You don't care if he doesn't call, because you can win the pot right there, without the risk of having your opponent further improve and outdraw you on a later street.

A lot of times when you check raise and your opponent continues playing the hand, you will still be the favorite over him *if* you have paired. However, if you catch a connector and are back on the straight draw, such is not the case. With two cards to come, your odds of winning against one higher pair will be fairly close. So you may consider betting into your opponent with a high board and four to the straight, particularly if your straight is open-ended, hoping he will fold when you make your semi-bluff bet. Seldom check raise in this situation unless you are up against a tight player whom you are positive will pass unless he has a second, concealed pair. In this case, a semi-bluff check raise is in order.

If you have four to a straight on fourth street, your chances of making your hand are not quite as good as they would be if you had a four-flush. But you still have about a 40-45 percent chance, depending on whether any of the eight cards you need to complete your straight are showing. With a reasonable hand, enough money in the pot, and overcards, you have adequate reason to play to the river—unless you think someone has either filled up, or has paired his doorcard with a strong potential to fill up, or has made a flush.

Be very leery when you are playing straight draws against flush draws in multiway pots. In tournaments, however, you often have only one or two active opponents in most pots, so you are usually getting enough incentive from the pot odds and your live hand to continue playing to the river.

Key Concept

What you are looking for in seven-card stud is either the best *starting* hand, which is usually the highest pair, or the best *drawing* hand, which is either three big straight cards or a three-flush with overcards to the raiser's doorcard. You want either one or the other: the best starting hand or the best drawing hand.

I caution tournament players, however, to remember this: playing too many drawing hands in tourneys is usually a mistake. I exact multiple criteria for my drawing hands, one of which is the possession of overcards so that, if I don't improve to the flush possibility I started with, at least I have a chance of making the best hand with a higher pair than my opponent(s).

If that isn't likely to happen, then playing a drawing hand will get you into trouble. You simply won't make them often enough to warrant putting a lot of money into the pot with them, unless you have other outs such as overcards. You will be in jeopardy of losing a substantial portion of your tournament chips when you don't make your draw. And usually, the price you have to pay is not worth that risk.

One of the most common complaints I hear from players who have busted out of seven-card tournaments is "I missed x-number of my straight or flush draws," or "My two small pair lost." They probably shouldn't have been in the hand with only a small pair to start with. Making two small pair often leads to death and destruction in seven-card stud. Not only are they often difficult to lay down, but also, if an opponent starts with a high pair and then makes a second pair, he will beat you unless you improve to trips or a full house.

Playing Pairs

There are far fewer multi-way pots in seven-card stud than there are in hold'em because most stud players do a lot of raising on third street to try to force out weaker pairs and marginal drawing hands. The reason is obvious: when you start with the best pair, you have a much better chance of winning *without improvement* if you are against only one or two opponents than you have against three or more opponents. What you hope to do is isolate and eliminate players so that you can play heads up with your big pair. Although it isn't always possible to accomplish this, you can at least punish people for trying to draw out on you by making them put extra money in "your" pot.

Sometimes your opponents will draw out on you because they don't put you on the correct hand, or because they think you are either bluffing or semi-bluffing. Other times, they may have a good pair themselves or a live overcard to your doorcard.

If you think you may have the worst pair, only one overcard makes any sense in prompting you to continue with the hand: an ace. If you have the ace overcard, it is better to have it buried for these reasons:

(1) Suppose you start with a buried pair of tens and an ace showing. You call someone who raises with a queen. On fourth street, you catch another ace. When you bet your aces, the queen isn't going to call you unless he can beat you, so you probably won't get any action on the hand, even when you make it (unless someone decides to call you with two lesser pair). Therefore, if you suspect your opponent has his doorcard pair on third street and your hidden pair is lower in rank, you are probably better off passing to begin with.

(2) If your ace is in the hole with one of your tens showing (and if your aces and your tens are both live), you can justify calling on third street, especially if you have some doubt that the raiser with the queen showing actually has the hand he is representing.

The situation changes drastically, however, if there is a raise and a reraise before the action gets to you. For example, say a 9 raises, the queen reraises, and you have the same split pair of tens (one down and one up) with an ace in the hole. Can you continue playing the hand? With nothing invested in the pot, the answer is a clear-cut and emphatic "no."

Now let's look at a slightly different scenario. The 9 raises, you see several high cards showing behind you, and so you decide to simply flat-call with your tens. Then the queen reraises and the 9 calls. Now you are getting a fair price to continue playing your hand, plus you have the buried ace as an extra out. Furthermore, if you hit the ace, your opponents will not put you on aces-up (the majority of the time), so you can get some action on your hand. And aces-up will win the pot in most cases.

Calling a double-bet *cold* is a totally different thing than calling that same double bet in two increments. Your hand must be much stronger to cold-call a double-bet than to call two separate bets.

But what happens if the 9 raises, you call with split tens and an ace in the hole, the player behind you reraises with the queen, and then the 9 fires in a third bet? Now what is your best move? With only one bet invested, you should pass. The raisers could have buried aces or be rolled-up (trip nines or queens). So why enter the pot with what is probably the third-best hand? You will be asking too much to hope to improve against two hands that are squeezing you in the middle—it's too expensive a proposition.

However, if you can play the hand for only a single bet, your cards are live, and your opponents don't show any visible improvement, you can continue playing the hand even to the river, so long as you are getting two-to-one on your money. Since there are a lot of "ifs, ands, and buts" in this situation, you need a fairly accurate read on your opponents and you should be reasonably certain that improving to either aces-up or three tens will give you the best hand. If you aren't certain of this, or if you are in jeopardy of being raised after calling a bet, you will have to pass. All these criteria need to be met before it is correct to continue playing the hand.

Now suppose you are heads up at the start, or you are probably going to be heads up, with your 10-10-A. If you are reasonably certain your opponent has a bigger starting pair than yours, it is not correct to continue playing, even though you have the ace working for you. In the long run, you won't be able to draw out often enough to justify playing. At best you will have only about a 40 percent win rate, so heads-up play with this type of hand can become very expensive.

Playing Pair Against Pair

Suppose you begin with what you think is the best starting pair and your opponent catches up with you when he makes an open pair (but one that does not pair his doorcard). For example, say you raised with a 9 and have been called by a player with an 8. On fourth street, he catches a 6 while you catch a random jack that doesn't help you. On fifth street, your opponent draws another 6 and you catch a deuce. You believe he now holds eights and sixes. Your starting pair of nines with a 7 kicker has been augmented by only a jack and a deuce. What should you do against your opponent's probable two pairs? So long as you are sure your opponent has made no better than 8s and 6s, you can continue playing. You are hoping to make either a second pair or trips, which will give you the winning hand provided your opponent gets no further help.

Of course, you can no longer play aggressively, taking a more defensive posture by just calling. If your opponent bets into you on the river, you would have a tough call with only one pair because the only hand you could beat would be a busted draw and the one open pair he's betting. In this case, it is correct to fold on the river unless you have a very good read on your opponent as having only the one pair with a busted flush or straight draw. But that would be a risky call which you wouldn't want to make very often.

Now suppose you have made two pair and your opponent bets into you on the river. Normally, you should just call because you cannot be certain he hasn't made either trips or is holding a big pocket pair such as aces or kings which he has been value betting. Of course, against an aggressive player whom you think is capable of betting 8s and 6s, you should consider a raise, which can be a very close judgment call.

When a Doorcard Pairs

When someone pairs his doorcard, he has made trips the majority of the time, if he started with a pair. This becomes an especially dangerous situation if the pot has been raised on third street: he must have had a good hand to have called. Even though your opponent may have called with a three-flush rather than a pair, the chances that he has made trips occurs often enough to make calling him dangerous, even if you started with a premium pair. If you notice that one of his doorcards has appeared on the board, you may assume he is on a drawing hand rather than trips. But if none of his doorcards are showing, you must make an educated guess about what he has. In most cases, you will just have to pass.

While I have said previously that the strongest play in stud may be raising and then pairing your doorcard, the second strongest play is calling a raise and then pairing your doorcard. So, be very selective about continuing to play in these situations.

If an opponent pairs his doorcard in a later round, you may have improved your hand enough to justify taking the risk of calling. This usually occurs when you have made two pairs, each of which is higher than his doorcard pair; or when one of your two pairs is very high (you started with kings and now also have a pair of fours against his pair of sevens). It is usually correct to continue with kings-up, but in a defensive posture. You can even make a crying call with two middle pairs such as nines and eights, so long as they are still live. (However, you would still be better off passing with your two pair on *fourth* street against his paired doorcard 7).

Playing Rolled-Up Trips

This is a hand that will win you a lot of money when you are fortunate enough to get it, but it can also be very expensive when you lose with it. The following tips will help your to maximize your chances of winning with rolled-up trips.

First of all, remember that in tournaments, you are not usually trying to get full value from each potentially good starting hand, as you would be trying to do in a side game. Survival is more important than squeezing an extra bet from your premium hands. It is better to win a smaller pot than it is to risk getting drawn out on in a large pot.

This concept is more important in the later stages than in the early stages of tournaments, when you still have enough time and chips to recover when you suffer a bad beat. So, you can gamble a little bit more with rolled-up trips in the early stages than you can later on. With small trips such as deuces, treys, fours or fives, if the pot is shaping up as a multi-way contest, you will be in greater jeopardy of being drawn out on than you would be in a two or three way pot. Therefore, if you have limped in with your small trips, which is usually the correct thing to do, you may want to raise or check-raise on fourth or fifth street in an attempt to limit the field of contenders. Base your strategy on your betting objectives. If your objective is to eliminate players from a multi-way pot, you will probably have to raise to achieve that goal.

If your trips are aces or kings rather than fives (for example), you need not be as concerned about limiting the field because it is less likely that you will be drawn out on. So you can play the bigger trips with somewhat more safety. Slow-playing these high trips is probably worth the risk if the pot is not multiway. Since you don't get them very often, you want to make some money with your trips. They will usually win the pot in heads-up or three-way action without further improvement. Sometimes, you can even delay raising with them until sixth street because sharp players are capable of making a laydown on fifth street if they think you're slow-playing a big hand. However, if there has been a bet every step of the way, they will probably find it far more difficult to fold because the pot has increased to much larger proportions by then. This is a particularly strong play when you are heads up.

If you are against two or more opponents on fifth street and are last to act when someone has bet in front of you, you should be far more inclined to raise with your trips than to smooth call. The reason for this is that, with two or three other opponents, the pot has probably already reached a sizable amount—and the bigger the pot, the less reason to disguise your hand. In this case, you can take off the wraps because it is more desirable to win the current, adequate-sized pot than it is to take the risk of waiting for a mega-pot before you make your move.

Sometimes, it may even be best to wait until seventh street before you bet your trips, because the pot is often so large that your opponent will probably have to pay you off with just a marginal hand. He may not be sure about your strength, especially if your board looks ragged, and if he has taken the lead all the way, you can be fairly sure he will call your bet or raise on the river.

Occasionally, you get a bad break when you catch suited cards on fourth and fifth streets. While, in fact, you have rolled-up trips, it appears that you have a potential flush, which may scare your opponents. In this case, what do you do? Against only one opponent, try a slow play. Giving him a free card on fifth street may allow him to catch up a little bit. But if he again checks to you on sixth street, go ahead and bet. One freebie is enough. Against two opponents, be more inclined to bet your suited board on fifth street because it is more likely that one of them will call, although he may be suspicious of your apparent flush.

An exception to this strategy occurs when both your opponents' boards look ragged and you are convinced they will fold if you bet. In this case, you may give them a free fifth-street card in hopes of getting some action on sixth street. This play is more successful against weaker players than it is against stronger players. The better players will suspect a trap, so even if they have improved, they will probably be reluctant to bet into you. Against these sophisticated opponents, it is often better to just bet your hand rather than trying to be too tricky; they simply won't fall for your ruse.

Now suppose you have started with rolled-up queens in a multi-way pot. You limped in on third street and then catch a 10 on fourth street. One of your opponents started with 9♥ showing and has caught 8♥. Should you slow-play your queens? No, in this scenario you should bet. You have a good chance of filling up against his apparent flush draw, and you already have the best hand on fourth street. If your opponent indeed has a four-flush, he will probably call you. Nothing is sweeter than making a full house against a flush, so you can reasonably start gambling against his four flush with a raise or even a reraise if he bets into you.

Sometimes, a bit of deception pays dividends. If your opponent catches an ace or king on fourth street and bets into you, raise him. And if he raises you back, just flat call. But if he checks to you, you bet, and he check-raises with the high card on board, just wait until fifth street to raise when he bets into you. If he has caught a card such as a suited connector, he won't be expecting you to raise because of his check-raise against you on fourth street.

Key Concept

Based on your evaluation of your opponent, play rolled-up trips with the strategy you think will get the most money into the pot. If you think slow playing on fourth street and then raising on fifth street will do it, play that strategy. Or if you think it would it be best to wait until sixth street, do that.

Now suppose that you have played the strategy you decided would get the most money into the pot and maximize your chances of cashing in on your trips. Then an *aggressive* opponent catches a third suited card and fires a bet into you. What should you do? You should probably put on the brakes. There is no reason to throw away your hand, but there is also no cause to raise him, either. In this situation, you will need to play somewhat more defensively, rather than offensively, as you did against the three-flush, non-aggressive player previously mentioned. (Two big pairs may be played the same way.)

One situation I like to be in is holding high trips when the big overpairs start raising wars against each other. In this case, I take the gloves off sooner because, once again, the bigger the pot, the less reason I have to disguise my hand. I may reraise on fifth street when there has been a lot of betting on third and fourth streets. I may even cap the pot on third or fourth streets if a raising war seems to be developing because, once people call a raise and a reraise, they aren't likely to throw away their hands when someone puts in another raise behind them.

Middle Stage

Your stack size relative to that of your opponents becomes an important factor in the middle stages. Be more willing to gamble against short stacks that have only enough chips for one or two more bets. With small to medium pairs, be more willing to gamble against a short stack. What you want to avoid is giving action to a small stack when a *third* player is involved in the hand, especially if he is sitting behind you with a threatening-looking card and could raise, in which case you could be holding the third best hand. So be reasonably certain you will be heads up against a short stack before you do battle with him.

Heads up against a short stack, I will deliberately give some loose action with the worst pair. It won't hurt me very much and I have a reasonable chance of drawing out against him. I am inclined to gamble with hands such as three-straights or small three-flushes that I might fold in other circumstances.

Be careful about the types of drawing hands you play in these middle stages—even more careful than you were in the early stages when it didn't cost you as much of your stack if you failed to make your draw. You may have to expend one third or more of your stack to play a drawing hand in the middle stage, and you want to avoid doing that if you possibly can. *Be very selective with drawing hands in tournaments.*

Playing Four-Flushes and Straights

A student in one of my seminars asked me, "If your first four cards are a flush or an open-end straight draw, should you play to the river against someone who pairs his doorcard?" The answer depends upon whether you think your opponent has trips. If you are reasonably sure he has trips, you should fold. If you doubt he is tripped-up, you can go to the river unless he makes another open pair, in which case you should pass.

If you make your straight or flush, you can raise with it, but be very leery of a reraise. Suppose, for example, it becomes apparent that you have made your flush (three or four of your suit are showing) and your opponent raises you anyway. He has probably filled up and you are drawing dead; therefore, you should pass. It takes a very gutsy player to reraise with less than a full house unless he is confused or lost in the hand. If you think he is confused, just call him down. But if you think he is a solid player, fold because it is very rare that a player will reraise on a bluff.

Now suppose you have two high pair and your opponent pairs his door card—do you go to the river? Generally, yes, unless you are positive he has trips, in which case you should pass. But if you doubt that he has trips, you can usually go to the river if you have a minimum of queens-up. Ideally, both your pairs should be higher than the raiser's door card pair, and all four of your out-cards should be live.

Suppose an opponent has limped in with a 6 showing, for example, and you have raised with a pair of queens. On fourth street, you catch a deuce, which is your side card, making two pair and he catches another 6. At this point, you have to use very good judgment. I would feel much more comfortable if I had made queens and sevens, for example. Or suppose he catches something like a jack on fourth street and calls your bet. Then on fifth street, he catches another 6 and check-raises your bet with queens-up. It is very likely he has tripped, and you should pass.

Playing Big Stacks

With a large to medium stack, use a solid approach to every hand. Prefer to play more on the side of caution, except against a very tight, passive opponent. Then you can try to capitalize on his tight posture by playing somewhat more liberally: perhaps putting in a raise with a medium pair, semi-bluffing, and trying an occasional ante-steal.

But when you have a short stack and are up against a tall stack, you cannot afford to jeopardize yourself with a weak drawing hand; you must wait for something better, especially when you have enough chips left to post the ante for two more rounds. Short stacks are more likely to get called by tall stacks because it won't cost them very much to try to eliminate a player. So if you're the short stack, use your best judgment about when to commit your chips. Naturally, you would rather commit with a split pair and an ace kicker than you would with a small three-flush. Your chances of either having the best hand at the start or of improving to the best hand with your ace kicker are much better than you would have with your three-flush or three-straight.

Key Concept

Don't lose patience when you have a short stack in the middle rounds. Pick your spot—usually, with three high cards or a good pair. If you have only enough for one or two bets, it is probably better to be aggressive early with your pair and simply go all-in. But if you have been forced to play a drawing hand with only enough chips left for two or three bets, you may not want to fully commit on third street. If you don't improve on fourth street, you can still escape with enough chips for a few more antes, a few more opportunities to make a comeback.

Personally, I don't like taking these halfway measures. I prefer being the aggressor and getting heads-up against the low card with my short stack and a reasonable hand. So I usually give it my best shot with a raise to try to win it right then, or to at least get one on one. Of course, I know I am much more likely to be called by a tall stack if I have only one or two bets left. That is why I like to wait for good pairs before taking my stand.

The middle stage is a very good time to take advantage of the table image you have created for yourself. If you have a tight image, capitalize on that: ante steal more often. If your image is loose (you've given your opponents the illusion of action that I mentioned earlier), play somewhat more conservatively. Try to maneuver your table image in such a way that your opponents will do what *you* want them to do. If you're looking for calls with your loose image, make an aggressive raise. If your image is tight, make more positional plays (such as stealing the antes).

With a medium or large stack, try to avoid playing small pairs against other medium to large stacks. (If you have such a short stack that you think your pair may be the best hand you're going to get, then play it, of course.) Most of the time, abandon small pairs unless it will cost you only one or two bets and will put you heads up against a short stack.

In tournaments, it is often correct to put in a bet with a negative expectation. For example, when you have a hand that may not be the favorite to win, but it will win just often enough to make it correct for you to play against a short stack. With a little luck, you may be able to draw out on him at minimal expense. It is important to put players all-in at every opportunity in the middle stages because, even with a short stack, they can make inroads quickly. Since the limits are higher, a player could rebound in only two or three hands. So when you have a short stack down, step on him, even if you have to play a mediocre hand to do it.

Be wary, however, about giving too much action with a truly terrible hand. For example, if you made the forced bet with a deuce showing and have 3-7 in the hole, it isn't worth it to call an all-in bettor who raises with a 5 showing. But if your cards were 4-5-6, for example, you would have a reasonable chance to improve and may consider making the call. Another type of hand with which you might call one extra bet against the short stack is A-K in the hole, because you have two overcards and you could outdraw him if you get lucky.

Talking about getting lucky may not sound very scientific. But so often, you *allow yourself to get lucky* by solid play that enables you to survive and accumulate enough chips so that you can take a few gambles such as this in select situations. It is your good, solid play in other stages of the tournament that has set the stage for you to get lucky when you think it is necessary to occasionally take the worst of it.

Late Stage

You will need to raise far more often than you call in the later stages of a tournament. The vast majority of the time, you should be trying to take the lead yourself, or isolate the action heads-up with one other player. With judicious raising and a good sense of timing, you can also pick up some additional antes.

Taking advantage of tight play in the late stage is crucial. It gives the chance to jockey yourself into position to make the last table with a reasonable number of chips. The antes are usually quite high, making it worth the extra risk to pick up a few pots against tight players.

However, you must also be ready to put on the brakes. Getting caught once in a bluff or semi-bluff is not usually enough to slow me down completely. Although I may have to wait an entire round, I will try it again. But if I get caught a second time, I am going to be more cautious. I may be tipping my hand, or showing a tell, or simply timing my plays badly. I will then kick in with better judgment about when I try a steal.

Ante Stealing

Suppose you have a king showing with A-8 in the hole. Your king is the highest upcard and all your cards are live. Only one or two other players are yet to act. You try an ante-steal and get caught by a 4 showing, who calls. What should you do on fourth street when your opponent catches what appears to be a bad card (in this example, a 9) and you catch a scary looking card such as a jack or 10 which doesn't really help you? Fire a bet with your two high cards showing in hopes of picking up the pot.

If he again calls with a raggedy front like 9-4, you are faced with a judgment decision as to what to do on fifth street. If you catch another scare card such as a queen (giving you an inside straight draw) and he catches a random 7, for example, go ahead and make another bet. If he calls you this time—or worse yet, if he raises—you must seriously evaluate your next move. If he raises, you are in a very bad situation with only an inside straight draw against a hand that probably has a minimum of one big pair and possibly two pairs or even trips. Your opponent would have to be very brave to put in a total bluff on fifth street with his ragged-looking board cards against your strong front.

Now suppose your adversary catches a suited connector to his doorcard on fifth street, for example, and you catch a bad card like a deuce or trey. You must check to him, hope for a free card, and just pass if he bets. In this situation, it makes no sense to continue representing strength you don't have.

The Delayed Steal

When you are playing heads-up against an aggressive opponent, you can occasionally limp in with the higher upcard and nothing in the hole. You are hoping to catch a threatening card such as a suited connector or a face card on fourth street, and then bet into him on the strength of your board. Naturally, this will work better if he catches a blank or a non-threatening card.

If you have been making frequent raises against the low card, the "delayed steal" will often prevent your opponent from making too many resteals against your third-street raises. Because you only limped in on third street rather than raising his low card, you may create some confusion in his mind regarding the strength of your hand.

For example, if I have a 10 showing against the low card's deuce, trey or four, I will sometimes limp in rather than raise him. Then if I catch a face card on fourth street, and he catches an 8 or other non-threatening card, I will now bet into him, which will probably allow me to steal the pot.

Seven-card stud is a game of strong looking boards. Be reluctant to continue playing against such a board in the late stages, and especially against several opponents. You would need a very strong hand yourself to continue. Therefore, even if you suspect a player is on a bluff or semi-bluff, if he catches two powerful looking face cards to go with the unmatched one he already has, you're taking too much of a risk to continue playing hands such as medium pairs, for example.

You can't afford to be a sheriff in a tournament, trying to keep the other players honest. You can't even afford it in a ring game, constantly checking people out to be sure you haven't been bluffed so you can sleep better at night!

The best players in the world get bluffed more frequently than their weaker compatriots because they are more capable of making a big laydown. So in the late stages, you can capitalize on the play of a conservative player who will make such a laydown when he believes you may have him beaten. But if you see that your opponents are willing to defend smaller cards with medium strength hands, you had better have a hand that is at least as good as the one they are defending with before you begin splashing around too often.

The Final Table

If you have arrived at the final table with a short or medium stack against several tall stacks, you will need to put your patience to the test by waiting for the best situation possible to put in your money. If your back is to the wall and you're down to only one or two bets, you will probably need to throw them in on a medium pair, three big cards or a strong looking three-flush that is fairly live.

In very few seven-card stud tourneys do you ever ante yourself broke. The antes are usually small enough in relation to future bets that you can wait awhile for a premium hand. But once you decide to make your final commitment with a short stack, put the heat on as early as possible. You hope to either eliminate players or to make your opponents put in their money early rather than later so that if you end up with the best hand, you can get full value from the pot. With a short stack, it is a bad play to put in only the minimum bet when you know you will need to go all-in on a later street, no matter what your opponents do. Also, if you just call, the opponents left to act behind you can get away from their hands on fourth street, for example, without putting in any extra chips.

When the table is down to either three players or you are heads-up against only one opponent, you will have to do far more ante stealing than you have previously done. You must also be prepared to put on the brakes more quickly, because your opponents won't continue to let you bully them without taking a stand. When you get caught in a bluff or semi-bluff, then, be prepared to muck your hand quickly.

If you are on a semi-bluff and get called, whether you fold on fourth street depends upon your style of play. If you are on a three-flush, for example, catch nothing at all on fourth street, and don't have a frightening front, you are better off to pass, even if your opponent's front also looks weak. If he was willing to call you on third street with a small pair, for example, if you can't even beat that, give it up.

On the other hand, if you are semi-bluffing and catch a card that pairs you, or gives you either a four-flush or a four-straight, so long as you have overcards, you can continue to play the hand. You may continue betting into your opponent, if you are first to act. If you're against a very aggressive player, be selective about when you take a stand. If he seems willing to mix it up with you, you may try a reraise bluff or semi-bluff, although they are very risky moves. But if it doesn't look as though anything will slow him down, you should wait and try to pick him off with better cards. It won't do him much good to steal four antes in a row and then lose the fifth hand he plays if it goes to the river.

I like to play all my hands the same way—whether I am bluffing, semi-bluffing, or holding a big hand—and bring it in with a raise shorthanded. After you have bluffed your opponents and have stolen a few antes, it can be very sweet to show down a legitimate hand for which they haven't given you credit.

Heads-up play requires a fairly accurate evaluation of your opponent. By this stage of the tournament, you should be able to read him rather well: his style, what's going through his mind, and so on. Once again, remember that it takes far less strength to get involved in a pot heads-up than it does when even as few as three or four players are left.

"Raise and take it" will probably become the order of the day with the high upcard raising the smaller one. Suppose the low upcard is a deuce and you have a jack showing. You probably have a far greater chance of taking the pot with a raise than you would if the low card were an 8 and you held a 9. When you have nothing at all, you are better off just passing.

There are two occasions when you can limp in heads-up rather than raise. One is with a marginal hand such as a 9 up against an 8. If you have 7-10 in the hole, for example, you may want to take off a card. Although you are looking for that perfect 8, you might also catch one of your overcards, a 9 or 10, and end up with the best pair. Another time you may want to flat-call with such a marginal hand is when you hold a three-flush and only your upcard is higher than your opponent's doorcard. You hope to either pair your high card or catch a fourth flush card; if you don't, you quickly give it up if your opponent bets into you.

Strong boards are often the key to whether you semi-bluff, bluff, or continue with a hand in heads-up play. The ultimate in personal judgment is always required in deciding how to best proceed with your hand in seven-card stud. ♠

Chapter 12

SEVEN-CARD STUD HIGH-LOW SPLIT
(8 or Better)

Seven-card stud high-low split is not for the faint of heart. It is one of the more difficult games to *read* players because, so many times, you cannot know for sure what they are representing: have they paired their low card or do they have a solid hand?

Good card memory is very important in this game. You need to recall what has been folded early in the betting, particularly which *low* cards have disappeared from the board, and which *key* cards (those that affect both your hand and your opponents' hands) have been folded.

Seven-card stud high-low is a game of strong boards throughout all stages of a tournament. You must make your maximum effort at always paying close attention because so much is going on at every stage of the game.

In split games, you often begin with a good starting hand which improves just enough for you to continue getting sucked in. Sometimes you escape with half the pot, other times you don't. This is one reason why I prefer playing games that are high only or low only where every single pot is a scoop pot.

Hand Selection

Ideal starting hands contain three low cards such as 3-4-5, preferably suited or with a two-flush. Such a hand is worth a raise or even a reraise. Another excellent starting hand is split aces with a baby such as a deuce or trey. In this case, you have not only the probable best high starting hand, but also some potential for low. When you are showing an ace up with an ace and a baby in the hole, your opponents will have difficulty playing against you because they're not sure whether you are going high or low.

"The almighty ace: don't leave home without one," is an old saying in seven-card stud, high-low split. Although this doesn't always hold true, if you have gaps in your hand, you are far better off if it also contains an ace. Even with cards such as A-3-8, in which the 8 makes it a borderline start, if there are no other aces showing, you have a marginally playable hand, especially if there are no other aces showing.

Any three low cards with straight potential have some value, even a hand with a rough low such as 6-7-8 unsuited. Even though you may not have the best low at the start, your hand has some merit because it has some high possibilities. But you don't want to play it if it becomes too expensive; for example, there is a raise or a reraise. A hand such as 7-8-9 is simply not playable because you have only two weak low cards and if you do make a straight, you'll probably have to split with the low hands because your low (assuming you make a rough 8) will not be good enough to scoop the entire pot.

Even though there may be gaps, any three cards below an 8 that also have straight potential are playable if you can get in cheap (7-5-4 or even 8-6-4, for example). Unless you are semi-bluffing heads-up against one other random low card who has bet first, you should not be raising with this type of hand. If anyone else enters the pot, your hand is very marginal at best, and you would hope to draw another low card, which would give you four to the straight, on fourth street, while your opponent catches an unfavorable card. If you both catch good and your opponent appears to have a better low draw, at least you have both a low draw and some straight potential, then you can take off another card.

Sometimes your hand will show a movement from low to high. For example, you begin with three small cards such as A-4-5 that have some straight potential. You pair the 4 on the turn, and you take off another card. It is a 5. Now your two-pair hand has more high potential than low. If you're up against a player with a high pair, your hand has the possibility of beating his hand while still retaining its low potential. If you're playing against someone with a low hand, you have now shifted into the high end of the spectrum, have paired two cards which he probably needs to make a straight, and you have a very good chance to make at least the high end of the pot and possibly scooping it. You can take a very aggressive posture in these types of circumstances.

However, if more than two people are in the pot while you hold this hand, you will be in a rather marginal situation. You have the best high hand at the moment, your low-draw opponent has a better low hand, and your high-draw opponent could make a second pair to beat your two low pairs.

Early Stage

In the first round of high-low split tournaments, you can be somewhat more liberal with your starting hand standards: you can tolerate a few more gaps for your low hands. With holdings such as 2-3-7 or 3-4-7, you can call for the minimum bet or call a raise if someone raises behind you, provided the pot doesn't get jammed before it comes back to you. If you catch bad on the turn, you should usually fold, even if your opponent has caught bad, unless you also have three flush cards working. Otherwise, you can get sucked into the pot, catch a low card on fifth street, pair up on sixth, and then catch a paint on the river, ending up with only one small pair and no low. You can avoid this type of trap by giving up your hand on fourth street when you don't get a helping card.

If you are holding a low starting hand such as 2-3-7 unsuited in the tournament's early stages, there should be other hands competing for the pot to make it worth your while to play. Going heads-up against a high hand only is not a good spot for you to be in because your hand has virtually no high potential. If someone with an upcard such as a jack or queen brings it in for a raise and it looks as though you will have to play the hand heads up, you have only a marginal call at best.

If you decide to take off one card and you don't improve, then you must pass on fourth street. Too often, what happens is that you get some improvement if you catch a small card (such as an 8). Your hand may look good at this point, but even if you make it, you will still win only half the pot. Without an overcard such as an ace, hands such as these have only limited value.

You're much better off playing against one high hand and two other low hands. Even then, you have to use both caution and discretion, because the other low hands may have a better start than you do, with high potential as well. So if you limped in along with a couple of other low hands against a king or queen who raises the pot (probably meaning they have another card to match their door card), you can take off a card because, with two other low callers, you have justifiable pot odds. Any hand that has an 8 in it is very marginal in seven-stud high-low split and should either be folded immediately or played cautiously.

When you start with 2-3-7, if you're fortunate enough to catch inside the 7 (A, 4, 5 or 6), which gives you at least some straight potential plus a good four-card low to draw to, you can continue playing the hand. However, if you catch only moderately good (such as an 8), or if you have either paired or caught a face card, you probably cannot continue playing past fourth street, especially if one or more of your opponents has caught a good low card and either bets first or raises the high card's bet. When you're drawing for only half the pot, you must be sure you have the best draw.

Playing High Pairs

Big pairs other than aces are often in jeopardy in high-low split games. Playing them correctly requires excellent judgment, especially in the opening rounds of the tournaments when people are usually playing very solid hands. High pairs—kings, queens, jacks, tens (and even nines or eights if they seem to be higher than any pair your opponents are likely to hold)—play best against the fewest possible number of opponents. These types of hands hold up better against a single low draw or one other high opponent with a pair that appears to be lower than yours.

The betting rounds, of course, double from fifth street on, and even with open pairs on fourth street, the bet remains fixed, in contrast to seven-card stud where a player with an open pair has the option of betting either the smaller limit or the upper limit.

Quite often, a high pair such as kings will have to be pitched into the muck on fourth or fifth street. One reason is because many players will not enter a pot without an ace in their hands. Therefore, when an ace shows up on fourth or fifth street, it is almost certain to help someone else by either pairing them, or by assisting their low draw. If the ace pairs them, your kings are beaten; if it assists their low draw, you will probably have to split the pot with them.

However, if you are holding aces and another ace falls in someone else's board, you still remain in good status because the two aces in your hand diminish the chances that your opponent will also have an ace in the hole. It is more likely that he has improved his low draw. But if several players have already entered the pot, you are probably better off to simply throw away your high pair. When four or five people limp into a pot with low hands, they could easily have low straight draws, or make two low pairs, making you a dog against them.

With only one or two other opponents, however, you have some chance of success, although you still must use good judgment in playing your hand. All too frequently, with a hand such as kings-up, you will find yourself reduced to calling-hand-only status from fifth street on, especially when an opponent shows a board such as 4-5-6. In these cases, you are only hoping your two high pair can withstand his possible straight draw and win half the pot. Only one high pair, of course, is even more vulnerable.

When I am dealt a high pair, I will usually raise or reraise early, if the pot has not been bet or raised by an ace. If someone raises with an ace, you simply don't know what type of hand he's holding: a low draw or a pair of aces? If he has a low hand, you'll be on the defensive throughout the hand if he catches another low card on fourth street. Quite frequently, however, he's starting with two aces. So again, a great deal of judgment has to be exercised. Therefore, I don't want to invest too much money with kings or queens against more than one opponent.

However, if I can isolate the hand against one opponent, my chances of winning the whole pot are improved (or at least winning the high end of it). So my general strategy is that if no one has yet entered the pot except the forced bet, and if I have a good card showing (such as a king with another king in the hole), I'll raise and see what happens. Since I haven't yet invested much in the pot, if I get too many callers behind me, I'll evaluate what cards come out on fourth street to decide whether to continue playing the hand.

High hands are very vulnerable when the dreaded ace falls in one of your opponent's hands, so you have to use good judgment. If I had a choice between a premium high pair such as kings or a premium low hand such as 3-4-5-, I would take the 3-4-5 because it has a lot of scooping potential, whereas the two kings are relegated to a high-only potential.

Key Concept

Your goal in seven-card stud high-low split is to win the whole pot, so you have to develop hands that can do that: these are usually low hands with straight or flush potential. A three-flush that contains two high cards such as A-K with another low card such as a 5, for example, are certainly worth taking a card off with, even in a raised pot.

In fact, if a couple of people have already passed, I might even try to steal the antes by semi-bluff raising in middle position with, for example, A♥ suited to my two hole cards. Even if I am called, I have a hand with a lot of deceptive value because players won't be certain whether I am going high or low. In reality, I could go in either direction, and maybe even in both.

Of course, what you hope to catch with this hand is another baby heart, giving you three low cards, plus the four-flush. If you catch something like a black 6 on fourth street against a single opponent with a 4 showing who catches a face card, you can probably pick up the pot at this point without even bluffing—because your ace high three-flush is probably better than what he's holding. Even if he has a small pair (4s with a 3 kicker, for example), he's almost forced to pass when you catch another low card which looks as though it has improved your hand. Deception is always helpful in a hand

Key Concept

Avoid playing in totally predictable patterns: that's why deception is important in all stages of the tournament. If you can deceive your opponents in the early rounds, they may make mistakes against you in the middle and late stages by not reading you correctly. Their wrong decisions will benefit you. So if you can deceive them early with tricky and deceptive maneuvers, you're that much better off.

This game requires both judgment and reading skills, because you can't always know with certainty whether your opponents are playing for low or for high. Sometimes, with a low card showing, they will have a big pair of Ks or Qs in the hole, but you won't find that out until later in the hand, although occasionally, you can figure it out earlier.

For example, suppose a 3 or 4 has raised the pot and then catches a jack on fourth street and a 10 on fifth street. If they continue betting, you can be fairly sure they must be going high because they have caught two cards which cannot possibly help them for low and yet they are still in the pot. Since they must be betting on something, you have to put them on either a big pair or trips.

Any rolled-up trips is a nice hand to start with in high-low split. Because of the split-pot nature of the game, I would usually play them very aggressively from the start. The exception is trip aces. Because they are such key cards in other opponents' hands, if you've tied up three of them, they're far less likely to make their lows if they're going in that direction. Therefore, slow-playing them may net more money than playing them aggressively. However, an aggressive posture is almost always correct for other sets of trips.

There is less need to play rolled-up trips deceptively in high-low split because, if you have a king showing with two in the hole, for example, opponents will put you on two kings rather than trips. You have little to gain by being deceptive since they already know you have a high hand. Therefore, you may as well bring it in for a raise because they won't be giving you credit for three kings anyway. Another advantage to raising is that you can "tax to the max" the low draws.

You can add some deceptive quality to your hand by also playing low rolled-up trips aggressively. Since it is not unusual for a three-card straight draw to raise the pot, your opponents are more likely to put you on the straight draw than on trips, and thus misread your hand.

Key Concept

High pairs can usually be played aggressively to start with. If three or more players call your raise and at least two of them subsequently catch threatening low cards, be prepared to abandon ship.

Key Concept

Hands such as 5-6-7 are better than 2-3-4 or 4-5-6 because your pair possibilities are higher when you are up against smaller low draws. Also, hands such 7-7-2 are much stronger than 2-2-7.

Middle Stage

In the third and fourth rounds of the tournament, many of the short stacks will be trying to play somewhat more conservatively. You can take a few more liberties against them because they will be less than anxious to enter the pot without a premium hand, preferring to wait for a good solid raising hand before they come in. Their tight play will give you some semi-bluffing opportunities when you have a reasonable hand—for instance, a borderline hand with its marginal cards buried—and you would prefer playing for just the antes and the forced bring-in bet.

For example, you are last to act against the low card, a deuce, who brought it in for the forced bet. You have a 5 showing, with an 8-3 offsuit in the hole. Actually, your hand is not too bad. If your opponent has only a two-card low (2-3-J, for example), or if he has an 8 in the hole, he may very well just give it up because he would have a hard time defending.

Even if you are in middle position, and the cards behind you are not that threatening (for example, a nine and two eights), you can raise with any three-card low and perhaps pick up the pot right there. (Of course, if you have an 8, it should be hidden.) It's probably no great tragedy if you are called because you'll most likely be fairly close to equal with the caller.

If you're competing at a table where the players are mixing it up with a large assortment of hands, this play won't work. But if you're fortunate enough to be playing at a table where a lot of players are playing two-card hands (such as A♦2♥K♣) , you can successfully value bet more often. These types of opponents often get involved with a raise on third street, and make a big mistake by playing the pot with shaky hands. Therefore, when you value bet against such players, especially with marginal low hands against weaker looking draws, you can expect to get action. Although it doesn't happen very often, this gives you an edge.

Key Concept
Cut your losses on fourth street when you catch bad and your opponent catches good. Save those precious chips for a better situation.

Late Stage
As the tournament progresses and you have accumulated a large stack of chips, it is quite reasonable to try to break a short stack with a slightly inferior hand you wouldn't normally play in a side-action game. This is common throughout tournament poker, not just high-low split, but many times you can justify more marginal hands in high-low split.

For example, I might be aggressive with the A-2-K (referred to earlier in such derogatory terms) against a short stack to get him to fully commit all his chips, even though I would clearly pass this hand in a normal side-action game. It is quite correct in tournaments to play a hand that is slightly worse, but which has some potential to develop into the best hand (although it has an overall negative expectation), when you are trying to break a shorter stack.

With a short to medium stack you're jockeying for position in the later stage of the tournament, when there are only two or three tables left and you're trying to survive to the money table. Actually, you are looking for really decent solid starting hands or situations in which you can play a medium-strength hand against the low-card bring-in only.

You have to be jockeying for position at this stage, just like the rest of your colleagues. However, if you've already built a big stack and you're fairly sure of a money finish, you can be a bit more aggressive in trying to pick up a few antes with marginal hands, *if* you are playing against opponents who are playing more cautiously.

In all phases of seven-card stud high-low split, when there are several people in the pot, some of whom have gone all-in, there is less reason to disguise the strength of your hand. You don't want to protect the all-in players you're trying to eliminate. So many times, you'll just want to check-call medium strength hands rather than raise with them to give the all-in players protection. Naturally, if you have a premium hand, you can raise to extract maximum money from the remaining players contesting the pot. But you should be sure you're a big favorite to win the pot before you protect an all-in player.

In my earlier book on tournament play, I said that if you have a short stack and are forced to commit, just go ahead and do it without second-guessing yourself. This strategy certainly applies to high-low split. If I have a hand such as 4-5-6, two-suited or even three-suited, I will raise and reraise to get all my chips in early and then just hope for the best. Hands such as two aces would play the same way.

You are less likely to have several people contesting the pot when people are jockeying for the money payoffs. Therefore, I would be far more likely to commit with the same two kings or queens I would have passed earlier (or would have played for only one or two bets), because they are less vulnerable against a single opponent or in a shorthanded pot than they are against multiple opponents. Even if the dreaded ace falls in another player's board, I will raise with my high pair, provided I think that the raise will get me heads-up with a single opponent.

Desperate men do desperate deeds. When you have a short stack, sometimes you just have to play a hand you may not have played earlier—and play it aggressively to try to maximize your chances of winning with it. A more conservative approach simply won't do you any good. You've played as conservatively as you can for as long as you can just to survive with a short stack, but sooner or later you're going to have to commit with less than the nuts. Naturally, it requires good judgment to decide when that time has arrived.

Key Concept

Avoid traps when you don't have either the best high hand or the best low hand to draw to. You must avoid being in the middle of a raising war if you are not drawing to the best hand in at least one direction.

The Final Table

When you are at the final table with only two-to-four players remaining, you will have to play more hands. You will also have to represent hands that you don't always have, which means occasionally raising with an ace showing and weak cards (such as 9-8 offsuit) in the hole in an attempt to win the antes and forced bring-in bet against the low card. It is usually worth a raise because, even if your opponent tries to defend his low bring-in bet, if he catches a bad card such as a jack or 10 on the turn card, you can bet again if you have caught any card 8 or lower. Since you will be representing a stronger low hand than his, you can probably win the pot right there.

Of course, this type of play will not work against a stubborn or liberal player (although these types of players have usually eliminated themselves with their loose playing habits before the final table action begins). In most cases, at the final table, you will be competing against solid players, who will not jeopardize their chips, even if they suspect you are bluffing or semi-bluffing with a weak starting hand.

Many times, if you have a rough 8 with no straight potential against what looks like a better low hand (even though it may be paired up), you will have to play the hand very slowly with check-calls, or even give it up. It is simply too dangerous to continue playing when you could be against a better low.

If I don't have a pair and am playing against a hand that does have one, even though he may be drawing to a better low, I will sometimes make a crying call with a rough 8 on fifth street. Then, if I catch bad while my opponent catches a scare card on sixth street, I will fold. In fact, you may find yourself making a lot of sixth street lay-downs throughout a seven-card stud high-low tournament. But, of course, so will your opponents, so it works both ways.

Seven-card stud high-low split is a game of strong boards throughout all stages of a tournament. Try to add deception to your own hand when you have a strong board, but do not have the hand you are representing. For example, suppose your opponent catches a bad card on sixth street and you catch a good looking card, when in fact you have two pairs and an incomplete low draw working. Even though he may already have made his low hand, it's a great coup for you if your bet or raise can get him to fold, thus allowing you to win the whole pot. You can set up such a play by betting on fifth street, even though you have not yet made your hand, *if* your board makes it appear to your opponent that you *have* made it.

Key Concept

The bottom line is this: at the final table when the game is shorthanded, you will have to do more raising than calling in order to take command of as many pots as possible, as early as possible. As winning tournament player John Bonetti said, "Lots of players can get to the wall (the final table), but not many can climb over the wall (win the tournament). I can." ♠

Chapter 13
SEVEN-CARD RAZZ

Razz has always been a favorite of mine because it is the only game in which I have made it to the final table three times at the World Series of Poker. In 1986, I won the razz title and have finished in the top eight two other times.

Although it is not nearly as complicated to play as seven-card stud or Texas hold'em, razz can be far more frustrating. It is a game designed to aggravate people and put them on tilt. In fact, the description of razz that circulated around cardrooms in the 1980s when it was far more popular than it is now, may be fairly accurate: "Razz is not a poker game, it's a disease."

Some players are making the same comment today about Omaha high-low split, which is another game in which you can enter the pot with the best hand, and frequently see a much weaker hand beat you on the river. This kind of frustration can drive any rational, intelligent, reasonably solid poker player to distraction after a while. That's why it is especially important not to lose your cool when things go bad in razz.

Razz has a unique way of making players expose their true colors. It's a great game to study the character of your opponents—how they handle adversity and what their tilt factor is. Even when you start with three perfect cards such as A-2-3, you're still on a draw, *even if* you catch that perfect 4 on fourth street. And many times, you're going to lose with this perfect start because you need *five* cards for a complete hand. Catching a face card or pairing a couple of times can throw some of the most solid players on tilt.

But razz can also be a very profitable game to play, particularly against opponents who are willing to start with one bad card in their hand; in other words, they're starting with a lot of two-card hands. Their loose style of play can be especially lucrative for you in tournaments, where it is very important to pay attention to the quality of hands your opponents are turning up on the river. For example, if you notice that a player often starts with a 9 showing, or in his down cards, you can reasonably assume that he opens with weak starting hands. (With a 9 showing, he will usually have very good low cards in the hole, of course.)

It seems like I have seen more people make open trips in razz than I ever have in stud. I've even witnessed three players going to the river in razz, with everyone making a full house. That's pretty bizarre, but it does happen. I once thought I would bluff when I made a fullhouse at the river—my opponents had a couple of face cards showing and I was hoping they hadn't made their hands, so I thought I could successfully pull it off. I never dreamed I had the best hand, but when each of them showed me an even bigger full house, we all laughed together. I was bluffing with the best hand!

Razz requires a lot of patience, good judgment in spots, and an accurate read on your opponents, although it isn't as difficult to read hands in razz as it is in seven-card stud or Texas hold'em. Razz also requires that you remember the key cards that are out that will affect both your hand and your opponents' hands, especially the babies, seven or below. A quick inventory of these cards is imperative—you can't just sit there like a lazy lump in tournaments.

Hand Selection

What you hope for in razz is the best starting hand with the best draw. In tournaments, if your opponents are playing the way they should—starting with solid three-card 7s—you have to be somewhat cautious when you enter the pot. Most of the time, you should be in there with three "babies," three unpaired cards 7 or lower. Although there are times when starting with a rough 8 or even a 9 may be the right play, you will not want to enter most pots with anything less than a premium three-card hand.

With any three-card 7 starting hand, you can call a raise or even a reraise. One exception to this is when you have a very rough three-card-7 (7-6-5, for example), and several of the cards you need (such as a deuce and a couple of 3s) are showing in other players' boards, and they are either betting or raising with them. But as a general rule, so long as three or more of your key cards are not showing, you can call a raise or a reraise, or even raise yourself, with any premium three-card 7.

You need not be too concerned if you're taking slightly the worst of it, either. Even if an opponent starts with a three-card wheel draw or a three-card 6, although he's definitely a favorite over you, you're not that far behind—you're in the ballpark. Those are the hands I like to gamble with. In fact, you might start with a slightly worse three-card hand, but still be a substantial favorite over the original raiser simply because your cards are more *live* than his cards.

For example, suppose a player raises with a 6, which you are fairly certain is a three-card 6, and you are holding A-2-7. You don't see any other fours or fives out, which are key cards for your hand, but you do see some twos and sevens, which are some of the cards your opponent can probably use. These are cards which are likely to affect his hand, but are not as likely to affect yours because you already have them to start with. In this situation, you can usually reraise the 6.

With a start such as 2-3-7, if you see two deuces and a trey showing in other players' hands, you are less likely to get paired. And yet your opponent is probably going to need a 2 or 3 to help his hand. Therefore, even though he starts with a three-card 6 or 7, your hand is actually more *live* than his, because you have more cards to draw from that will help your hand than he does.

Even if your start is slightly worse, then, you actually have more winning possibilities than your opponent. These are the situations in which I will sometimes jam the pot in the early stages of a tournament.

Because razz is a game in which people can catch up very quickly, you probably will not want to slow play very often in tournaments. With a premium three-card hand, so long as your cards look *live*, you can raise or even reraise. For example, if I start with a hand such as the 2-3-7 mentioned earlier, my key cards are aces, fours, fives and sixes. If I don't see too many of them in other people's boards, I'll raise because I have a very live hand with good winning potential.

As a general rule, you can play for a raise or reraise with virtually any three-card 7 starting hand, even if your opponents' start is slightly better. Again, you can catch up fairly quickly in razz, even if your opponents begin with slightly better starting hands.

Early Stage

Razz tournament strategy requires that you play a generally solid game, not tight, not loose, just solid. This means you will be passing most of the time, but when you do enter a pot, you will be selectively aggressive.

Play the first round in about the same manner as you would in a side game, except that you might be slightly more conservative to start with. For example, you might not put in a reraise with a premium 3-card hand if it is the first hand you get involved with, and there's jamming from the start, you don't necessarily have to put in the third bet. Instead, just call, even though you think you have slightly the best of it. Hold off and see what fourth street brings, and then decide how to continue playing.

Actually, I am not much of a believer in just calling most of the time. That is why I like to reraise (if my cards are live) with a solid three-card 7, even though I might be against a slightly better hand. Solid, selectively aggressive play is essential for survival to maximize your winning hands. Of course, reading players properly and making correct lay-downs are also very important.

Occasionally you will be in a game against opponents who are playing faster than normal, with a lot of raising and reraising on third street. If that is the case, they are probably gambling with reasonable hands. They may be raising with a three-card 8 with the 8 buried in the hole, or even a three-card 9, hoping to pick up the antes by representing a hand they may not have. But if your opponents are starting with solid three-card 7 hands or better with an occasional 8, be careful about entering the pot with anything less than a premium hand.

Of course, there are times when starting with a 9 may be the correct play. For instance, when you have a three-card 9 and all the remaining exposed cards on third street are bigger, you actually have a *raising* hand. But if the pot has already been raised and there are some other babies out, including people to act behind you with low cards showing, you should fold most nines and some of your rough eights.

For example, with a hand such as 8-7-5, if the pot has been raised by a 2, called by a 3, and several low cards are yet to act behind you, you cannot play your rough 8. Even though you might have *one* of them beat, you won't have *all* of them beat. You might even be subjected to a reraise behind you, trapping you for extra bets and forcing you, if you improve and help your hand, to probably take the worst of it throughout the entire hand. Therefore, although there are times when you can do it, you have to be very selective when you enter the pot with a rough 8 or 9.

Your decision will require both good judgment and *patience*. Although it is tough to get a whole lot of premium three-card starting hands, you simply must wait for them as long as you can. Once you start losing your patience and begin slipping in with 9s and 10s or even worse, you are on the road to tournament death and destruction.

On the other hand, players who continually play 10s and 9s against raises, even when they catch mediocre or bad on fourth street, can be a great source of profit and will fatten up your stack. Even though it may be frustrating to lose to these players, you'll get a great boost from them when your hand holds up in tournament action.

As a good rule of thumb, if you start out playing a marginal hand (such as a rough 8 or 9) cheaply in an unraised pot and catch bad on fourth street, even if your opponent doesn't seem to catch any better, if he fires a bet at you, you are usually better off folding your hand than chasing the pot.

Razz is a game where you can catch up fast, but you can also lose ground fast, especially if it's debatable whether you started with the best hand. It is often better to just pass while the pot is still small. This is a tournament strategy which might be different from how you would play in side action games.

Sometimes, however, when your chip position has eroded and you're down to just a few chips, you may have to play a starting hand such as 9-3-2. In fact, sometimes you are forced to go all in with this kind of hand because you're just not likely to see anything better before the antes devour the rest of your stack. But in the early stages of the tournament, this is not usually the case. So, why jeopardize yourself in a raised pot with cards that are almost certainly going to be getting the worst of it?

Key Concept

Razz offers many opportunities for representation, especially in the opening rounds. For example, suppose you're paired up twice, but your opponent doesn't know it because both your pairs are split. If your board looks solid, you can *represent* a premium hand you don't have.

Suppose you start with a three-card 7 with the 7 on top and A-2 in the hole. You catch another 2 on fourth street, while your opponent catches a 10. Even though you have paired, you should continue to bet. If your opponent calls, you still have a chance to steal the pot on fifth street if you catch another scary looking card, or even if you don't, but he catches bad. Although he actually has the best hand, he doesn't know that for sure.

Now, you catch an ace on fifth street so that your board is showing A-2-7, and he catches a jack. How can he call? He just can't do it, even if he suspects you have paired. Although he has the best hand at the moment, he probably knows that if you are paired only once, you are still the favorite over his made J-10. Plus, he virtually can never play the hand strongly from fifth street onward, even though he has the best hand. Even if you catch bad on sixth street, if he also catches another bad card, he can't very likely bet into you. In fact, he is probably forced to fold.

Actually, many players will call on fifth street with a hand such as 7-J-10 against a 2-3-7. Against such an opponent, if your 2-3-7 catches a face card on sixth street, you can expect the 7-J-10 to probably continue playing the hand, whether or not he has caught another bad card. So be careful with your betting tactics on sixth street in these types of circumstances.

Middle Stage

In razz tournaments, the action will frequently be hand again hand. If you and your opponent both start with premium three-card hands, and you've both caught good or you've both caught bad, you have every reason to continue playing because no one has a discernible advantage at this point. This is when your card reading abilities become very important.

If I think my opponent is paired up, for example, and I have a pretty good four-card hand, I may very well test him with a raise. Other times, however, I will take a more conservative approach. If both hands look about equal, but my opponent has a slightly better board and is betting into me, I will usually just call, with a few exceptions.

For example, suppose I have made a good read of the exposed cards on third street and have locked them into my memory. In my opinion, some of the cards my opponent needs have already appeared in other people's hands, making it more likely that he will pair when he catches another low card. He bets into me with his low board, hoping that maybe I am paired and will give it up. If I suspect that he has paired (and I haven't), I will raise him. If he raises me back, I have to assume he is not paired. I will just call his raise and proceed cautiously.

Then, if he catches a card which appears to make his hand, I will usually consider passing if I am not drawing to a better hand than what I think is the best hand he could have made. In this situation, I have tested my opponent with a raise and he has played back at me. I have to give him credit for the hand he is representing, because it becomes pretty risky to continue playing the hand on the off chance that his fifth card has paired him.

If you're up against a real action player who is quite capable of putting in a reraise with a hand that's no better than yours (or is even slightly worse), that's a little different. Sometimes, aggressive players get more action than they deserve because they give you a lot of action. In tournaments, however, it is quite rare for a player to put in a reraise bluff on fourth street when you have both caught good cards.

Suppose your hands are about equal. On fifth street, you both catch good. Maybe you have made a 7-6-5-4-2, for example, and are looking at a 7-2-3 in your opponent's three upcards. He bets into you. In this situation, you might decide to see if he has made his hand; or whether any one of those cards has paired him; or whether he started with an 8 in the hole. To find out this information, you can put in a raise.

If he reraises, be very careful about how you play the hand from that point on. You don't necessarily have to pass your five-card 7, but you're forced to play defensively unless you improve to a 6 or better. And you want to be very sure that you're still drawing *live*. The pot has usually reached such a large size at this stage that even if you think you're beat, if you're drawing live, you can continue playing the hand.

But you must play defensively: just check and call. For example, if you catch a card that appears to help you, although it has actually paired you, and if it becomes the low hand on board (because your opponent has caught a higher card), you still cannot take the chance of betting into him with your rough 7. You will often get raised again. However, you don't have to throw your hand away either. You may call. Now suppose he catches a 9 or 10 on the fourth upcard, while you actually improve your hand to a 6. If the best hand he can have is a 7, naturally you can bet into him with a 6.

In another scenario, suppose the pot has been raised on third street. You call and now you are heads-up. On fourth street, he catches good while you catch bad. If you are not absolutely sure he has paired, it is a clear-cut pass. Don't continue playing the hand if you each have only one single bet in the pot. It simply isn't worth it.

If it is multiway action between three or four of you, you can call the raise. Now if you catch a bad card on fourth street and two of your adversaries catch good cards, leaving you in-between two players who may or may not raise, you clearly must pass your hand. It doesn't matter that you started with A-2-3. If you catch a 10 or jack, for example, and one of your opponents has called with a 7 and then catches a 4—while the other one called with a 6 and now catches a 5—you can't take a chance on calling because the 7-4 might decide to raise behind you. Then you would be wasting your bet because the 6-5 may decide to reraise, and you just can't take the heat.

It would still be a bad situation even if he didn't reraise. If the 6-5 bets, you call, and the 7-4 just calls with his four-card rough 7, it is still just too risky to continue playing this hand on fourth street.

However, if only one other player catches good, and it's not clear whether he has paired, even if the other three of you have caught bad, you may very well stay for another card because the pot odds warrant it. In this situation, if your hand is reasonably live, and if you started with a premium three-card 7 or better, you can justify seeing another card. But you must play with some degree of caution.

Again, the smaller the pot and the fewer the number of opponents on third street, the less reason to continue playing the hand when you catch bad on fourth street and your opponent catches a good card. Conversely, the more money in the pot, the more reason you have to contest it if only one opponent has caught good.

Now suppose you have a three-card 7 starting hand against an aggressive player with an 8 showing. On fourth street, you catch another baby and so does he. You bet and he calls. Then on fifth street, you catch perfectly to complete your pat 7, and he also catches an unpaired baby.

If you are against an aggressive opponent, this may be a good time to try a check-raise. Thinking that you have probably paired, your opponent will most likely bet when you check. When you raise his bet, you actually don't care whether he calls or folds: either way, you have gotten his chips into the pot. This is just another ploy you can use to try to build your chips during the middle stage to put yourself in a competitive position for the late stage of the tourney.

Raising with the Second-Best Hand

One intriguing aspect of play in razz occurs when the second-best hand raises the best hand to drive out the third-best hand. In my opinion, this play is overdone by many players. However, when the (presumably) second-best hand looks very close to the best hand, it is sometimes correct to put the heat on the pot and try to drive out the third-best hand. An example of this ploy is as follows: You start with a 4-2-7, which you bring in for a raise. The pot is either reraised or called by two players, one with an ace showing and the other with a 6 up. You know they are both solid players and your hands are very close. Perhaps you may even have slightly the worst of it, but not by much. In this case, the second-best hand may raise the best hand to drive out the third-best hand.

You catch a 5 on the turn. The 6 catches a 4 and the ace catches a 10. The 6-4 leads out. You are next and you raise with your 7-5 showing to force out the player who caught the 10 on the turn. This play is especially powerful when there have been two bets on third street. Say, for example, you raise and were reraised by the 6 and cold-called by the ace. You can fairly well assume that the 6 started with a three-card 6, and the ace started with a wheel card and no worse than a 7. But when you catch the 5, you are probably close enough to the opponent holding the 6-4 to raise in an attempt to drive out the A-10. This is an especially good strategy in tournaments when people are playing more conservatively than they would in a ring game.

However, I don't believe this strategy is correct when, for example, the player holding the ace who cold-called the double bet on third street catches an 8 on fourth street. In this case, it is probably not in your best interests to raise with your 7-5 because there isn't that much difference between the three (apparent) hands in play, whereas it is clearly correct to raise when the ace catches a 10 or worse card.

If you raise to force out the A-8, your raise probably won't work anyway, and you may be opening the flood gate for a reraise from the 6-4 if he thinks he has the best of it. Then you may be forced to put in a third bet without accomplishing your goal of eliminating the third-best hand. If the ace catches a 7 on fourth street, you definitely should not raise. The ace needs to catch slightly worse than both you and your other opponent, which usually means a 10 or worse, or possibly a 9.

To summarize the concept of the second-best hand raising to force out the third-best hand, you definitely want to see the third-best hand catch a card which is a gap or two worse than your hand in order to justify the play. If there is only a one-gap difference, it could prove to be too expensive. In the example above, an 8 is shaky; a 10 is much better; and a 9 is on the borderline.

Calling a Raise When You Are the High Card

Suppose you make the forced opening bet with the high card, a low card raises, and a couple of other low cards call, even though they are only average (eights or sevens, for example). The action is now back to you and you have only a partial bet in the pot.

Say you started with $500 and you are in the $15-$30 round. You bring in the pot for $5 with you high card. A deuce raises the pot, and both a 7 and an 8 call. You can safely assume that the best they can have are three-card sevens or eights, with only average strength, but the deuce probably has something that is definitely better than that. Now what do you do?

You may be thinking, "Gee, I'm getting 3-to-1 on my money and can't get reraised. Why not take off a card?" This is faulty thinking. Taking off a card is a terrible decision because you will have to outdraw three other players, not just one. It is very unrealistic to think they will all catch bad and you will catch good. In fact, even if that does happen, the only result is that you have put yourself in an even-money situation with the other hands. Suppose, for instance, you brought in the pot with a king on top and A-2 in the hole. You catch a perfect 3 on fourth street while your opponents all catch bad. You are still a 3-to-1 underdog.

There are occasions, however, when I will defend. Say I am the high card with a jack. Everybody passes except a 9 or 8, who raises the pot. If I have two cards in the hole which are below his 9 or 8, I may very well take off a card. Another instance is when the last player to act when everybody else has passed raises my high card and I have two cards below the raiser's door card. Suppose he raises with a 7: I have a 6 and a 5 in the hole (or any two cards below a 7). In this situation, I may defend because almost any player will automatically raise when he has a low card up and is heads-up against the high card. In this case, it not clearly evident that the raiser has a premium three-card hand, and so I will usually call the raise so long as my criteria have been met.

However, if the raiser has raised through several other low cards (he has a 4 showing with a 2 and a 3 yet to act behind him), I know he has a good three-card hand because he has raised against two babies behind him. In this case, I will give him credit for a good hand and will fold, even though I may be able to play heads-up.

Sometimes you will see this type of play: Everybody has passed, a 5 raises, a jack on your immediate right cold calls the raise, and the action is up to you. You have brought in the pot with a queen and have two babies in the hole. In this case, you can call, since the 5, who raised into only two high-card hands, may not have a premium three-card low. Since your queen is fairly equal to the jack who cold-called and the raiser did not need to have a three-card low, your call with two babies in the hole can be justified. Your two low hole cards can even be 6-2, for example, but you would not want to call with a 6 and 7 in the hole, even though the other high card has called. The 7-6 is too shaky against the 5 and another high card who probably has better hole cards than you have.

The higher the door card of the caller, the smoother his hole cards usually are. So you would not expect the jack to be calling with a 7-6 or worse; his hole cards are probably very smooth, which means that even if you have the raiser beat, you probably don't have the jack beat.

Late Stage

Bluffs and semi-bluffs take on added importance in the later rounds of tournaments. Usually, the best time to bluff or semi-bluff, particularly on the first three cards, is when there are only one or two little cards remaining to act behind you.

Suppose there are only 18 or 19 players remaining in a tournament which pays 16 spots. You have a 7 showing but have a 10 or even two bad cards in the hole. If you believe the players left to act behind you are playing a very tight game and would not enter a pot without three wheel cards—because they want to ensure a money finish—use that information to your advantage and bet your hand in an effort to steal the antes.

This doesn't mean that players won't play their premium hands; of course, they still will. But with a marginal hand, you can take a few more liberties against them. However, if your opening raise with a marginal hand gets called and you subsequently don't catch good on fourth street, give it up immediately against a bet. Don't continue representing something you don't have. If you both catch bad, check and go for a free card even if you are the last to act. Sometimes you can steal on fifth street if you catch bad and your opponent also catches bad. The general rule is that when a tight player continues to bet, give him credit for a hand.

If you have a premium hand, you don't care who you play against. In fact, you would prefer playing it against someone who has a lot of chips because you have a chance to put a serious dent in his stack. But if you have a more marginal hand, such as a three-card 8, you would rather play against shorter stacks who cannot do as much damage to you as a tall stack could. With marginal hands, avoid major confrontations with big stacks whenever possible.

Key Concept

Players sometimes change their strategy in the late stages when: (1) they have a big stack and loosen up their play; (2) the limits rise—for example, from $300-$600 to $500-$1,000, which can reduce what was an average stack entering the round to a short stack during the round, because of the higher limit; (3) they have a short stack and are playing ultra tight. Be aware of these possible changes and alter your play to reflect current playing conditions.

For example, suppose you have a three-card 9 with the 9 in the hole. The high card has brought in the forced bet, four people have passed, and two are yet to act behind you. One of them has an 8 showing and the other has a 9. This is a perfect spot to raise with your buried 9. It wouldn't be a tragedy, either, if one of them calls you because you are at least equal to the other 9 and only a slight underdog against the 8. So be aggressive in these situations, rather than allowing the antes to erode your stack in these late rounds of play.

Playing on Fifth Street

Suppose you are drawing to a 7 or better on fifth street (when the betting limits are double what they were on fourth street) and your opponent bets a made 9 or 8 into you. What do you do?

For example, you started with A-2-4, raised the pot, and got called by a 9. On fourth street, you catch a 7 and your opponent catches an 8. You bet and once again get called, so you can safely assume that your opponent has two low cards in the hole. On fifth street, you catch a king and your opponent catches a 5, giving him a 9-8-5 showing against your A-2-4-7-K. With two cards to come, you are a slight favorite against the made 9-8-5.

The best your opponent can improve to at this point is an 8, whereas you can improve to a 7 by catching either a 3, 5 or 6, with 11 cards that would make your hand (or 10 if your opponent has a duplicate of one of your cards in the hole). You could also make an 8, of course, increasing the number of cards that would make your hand from 10 or 11, to 12 or 13. Depending on how live the cards you need to complete your hand are, you are at least even money and probably a slight favorite over your adversary. Therefore, I will often raise my opponent in this situation. Then if I catch a good card on sixth street (even if it pairs me), he will probably have to give up his hand when I bet into him. He cannot take the chance that I have a made 7, for example, while the best hand he can make is an 8.

Of course, your opponents won't always fold, even if they have to draw on both sixth and seventh streets (if they call sixth street, they will invariably call on seventh). So if your sixth street bet doesn't make him lay down his hand, only bet on seventh street if you have made a 7 or better, because the chances are that a rough 8 won't win it for you.

Now suppose that on sixth street, he improves to a slightly better hand than you. For example, you catch the king on fifth street and he catches a 10, which he checks to you. You value bet and he calls. Then on sixth street, you catch another bad card, a queen. He catches a 6, giving him a probable made 9 (9-8-10-6) with one card to come against your four-card 7. At this point, your hands are fairly close in value. If he bets into you, you probably should not raise with only one card to come. Instead, just call and try to draw out on the river.

Final Table

During the very late action when there are only four or five players remaining, both you and your opponents will catch fewer premium starting hands. This means that you must pick up more antes and represent more starting hands than you are actually getting, so long as your weakness is disguised.

For example, suppose your start is K-4 in the hole with a 2 showing. A jack makes the forced bring-in bet and a 9 folds. You are next to act, with a 7 behind you. A raise is in order in such a situation because the 7 will probably not call without two babies in the hole. If he does call, you must give him credit for a hand.

Then if you catch good and he catches bad on fourth street, you have a very good chance of picking up the pot with a bet. But even if he calls, you are probably still in an even-money situation at the worst.

If you again catch a good card on fifth street (even though it may pair one of your hole cards), and if he catches another bad card, you can easily win the pot with a bet. After all, your opponent is looking at three babies in your board, and he has caught bad cards twice. What he doesn't know is that your hands are approximately equal, but he cannot take a chance on calling and risk diminishing his chances for a higher money finish.

Playing judiciously and courageously in final table situations such as these will often bring you the results you desire, while playing too cautiously, too timidly, or too tight just won't win the money.

When you have already completed a yeoman's job—you're among the final three or four players—

tight play just won't get you there. With the antes and the bring-in bet very high, you cannot afford to just sit there and allow your opponents to run over you. Your job is not over yet—in fact, it has just begun. ♠

Chapter 14
STRATEGIES FOR LOW-LIMIT REBUY TOURNAMENTS
by Shane Smith, Author

Poker Tournament Tips From The Pros

The techniques in this chapter are geared to the popular low-limit rebuy events conducted by casinos and online gaming sites across the world. Low-limit poker tournaments are good training grounds for players who want to eventually move up to the big-time tournaments featured on television. Most big-league tournament champions began their tournament careers playing low-limit rebuy events.

The type of tournament you enter determines a major part of your playing strategy. In freezeout tourneys, for example, your strategy will most likely be more conservative than it would be if you could replenish your chips with a timely rebuy if you go broke. But most low-stakes tournaments are not freezeouts (the format used at the World Series of Poker). Low buy-in casino tournaments allow multiple rebuys, either when you get broke or when you fall beneath a minimum chip count, plus an add-on at the end of the rebuy period. With all these opportunities for refilling your canteen at the oasis, your strategy for traversing the occasionally arid desert of rebuy tournaments will definitely differ from freezeout tourneys. On the following pages are some tips that will help you cross the desert with a full canteen and saddlebags full of cash.

Rebuying and Adding on

If you plan to win a rebuy tournament, enter it with enough money to make several rebuys. In most cases, you'll need to take advantage of this rebuy option to be one of the top finishers. If you are on a limited bankroll, it may be better to save your funds for ring play or for a freezeout tourney, because your insufficient bankroll can become a significant drawback in playing optimal rebuy tournament strategy.

When you go broke, it is usually correct to rebuy. If your winning expectation seems to be favorable—you are one of the stronger players in the tournament and there will be a big payoff—rebuy so long as you feel comfortable with the number of times you do so. Although I have seen players make as many as five rebuys, I believe they probably should have accepted the decision of the poker gods who simply did not smile on them that day, and bow out of the fray.

Deciding whether to add on is a major decision in rebuy tourneys. The add-on option is usually offered at the end of the third round, and is your last opportunity to buy additional chips. If for the price of a single rebuy, you get twice the number of chips you would ordinarily receive, making the add-on a sort of "two-for-one" special, it is correct to add-on.

Tom McEvoy believes you should always add on because of the extra leverage the add-on gives you, if it is a two-for-one special. Also, the price of the add-on in low-limit rebuy tourneys is very small compared to the pay-out for first place. For example, in a rebuy tournament that costs $20 to enter with $10 rebuys and a $10 add-on, the add-on usually gives you an additional $200 in chips with which to compete for the top money. The prize for first place usually exceed $800 in a typical Las Vegas tournament with 60 or more entrants.

Other tournament experts have different opinions. Some believe that adding-on should be determined by two factors: your chip position, and the strength of the players who are in top chip status when the rebuy option comes up. Following the chip-position guidelines, if you are very low on chips, add on. If you are the tournament leader, there is little need to add on. And if you are in a middle chip position, it probably doesn't matter much one way or the other.

Using "who has the chips" as a factor in deciding whether to add on, it is probably wise to take the add-on option if you see that a very weak player who has been on a lucky streak holds top or near-top chip position. You may need the additional ammunition to take advantage of his weak (and often loose) play. But if a very strong player holds top spot and you have a mid-sized stack, it probably will not increase your chances of a win enough to justify the add-on. In tournaments with a lot of entrants (over fifty), it is more difficult to determine the strength of the players with top chip position. Use your best judgment in these circumstances.

Tournament leaders often say they buy the extra chips for insurance, which is a viable strategy, but I suspect that fear also plays a part in their decision. The fear of losing the lead is a mental shadow which lurks in the dark corners of a leader's mind. Possibly the worst feeling I have ever experienced in tournament play is going to the final table as tournament leader armed with my add-on "insurance," playing very tight to protect my lead, and then finishing fourth in a three-way pay-out. "You choke when you get afraid and try to protect your lead," is the way the late Bill "Bulldog" Sykes put it.

Your real rebuy tournament nemesis is the experienced tournament player with a bankroll large enough to make multiple rebuys. If you find the competition just too tough for you to buck, back out in favor of buying into a tourney with an easier lineup, although an easy lineup is becoming tougher to find with the proliferation of tournaments across the world where you compete against the new breed of tournament junkies. In Las Vegas, these junkies enter almost every rebuy tournament in town, sometimes two a day. Avid online players can play even more than that from the comfort of their living rooms.

Decide in advance how much you're willing to invest in the tournament. You can use the projected pay-out in relation to the expected cost of the tournament in making your rebuy and add-on decisions. Some players, for instance, use a "ten times" yardstick: the probable payoff for first place must be at least ten times the amount they invest. Others insist on a twenty-times reward. You can project the payout by counting the number of entrants and estimating the probable rebuys, or by asking the tournament director what the usual payout is.

I recommend devising a strategy which you intend to follow *before* you enter any tournament, and then writing your reminders on a business card which you take to the table. You should include what you will do in specific situations, such as rebuying, adding on, playing the small blind in low stack status, attacking short stacks when you are leading, and so on. Your rebuy and add-on philosophy must become an integral part of your rebuy tournament strategy.

Play Assertively in the Early Stages

Some tournament players have a tendency to play too tight, waiting for optimal starting hands to survive to the last table (although every tourney also seems to have its share of kamikazes who try to torpedo you early-on). Although playing tight-early may be a viable strategy in a no-rebuy tournament, it is not an optimal strategy in rebuy events. (Of course, neither is loose-early.)

Some tight players are actually looking for an excuse to throw away their hands—yes!—perhaps to alleviate the stress of taking a big draw which may decimate their stacks. When an inveterate rock feels threatened by a big bet (usually by the middle stages of the tourney), you can often take advantage of his timidity with bold, assertive play—running an outright bluff or steal (easier to pull off in hold'em than in Omaha high-low or seven-card stud).

The advantage of playing fast (not loose) early in a rebuy tourney is that you can build a quantum stack to take into the later stages for a survival pad and for driving out the short stacks by intimidating them with strategic bluffs and steals. The disadvantage is that you stand to lose it all and you may need to rebuy several times.

If the risk you take when you play fast appears to have a positive expectation against the field you are facing, take it. But if the play-fast strategy isn't working for you, ease off and change gears. Maybe you're up against a weak player on a lucky streak, too many calling stations, or are being outplayed by a superior strategist. Or maybe you just aren't getting the cards you need to back up your assertive ploys.

Playing fast doesn't mean playing loose. Loose players enter pots with inferior or mediocre hands hoping to hit a flop with their rags. Fast players come in with good hands, calculate the pot odds on their drawing hands, and push their good draws to their fullest potential. When you play fast, you bet for value, raise, reraise, or whatever you need to do, to build a pot that will pay you maximum value. You want to win as many chips right now as you can, realizing that you can play looser while the rebuy stage is still in effect. Your goal is to build a big stack for the later stages when you can no longer rebuy. You build that competitive stack with good holdings and assertive play designed to squeeze out every drop of value—not with the maniac's reckless raises and loose play.

The late Tex Sheahan, noted Card Player columnist who was still winning tournaments at the age of 78, offered some solid advice on assertive fast play in the early stages of tournaments. "As to the actual playing style in the early stages, it's aggressive!" He suggested raising with a live top overcard in seven-card stud if you're in late position, or calling an aggressive player's raise with a premium pair or a small live pair with a good kicker. "You'll either live fast or die young. Rocks seldom win tournaments."

Caution is sometimes the better part of virtue, however. In his original book on tournament poker, Tom McEvoy stated, "In the beginning stages of a Fast Action tournament, players often tend to play too fast, especially in the smaller tournaments with a buy-in range from $25 to $45 with rebuys for the first hour." All low-limit rebuy tourneys fit the description of "fast action," because the betting rounds are usually only 20 to 30 minutes long. McEvoy suggests that you play more conservatively than your opponents, if you *don't* plan to rebuy. My observations of low-limit tournament players verify that many players do not draw a line between *loose* and *fast*, and a lot of them seem to put no limit on the number of rebuys they are willing to make to compensate for their loose play. (I hate playing against these guys because it is very hard to put them on a hand, although if they survive to the later stages, they can become major contributors to your wealth.)

On the flip side, if rebuying is part of your strategy, you can loosen up your starting requirements because theirs are also looser. "You might take a slightly inferior hand in Texas hold'em, like 8-7 suited, and gamble with it," McEvoy suggests. "It's likely that big pairs or high cards are out against you, which means the deck should be rich in middle cards."

There is more than one theory about how to play in a tournament's early stages. Some players push their *Charge!* buttons and never turn them off. Others think you just have to make the most of the cards you're dealt and play assertively with them. Some rocks sit and wait for the nuts 'til the squirrels come home. But probably neither squeaky-tight nor super-aggressive will do the trick. Ultimately, you must choose a style of play that is exactly right for you.

Track Your Stack

Always be aware of your stack status relative to that of your opponents, and of your playing position at the table. For example, if you have a very low stack with an average holding in a middle table position, be inclined to throw away your hand. Save your chips in hopes of catching a stronger hand in a later, more favorable position.

Suppose you are in the big blind in a hold'em game and have enough money left for only the small blind and perhaps two extra bets. The player on your left is very short on chips with only enough to meet the big and small blinds. A player in late position raises the pot. You may not wish to call the raise, but instead allow your left-elbow opponent the opportunity to go all-in on the next two rounds, thus possibly eliminating him, while avoiding jeopardizing your stack.

When you are in strong chip status and good position, attack the weak chip status blinds with a raise if you have a playable hand, especially if they are very tight. If they fold, you own their chips. If they call, you have the positional advantage to raise them all-in and possibly eliminate them from the tourney.

But if you are in good chip status and so is the player to your left, allow him to attack the blinds (provided he is a known aggressive player), and thus preserve your own checks. It is the *duty* of either you or him to get the blinds out of the game if either of them is in weak status. Taking out a competitor in the later stages is usually a one-man job.

If you are the tournament leader, try to eliminate the weak spots as often as possible, especially after the add-on option has expired, to reduce the competition and further enhance your chances of winning. I recall a tournament in which an experienced player complained because a tight-timid opponent with a tall stack piled in front of him did not take out a short stack when he had the chance. It was a justified complaint. That short stack rebuilt himself and took third place.

Watch the Clock

Most low-stakes limit poker tournaments increase the betting increments every twenty or thirty minutes. This often means that with ten players in your circle, you will get around it only once per increment increase.

Think of the tournament as a pie which is divided into as many pieces as there are time periods. Within each piece of the tournament pie, there are somewhat definable sequences of action. In Texas hold'em and Omaha high-low, you will probably face only one small blind and one large blind during a round; have late position or the button for about three hands; be in mid-position for about three flops; and be in front position for two hands (discounting the blinds). "If you can win one pot at each increment, you can sustain yourself," Sykes advised. I have found this to be solid advice.

You sometimes need to time your moves according to the movement of the clock's hands. For example, your goal may be to increase your stack by 50 percent or more during each betting-increment round. You look at your watch and see that the time is almost over in the round; you're in late position with a medium-strength hand; and so you decide to play your reasonable draw faster than you would otherwise play it. Why? Because the betting limits will double within the next two hands. You can take this opportunity to double-up while the bets are still at the less expensive rate, without taking the next round's higher monetary risk if you fail to make your hand. Experienced tournament players often use this ploy. (Do not feel pressured, however, into playing a very marginal hand under the time-pressure gun.)

In the middle stages of rebuy tournaments, if you have a short stack, McEvoy suggests that, "You have to double-up. Double-up or get up! You don't have to wait for a premium hand, so play that K-J with a raise, even from up front. Chances are you won't get any better cards in this round anyway."

Another time tactic to consider in hold'em and Omaha high-low is putting in a raise from late position just before the betting increments rise. Or if you are in short stack-status on the last hand before the final add-on, you may want to throw in those extra chips with a good, playable hand. This is advisable because all the odd lower-denomination chips are usually "raced off" the table on the first hand after the add-on option is over, giving you added value for your auction-block chips if you win the hand. (The highest dealt card either wins all the odd-chips on the table, or they are "rounded-up" to their full value.) In general, then, one of the optimum times to play fast or to bet aggressively is just before the increments increase to make full use of your chips at the lower current price.

Good tournament strategists track their stacks, observe the other players, and watch the clock. They also win their fair share of the gold and glory, those elusive butterflies of tournament play.

Practice, Practice!

Before you decide to enter a tournament with a big buy-in (say $100 to $1,000), play in as many low-limit tournaments as you can find. The buy-in for many small tournaments is $20 with $10 rebuys when you have fewer than 200 chips remaining in your stack. A $10 final add-on buys you 200 additional checks. First-place money in these events is often in excess of $1,000 when the field has 70-100 entrants. Seven-card stud tournaments generally have fewer contestants with payouts of about $600-$700. Most tournaments reward every player who makes it to the final table.

As the tournament buy-in increases, so does the sophistication of the entrants. Although the number of entrants is often smaller, the competition is usually stiffer in higher buy-in tournaments than it is in low buy-in tourneys. Get some mileage under your belt before you tackle the big boys. You can do this by beginning your tournament career in lower buy-in tourneys, gradually progressing through the medium ranks until you have enough expertise to compete for the highest stakes.

Another way to practice is to stand at the rail at some high stakes tournaments and observe how the opponents play. Take notes. Did they make some moves you can use in your next tourney? Are they doing things differently from the way players perform in low-limit tournaments? What? How? Why? You also can watch the World Poker Tour final table on television. Just be aware that final-table play is quite different from the way you play a tournament in the early or middle stages.

As a professional writer, I am attracted to Tom McEvoy's suggestion that you study poker books. You must be also or you wouldn't have invested in *Tournament Poker*. I believe that I have saved far more money from the valuable ideas I've read in poker books and *Card Player* magazine than I paid for them—and they are much less expensive teachers than experience alone. When you hear a loser say "I'm paying for my lessons," you can believe he's paying an expensive price.

My final suggestion involves mental rehearsal. Before you enter any tournament, mentally prepare yourself by designing your strategy, memorizing it, and affirming to yourself that you are capable of winning. Mike Caro's famous affirmation is, "I am a lucky player. A powerful winning force surrounds me." If it's good enough for Mike, it's sure good enough for me!

Believe you are a winner. See yourself raking in all the chips and receiving wads of $100-dollar bills for winning first place. Imagine carrying home a B-I-G trophy and celebrating with your friends in your glorious moment of victory. Napoleon Hill said it best in his classic *Think and Grow Rich* : "What the mind of man can perceive and believe, it can achieve."

The Ultimate Tournament Tip

No matter what ugly things happen to you in tournaments, keep a positive mental attitude. It doesn't matter if:

- Maniac draws out on you in a monster pot
- Aggressor's bluff causes you to fold the winning hand
- Slow-Play sucks you into calling his raise on the river
- Dealer mucks your winning pair of kings
- You get nothing but rags for the first two hours
- Never fall victim to the one adversary who beats you more often than any other, *yourself.* Be your own best ally, not your own worst enemy. You will always get drawn out on, fold a winner, and get dealt a bag of rags, but this is the only chance you'll ever get to win *this* tournament. A winning attitude is half the battle—the other half is winning strategy combined with luck! ♠

Chapter 15
SATELLITE STRATEGY

I am a great believer in satellites because if it were not for them, I never would have been able to play in the main event of the 1983 World Series of Poker. That was the first time a satellite victor won the $10,000 buy-in no limit hold'em tournament, although it has happened several times since then.

The Bingo Palace, now called Palace Station, sponsored four $110 buy-in satellites with fields of 100 players each. The four winners were each awarded an entry into the WSOP main event. Rod Peate, who finished second to me in '83, won one of them.

I also won a satellite, but it was a one-table event at Binion's Horseshoe which cost $1,135 to enter. Even though I had already won the limit hold'em event that year, I was still reluctant to put up the $10,000 buy-in for the main event, but I was willing to take a shot at a satellite. Since I had sold shares of my action in the limit hold'em tournament, one of my partners asked me to split the satellite entry fee with him so that I could take a crack at the title. If I hadn't won that satellite, I may not have entered the championship event and would not have had the chance to win it. Winning the championship is the highlight of my poker career.

When I got to the final table heads-up with Rod Peate, it was certain that for the first time ever, a satellite victor was going to win the world championship. I give Rod a lot of credit because he had to beat a 100-player field and I only had to defeat one table of opponents to get there. We were both professional players and were familiar with each other's style because we had played against one another in $10-$20 hold'em games around town. But to the rest of the poker world, we were virtual unknowns. Like me, Rod had played many tournaments in Las Vegas and had developed a solid tournament game. He had enough gamble in his system to take some risks and make intelligent gambles, plus he got lucky (as did I) and made it to the finals along with me.

But it was the satellite system that enabled us to get there. After that, satellites increased dramatically in popularity. In fact, they have become such big business since then that there are professional satellite players currently on the circuit at the big tournaments. These are players who compete in virtually no events except the satellites and then sell the seats they win.

I feel proud to be among the select group of 28 men who have won the main event at the World Series of Poker—like the Marines, "the few and the proud." Satellites are essential for people on limited budgets to be able to compete. Many formerly unheralded players have gone on to achieve great results because of their satellite wins. In back-to-back years, in fact, totally unknown players won the championship event. This happened in 2002 when Robert Varkonyi won the championship via a satellite win at the Horseshoe, and in 2003 when

Satellite Strategy

Chris Moneymaker won the championship via an online satellite win.

Characteristics of Satellites

Satellites are mini-tournaments. They can be fairly expensive to enter, even the one-table events. For example, the entry fee for a 10-seat WSOP satellite costs $165, which can be a fairly expensive proposition depending on how many you enter. The minimum buy-in for a WSOP tournament is $1,500. You need a successful satellite style to maximize your chances of winning one of those $1,500 seats.

Typical satellites last about an hour to an hour and fifteen minutes, and have only four or five increases before they are over. You start with fewer chips than in a regular tournament, where you may start with $500 with limits of $15-$30. But in a satellite, you may begin playing $15-$30 with only $300 chips. You start with so few chips that by the second round, you are already playing in the equivalent of the middle rounds of a regular tournament.

Sometimes, players are very aggressive in the first round of play and are willing to mix it up more and to bluff more. They approach the satellite with a different strategy than a regular tournament, and so they play far less conservatively.

Most satellites have only 15 to 20 minute betting rounds, sometimes even less. Occasionally, a satellite that is held 30 minutes before the tournament begins will have 5-minute rounds, which significantly adds to the "crap shoot" nature of such events. Naturally, the shorter the rounds, the more important the luck factor becomes. I don't recommend playing in these five-minute events except as a lark.

Sometimes, bad players win satellites. If they didn't book an occasional win, there would be no reason for these weaker contenders to continue losing their money to better players. They need the positive reinforcement of an occasional victory to keep them in the arena.

Satellites attract a lot of pleasure players as well as world class competitors. These pleasure players are not always gunning for a satellite win: sometimes, they just want some experience in playing against top cabin opponents. The satellites give them this opportunity without costing them an arm and a leg. For others, competing against the champions is a turn-on: they want to rub shoulders with the giants of poker. And that's great: it is part of the lure and excitement of tournament and satellite poker. Of course, I don't recommend this strategy if you are a competent player. Personally, I try to avoid world class opponents like the plague!

Your Satellite Game Plan

You need an intelligent and logical satellite plan, which usually means playing in satellites one or two days before the tournament begins. Quite frequently, the heavy emphasis on satellites is for the game being played the following day. If the Omaha high-low tourney is scheduled for Tuesday, most of the Omaha split satellites will be held on Monday, although other satellite games may also be played. The usual rule is that if you win a satellite seat, you can use it for any of the games in the tournament.

Satellite Strategy

I use what I call an "over-and-under system" for my satellite play. If I cannot justify the full buy-in of $1,500, for example, but I can justify some satellites, here is how I approach the situation: If I win my first satellite, I have a minimum investment and will play the tournament. If I don't win my first satellite but I believe it is an event that cries out to be played, I am willing to play a second satellite if I still don't think I can justify the full buy-in. Then if I bounce out again, I take a break to pace myself before I enter a third satellite. I believe most big tournaments are worth three satellite tries, but no more. Three is the over and under on satellites.

What if You Don't Win?

If you don't win any of the three, it has cost you about one-third the amount of the tournament buy-in. That's enough risk to take. I don't sweat it and just move forward. But some players let their discipline break down, and they enter a fourth and fifth satellite. They can't tolerate not entering the tourney so they go ahead and put up the entry fee. Now they have paid for four or five satellites, each of which they have lost, and so they have increased their entry costs by around 50 percent—plus, they have become aggravated with themselves and are probably not playing their best game in the tournament. Under these conditions, I don't think their chances of cashing in the tourney are very rosy.

Usually, if you have given yourself that many satellite opportunities and have lost them all, you are probably not playing an optimal satellite strategy, or your game itself is off kilter, or you are just not lucky, or maybe a combination of all three. If you think you are running that badly, you are better off cutting your losses. Occasionally you will have a bad satellite run, enter the tournament anyway, and win it. But that is the exception rather than the rule.

When I know that I am going to enter the tournament no matter what, I will enter one (or maybe two) satellites and call it a day. That's it! It is too easy to either stress yourself out or burn yourself out with an excessive amount of satellite play. Playing several satellites on the day of the tournament, followed by 14 to 16 hours of playing in the tourney, is a rugged hill to climb . . . it is unrealistic to expect to maintain a high level of performance for that long a time. This is the major reason why I believe it is far better to play satellites the day before the tournament. The goal is not to simply win a satellite: it is to perform well enough to win the tournament itself.

Satellite Strategy

The satellite success formula is a sort of hybrid between what works in regular tournaments and what works in shorthanded play. It is radically different from side game strategy. You can learn only so much about how to win satellites by studying; you have to combine your research with participation in them. (Steady nerves and good deal-making abilities are also helpful!)

This discussion of satellite strategy deals with one-table events, rather than the larger super satellites, which I will talk about later. Because the betting rounds in satellites are only 15 to 20 minutes long, you must play faster than you would in either a ring game or a regular tournament. With the exception of no-limit satellites, tight play is clearly unacceptable.

Steady but controlled aggression throughout the 15-minute satellite rounds, plus a lot of good judgement, is necessary to win. The luck factor is higher, which is why I am willing to gamble in multi-action pots with speculative hands. Chips are power and I want to win as many of them as I can as early as I possibly can.

Many of the most successful satellite contestants are players who eliminate themselves quite early in many of the events they enter. They gamble and mix it up liberally, and it doesn't matter much to them if they bomb out early because they intend to enter another satellite anyway. Their fearless approach and lack of concern about an early departure maximizes their chances of winning a lot of chips early and becoming the dominant force at the table. It is a thing of beauty to see a solid satellite player grab some chips in the early rounds and then watch him use those chips for maximum leverage to dominate the table the rest of the way.

Common sense tells you that in a typical 10-handed hold'em satellite, you have barely enough time to finish one round of approximately ten hands before the limits rise. I am not an advocate of playing a lot of trash hands, particularly in raised pots, but it only takes winning one hand in a raised multi-way pot to put you in a commanding chip position. Double-up your chips early and you will become a very strong force at the table.

Key Concept

Whether it's a one-table or a super satellite, survival skills are not nearly as important because of the satellite's fast action rounds and rapidly escalating blinds, antes and limits. You have to scramble more because you won't be dealt enough premium hands to play only A-K or better every time in hold'em, or big pairs in seven-card stud, or A-2-3-4 in Omaha split. You don't have enough time to wait for them before you get involved.

Some of the situations you are looking for in these fast-paced satellites are hands you can gamble with in a multi-way pot. These hands include suited connectors and small pairs in hold'em, which you might even play somewhat out of position if it looks as though there will be four or five way action, which sometimes happens in satellites.

In these cases, I will gamble with a weaker starting hand. I realize I'm taking the worst of it sometimes, but if I get lucky and win, I'll be in great chip position. And with good chip status, I will have increased leverage: I can tighten up if I need to, or attack the short stacks when I can, whatever is necessary. Don't take a hopeless hand like 8-2 offsuit to gamble with, of course, but you might play two unsuited connectors or very small pairs, even if the pot has been raised.

If it works and I win, my stack increases by fifty percent or more. But after I have done this one time, I will stop. Sometimes, players win a big multi-way pot and then continue to gamble. Don't do that. Put on the brakes immediately. Some of your opponents will be getting short-stacked, while you already have a good-sized stack of chips (as the result of your gamble) to wait for another premium opportunity. This doesn't mean that you won't play decent hands or take a few more calculated risks.

But you won't be gambling quite so much once your goal of doubling-up has been achieved.

If you lose the multiway pot and have jeopardized 25-35 percent of your stack, you will be looking for either another multiway pot or a heads-up situation. If you can't find either, simply tighten up and wait for one good solid hand before you push in your chips. If this also fails, you will be in bad shape and in danger of being eliminated shortly, but *never ever give up!*

Playing Big Hands

If I have a premium hand (a big pair or A-K), I am willing to raise or reraise in an effort to get the most money possible into the pot. I will play any big pair fast, whereas I may not put in the extra raise or reraise with them in a normal tournament where the rounds last 45 minutes. If I lose, so be it.

Even with two jacks, when I am about even money to see an overcard on the flop, I will raise or reraise to try to get either heads-up or three-way action. Because my other opponents are also playing fast, I will almost be forced to go all the way with my hand, even if an overcard comes on the flop.

But I am not implying that you should be suicidal or reckless. For example, suppose you have raised an opponent before the flop with your two jacks and the flop comes K-Q-5. Your opponent checks to you, you bet to see if he has anything, and then he raises. In this case, you should probably fold. Sometimes, however, the strength of your opponent's hand is not that clear to you. He may represent a hand he doesn't have or he may play aggressively on a draw. If you are fairly sure he does have a hand and you have only two outs to your pocket pair of jacks, for example, you had better give it up. If you are not sure, you sometimes just have to play it out.

Raising in Shorthanded Situations

Here is a question Phyllis Meyers (who is a very successful satellite player) asked me: "In either a hold'em or seven-card stud satellite, should you raise with any picture card when it is down to the last three players?"

You should be more inclined to raise with a doorcard king in a stud tournament than with K-3 offsuit (for example) in hold'em, especially if you are on the button with no investment in the pot, in which case you should just pass and wait for a better hand. But in seven-card stud, say the low card has a 3 and the other player has a 7 showing. In this case, you can raise with a picture card showing and nothing much in the hole. However, if you are against very liberal players who are willing to mix it up and defend their low cards, this play won't work and you are probably better off to just pass.

Whether you raise in stud somewhat depends on the comparative size of your door card. For example, if your opponent is the low card with an 8 and you have a 9 or 10 showing, be less inclined to raise unless you have cards such as a three-flush or three-straight that work with your 10. If you have an ace or king showing against a deuce or trey, be more likely to raise. With a jack showing against a 7 or 8, it is better to pass unless you also hold two additional overcards to the 7 or 8. Against a liberal opponent, you can sometimes just call and take off one card if you hold three random high cards that are not paired, although I will usually raise in this situation.

Big-Bet Satellite Games

In big-bet satellites such as pot limit and no limit, the pace is still faster than regular tournaments, but you don't have to take quite as many risks as you do in the limit events. You can wait for that one hand which will give you a significant lead. Remember that you don't need to win a series of hands like you usually have to do in limit poker, you just have to win one big pot.

Selective aggression is usually the correct strategy, especially in no limit. In a pot limit or no limit satellite, I try to hold back longer than I do in limit play because doubling through just one player in big bet poker is usually significant, whereas in limit games it usually takes a series of pots to make a difference. This part of my satellite strategy is the same as my regular tournament play, although a generally faster mode is correct throughout a satellite.

The Player Mix

There is usually a mixture of players in these one table satellites: some are far more willing to gamble early with medium strength hands such as A-J offsuit, while others will lay back and wait a while longer for a strong starting hand. It is important to be able to judge who is playing faster and who is not. I prefer laying back a bit myself trying to find my best possible opportunity to pick off one out-of-line player for all his chips.

In no-limit, if you don't know anything about your opponents beforehand, you might be willing to gamble all your chips with a hand such as A-K, A-Q or a pair of 10s. Don't worry about second-guessing yourself because you have only a limited amount of chips to play with and you have to double-up at some point anyway. So don't be too concerned about being the first player eliminated. Tenth place pays the same as second place in a 10-handed satellite: nothing. Try to be more flexible in your satellite play and do things you wouldn't normally do in a regular tournament, such as committing your chips early. Since there is only one winner, it is better to choose your best spot and go for it.

You can win far more in a tournament than you can in a side game, even against world class players. World class players occasionally go on tilt in a side game, at least for a hand or two, but they are much less likely to tilt during a tournament where patience and discipline are so important to survival.

Super Satellites

Super satellites are multi-table satellites which award seats in the main event to the finalists. The more money in the prize fund, the more seats are given away. Usually, but not always, the game is no-limit hold'em with buy-ins of either $125 or $225, plus rebuys for one hour and an add-on option.

Super satellites are not easy to win. You usually see a full range of talents and skills on display during them. No matter who you are, you won't win unless you catch more than your fair share of cards. A lot of the more famous players are handicapped, no matter how great their skills, by the fast-paced structure of the super satellite. You can learn how these world-class players handle big stacks, medium stacks, small stacks; how they use survival skills; and every ploy in between. In a compressed time span, you can get a valuable tournament education if you are alert.

Key Concept

In super satellites, multiple tournament seats are offered. Your idea is not to win the super satellite, it is to survive. Therefore you sometimes have to take chances to survive to the last table. When four or five seats are being awarded, you are not aiming to be the chip leader, you are aiming to come in fourth or fifth with just enough chips to win a seat.

Naturally, if you have the biggest stack with a substantial lead on your opponents, you have to take intelligent risks. Playing gigantic pots against other big stacks is absolutely taboo unless you have the nuts or close to it. I might consider laying down two aces before the flop when I'm not playing to win the satellite, I'm just playing to outlast one competitor. If I see three people going all-in, for example, and I would have to go all-in myself to play my aces, then I will fold them rather than take the risk of losing my standing.

Making a Save at the Final Table

If the winner gets a $1,500 seat, for example, and the loser gets nothing, it is often prudent to make a save, even if you have a 2-to-1 chip lead. Such an arrangement is sometimes made on a chip count basis where you determine how much of the seat share you win by what percentage of the chips you have won.

At the Horseshoe and Four Queens Classic tournaments, you are given special satellite chips worth $500 each. I have often seen players take one chip apiece and then play off for the third one, so that the winner gets two $500 chips and the loser wins one $500 chip. This way, the loser still makes a nice profit from a typical $165 buy-in ten-handed satellite. If the only way I can play the event is to either win the satellite or make enough of a deal to reduce the entry fee, I will often take slightly the worst of it just to guarantee my participation in the main event.

If you're playing for one seat only, it is often wise to consider going for a settlement. If you have an indomitable chip position, you may not need to deal, of course. Just ask yourself if your position is superior enough to withstand all challengers. If you are heads-up with a player who has a clear chip lead, ask for a settlement. Usually, he won't take it, but it never hurts to ask.

The Casino's Profit

Tournaments and satellites usually have an entry fee, which is the juice the casino receives for sponsoring the event. Although it is a perfectly legitimate charge, it has slowly escalated over the years. The casino's juice used to be much smaller for major tournaments, but $70 is today's standard for a $1,500 tournament, $60 for a $1,000 tourney, $40 for a $500 event, and $30 for a $200 tournament. Percentage-wise, the juice is higher in the smaller buy-in tournaments and lower in the higher buy-in events.

Juice considerations also apply to satellites. Casinos sometimes figure they are entitled to a minimum profit of $70 on every satellite. Sometimes, their profit margin is the same for a $1,500 seat as

Satellite Strategy

it is for a $500 seat. Naturally, you have more equity in a satellite where you can win a $1,500 seat than in a lesser one. If I think the juice is too high for the size of the buy-in, I will decline to play satellites for smaller events. ♠

Chapter 16
SPECIALTY TOURNAMENTS

I am a great believer in being a versatile pokersmith who is able to play more than one game competitively. Personally, I don't like being shut out of any tournament game, so I try to keep my skills up to par in all of them. In addition to limit hold'em, if you also are knowledgeable in seven-card stud, Omaha high-low and no-limit hold'em, you have more games to choose from in tournament competition and will have a better chance to win the combination-game or specialty events.

In general, the number of hold'em events in the big tourneys is about equal to the combined number of other types of events. In the smaller tournaments, as many as two-thirds of the contests are hold'em. The World Series of Poker offers a four-game event called S.H.O.E. that includes seven-card stud, limit hold'em, Omaha high-low, and seven-card stud high-low split. The Bicycle Club, Commerce Casino and Foxwoods Casino tournaments also hold combination game tournaments.

Half and Half Tournaments

Limit hold'em almost always is one of the games played in combination-game tournaments. The second game usually is either seven-card stud or Omaha high-low. Being a skilled hold'em player gives you an extra edge in most half and half events. However this is not necessarily the case in half hold'em/half stud tourneys, because stud is a game of equal or greater skill than hold'em and has five betting rounds, so that being proficient in stud is equally important to being proficient in hold'em. The key difference is that more multiway hands usually are played in hold'em than in seven-card stud.

Half Hold'em/Half Omaha High-Low

In half hold'em/half Omaha split tournaments, the emphasis shifts back to hold'em. Because of the split pot aspect of Omaha high-low, hands take longer to play and many pots are divided between the high and low hands. These two factors decrease the number of deals that can be completed during the Omaha high-low rounds. The chip movement then becomes less pronounced and less frequent than it is in hold'em.

A very solid, selectively aggressive approach to Omaha high-low is necessary in these half and half tournaments because Omaha split has four betting rounds during which you can get quartered or counterfeited and lose a lot of chips. Be less inclined to take an aggressive pre-flop approach when you have a medium or short stack; wait until after the flop to do your gambling. Remember that you are not nearly as likely to pick up the blinds by raising in Omaha high-low as in other games because there are so many card combinations that could justify defending the blinds.

Playing a strong hold'em game can set you up very nicely for the Omaha split segment, especially if you have frequently put your hold'em opponents on the defensive. If you have built up a large stack going into the Omaha high-low round, it is especially important to play the selectively aggressive strategy. With a short to medium stack, play more conservatively during Omaha split.

Half Hold'em/Half Seven-Card Stud

The ladies championship tournament at the World Series of Poker is a combination event, half limit hold'em and half seven-card stud. The games are eight-handed in these tournaments, in contrast to the nine-handed half hold'em/half Omaha high-low events. Having one less player is quite significant for two reasons: It alters your starting position requirements by one full player in hold'em; and when you lose a player, there will be only seven players instead of eight, which again reduces the number of hands out against you.

During the stud portion, when the table has gotten down to seven or six players, a lot more ante stealing occurs. And during the hold'em round, there will be fewer multiway pots and so small pairs and suited connectors will decrease in value while big cards escalate in value. You need to consider these factors in your general strategy.

In general, you should be limping less and raising more during the hold'em half from the early rounds on. In stud, once you have lost a player or two, you should be selectively aggressive and ante steal in the correct situations. For example, suppose the low card with a deuce up brings in the pot in a seven player game. Two people pass. You have the highest upcard, a queen, and the two players behind you have an 8 and a 5, respectively. Go ahead and raise. Of course, aggressive and tricky players who are capable of reraising on a bluff could put a damper on your ante stealing activities, but this usually won't happen because, even if one of them believes you are trying an ante-steal, they would have to be very cautious in reraising an attempted steal since they cannot replace their chips if they are wrong in a freezeout tournament.

Many times, too, you may have enough power against such a weak board to outdraw them, even if they start with a pair. So it takes a very crafty opponent to have an accurate enough correct read on you to make such an aggressive reraise. Therefore, you should have a fairly high success rate when you try an ante steal under the aforementioned circumstances.

In shorthanded seven-card stud tournament play, ante stealing is crucial to maintaining your chip status. Too conservative or too tight an approach will allow your opponents to become braver and try ante stealing more often, thus putting you on the defensive. But retaining an aggressive posture yourself, whether or not you have a hand, tends to keep your opponents off your back because it forces them to have some sort of decent hand to play against you. Since they know you are likely to be aggressive, they will probably be more reluctant to raise when you are sitting behind them.

Of course, you will also be raising with your legitimate hands. In fact, you will often get action on your good hands that you would not have gotten if you had been playing a more conservative strategy. When your opponents are accustomed to seeing you raise a lot of pots, they cannot accurately predict when you have a hand and when you don't, so they are forced to guess and play defensively. Any time you can force your opponents into that posture, you have that much more of an advantage over them.

When your opponents must continually guess what you are raising with, they tend to call too often. Naturally, if you force them into such a calling mode, you have to believe you hold the best hand in order to continue taking a strong posture. So when you are caught in one of your attempts to steal the antes, you must use good judgment about continuing your bluff, especially in seven-card stud. For example, suppose you raised with a king on top and a 10-9 in the hole. You have some limited straight potential and three fairly high cards. Your opponent calls you with an 8 showing and then catches a suited 9 while you catch an offsuit 4. You are better off to abandon your bluff immediately than to continue representing something you don't have.

At the final table when the play is shorthanded with only two or three players remaining, you will have to do considerably more raising than calling in both hold'em and stud. Just remember that seven-card stud is a game of strong boards so that a high upcard, especially the mighty ace, can become intimidating at times. Of course, you would prefer having something to go with it, such as one or two other big cards or two flush cards. But the ace alone can be enough to induce your opponents to fold when you play it aggressively.

Tag Team Events

In the same mold as half and half tournaments are tag team events in which one partner plays one game and the other plays a second game. In these tourneys, of course, you try to choose a partner who is strong in the game that you are not playing. If you are versatile, you can give your teammate his choice of games. Sometimes it is nice to recruit a specialist in one type of poker, such as Omaha high-low, while you play the hold'em rounds.

H.O.R.S.E. Events

A relatively new phenomenon on the poker scene are H.O.R.S.E. games, an acronym for hold'em, Omaha high-low split, razz, seven-card stud and eight-or-better stud. Each game is played limit. Basic tournament strategies still apply in these multi-game events, but the uniqueness of this format requires special observation skills at the table. Because certain opponents are more skilled at some games than others, you must determine how best to play against them in their best games as well as in their worst games. As in all forms of tournament poker, a selectively aggressive posture is essential.

Suppose you have decided to enter a H.O.R.S.E. event and you believe that razz is your weakest game. During the razz segment, you would play a more conservative game, being far more selective about which hands you enter pots with. In particular avoid playing marginal hands that require a lot of tricky judgements. In reality a lot of players who like to play multi-game events are weak in one or two of the games being played. This is why it is so important to use your skills of observation and be more conservative and selective in your own weakest game.

Other variations on the same theme are R.O.E., H.O.E. and H.O.S.E. games, which frequently are played in the highest limit side-action games. In fact the biggest pot-limit cash games currently being spread are half hold'em and half Omaha.

Bounty Tournaments

Popular on today's low-limit tournament scene are bounty tournaments where you win a bonus for each player that you eliminate from action. Many $20 daily tournaments award a $5 bounty on each player that you knock out. A slightly higher entry fee covers the casino's cost for awarding bounties. Naturally this format stimulates a lot of additional interest and fun on the part of players, who sometimes take a marginal hand and try to draw out on an opponent in order to win his bounty, many times fattening up the short stacks in the process. I do not suggest that you try this tactic yourself, but rather consider winning a bounty to be an added bonus. In other words, don't become a bounty hunter.

On a much grander scale is the annual Shooting Stars bounty tournament at Bay 101 in San Jose, California, which features a $1,500 bounty on each of the "stars." At each table there is a "star," usually a former World Series champion or a well known poker personality. Each of these stars has a $1,500 bounty placed upon his head. A lot of excitement is created by this format. You are awarded a tee-shirt with the name of the player that you busted emblazoned on it. (One local personally busted seven of the fifteen stars a few years ago!)

Incremental Rebuy Events

Another popular format on today's tournament circuit is the incremental rebuy event, in which you get more chips when you rebuy and add on than you did in your original stack. For example, you might get $500 in chips for your initial $120 buy-in, and $800 to $1,000 in chips when you rebuy. Basically, this type of event is telling you that although it costs only $120 to buy in, you should not play it if you aren't willing to invest $220 because you'll be taking so much the worst of it if you don't rebuy. There may be times when the deck runs over you and you won't have to rebuy, of course, but always be prepared to invest the maximum amount in incremental rebuy events. This often is the format in "second-chance" events, which generally are played in the evenings during major tournaments and have smaller buy-ins with only one incremental rebuy. ♠

Chapter 17
TOURNAMENT POKER 102: STRATEGIC CONCEPTS

Building Your Stack

Just as an architect needs a blueprint to build a house, you need a tournament game plan to build a competitive stack. Your building blocks are your chips; the more of them you have, the stronger your foundation. In most tournaments, you try to build your stack by about 25 percent during each round in the early and middle stages, and you hope to double-up in the later stages. In seven-card high-low, you accumulate chips very slowly, but in no limit or pot limit, you can double or triple your stack in one hand.

It takes money to make money, as the old saying goes. Chips are like that too. The more building blocks you have, the more likely it is you can expand them, gathering momentum as you go. When you have built your stack to a large size, other players are more afraid of confronting you. A big stack is very intimidating at all stages of a tourney, so that it takes greater strength in your opponents' hands for them to compete against you when you have a lot of chips.

Just as homeowners need insurance against natural disasters, you need a backup plan for meeting tournament emergencies. For example, how will you handle it if you get a big hand snapped off, leaving you short-stacked? Your disaster plan can help you avoid panic when you suffer big beats. It should also include what to do in other stressful situations and how to play different opponents. You are constantly trying to get inside your opponents' heads to give you guidelines to their philosophy and what kinds of hands they play.

As for taxes on your "house of chips," you can defer paying them by not playing recklessly or making incorrect calls. Instead, play a selectively aggressive game that will more adequately ensure you of a money finish.

On the Value of Suited Cards

The bigger the cards, the less the value of being suited. For instance, you will play A-K in hold'em, suited or not. You may play 9♥8♥ in position, but might pass with 9♥8♣ in the same position. So the smaller the cards, the more value the suits; the higher, the less value. The added value of suited cards is approximately 5 percent to 7 percent, according to the "mad genius of poker," Mike Caro. These figures are approximate, of course, and they may rise to 8 or 9 percent for suited connectors. This percentage may be the deciding factor in deciding whether to play a hand.

The Factors You Are Playing Against

You are always playing against your opponents, your chip position, and the clock. You must always play your opponents as much as you play your cards. Your chip position dictates your strategy through the tournament. The more chips you have, the more options are open to you. The fewer your chips, the more restricted you are in your choice of maneuvers. The smaller your chip count, the more the clock is to your detriment. The bigger your stack, the more the clock is in your favor.

At the Final Two or Three Tables

When I have made it to the final few tables, I get up from my seat and take a cruise around the other tables to see how many short stacks there are, and how many more players need to be eliminated before I can make it to the final table or two. Sometimes, this census will affect my final playing strategy. If I am on a short stack myself, for instance, and I see a couple of other players who are on even shorter stacks, I will have to find a very premium hand before I jeopardize myself, especially if the other short stacks are about to get eaten up by the blinds. Of course, I won't throw away aces or kings, because I will need not only enough chips to survive, but also enough to go all the way. I never lose sight of the big picture, which is to win the tournament. A good knowledge of the chips counts of my competitors at the other tables, the short stacks in particular, are definitely useful tools. It also helps to walk around and stretch, to loosen up a bit and relieve the tournament tension.

Middle Chip Position

In many situations, though not in all cases, you will be doing more check-calling with a mid-sized stack. Suppose I hold a marginal or medium-strength hand like top pair in hold'em. I entered a pot in late position with a hand like K-J and I flop a king, which is the highest upcard. If there are surrounding cards that look dangerous, such as a 10 or a 9, I could easily run into a second pair or a straight. So, although I may have been leading at the pot, if the river card is a connector which could make two pair or a straight for someone else, I will check-call if I think I may still have the best hand.

Whereas I may bet the pot in a side game, I will play more conservatively in a tournament rather than trying to get full value for my hand. This is why check-calling is often the correct strategy. It also may induce a bluff on the end from a player whose hand did not materialize.

Control

None of your attempts to control your opponents will bring you success if you cannot first control yourself, your emotions. Self-discipline is the key. You must be able to shrug off bad beats and any other adverse situations that occur during the tournament. Because I sometimes have a hard time doing that, I am constantly on guard to control my emotions, especially when a player I don't particularly like, someone who has been needling me or is obnoxious in general, is sitting at my table. Naturally, you would want to beat this person more than anyone else, but you must guard against your tendency to exercise any personal vendettas because that thinking can lead you to becoming involved in hands you should not play and giving too much loose action.

One mental exercise that can help you maintain your emotional equilibrium is to look for reasons *not* to get involved in a hand with your most irritating opponents, unless you have a premium hand. I look for excuses to stay out of their pots, quietly folding marginal hands, waiting for the best opportunity to put him on the defensive. Always try to control yourself first—and *then* your opponents.

Making the Right Decisions

To win a tournament, you must act correctly most of the time. You have to read your opponents with a reasonable amount of accuracy, which comes mostly through experience. After you have read an opponent, you must then act properly, based on your read. I cannot list the number of times I have seen seven-card stud players accurately read an opponent's hand and then call him down anyway. "I know you've got aces-up," they'll say after correctly reading the other hand when they were check-raised on fifth street. And they're right, their opponent does have aces-up! So why call? Reading players is important, yes—acting properly after the read is crucial to winning or losing. You need to read *and* make the right decisions 80 to 90 percent of the time to win a tournament.

Key Hands

The play of one hand in a tournament, particularly in the middle to late stages, can drastically affect the play of hands to follow. They often have a direct influence on how well you finish in the tournament. For example, if you lose a key pot when you are short-stacked, many of your options and weapons are taken away from you. You may have to take a stand with a hand you would not ordinarily play because you have lost a big pot and are on a short stack.

On the flip side of the coin, if you win a key pot that puts you in a strong chip status, you have more options. You may play some hands you would have folded with fewer chips, which could enable you to go on a big rush and move into a dominant chip position. In other words, key hands can work both ways. Virtually every tournament I have won or lost has had a key hand that came at a critical juncture and became a turning point in my tournament fortune.

Play Yourself as Well as Your Opponent

Playing your best game means staying calm, cool and collected in the heat of the tournament battle. Using insight into your opponents to give yourself the best opportunity to win is also an important ingredient in the success formula. Know your own limitations, your weaknesses and your strengths, and continually try to improve your play. Be introspective, constantly analyzing yourself, your game, and even your motives when you enter a pot.

Guard against making errors based upon your likes and dislikes of other players. If you are a nonsmoker, sitting next to a smoker can be an annoyance, but you must overcome your irritation. Don't give too much loose action to an opponent who irritates you or otherwise causes you discomfort.

Playing Marginal Hands

The way you play marginal hands makes a big difference in your tournament success. The major difference between the winners and the losers is how they play medium-strength hands. True champions know when to push a marginal hand and when to back away from it. They have a good sense for when a medium-strength hand can be turned into a profit maker and when it is a dog and can become a big loser.

This talent for when to play and when not to play marginal cards often separates the "wannabes" from the winners. Top professionals shine in their astute judgment and timing with these types of hands. A pro can not only beat you with his cards, but he can also beat you with *your* cards. In other words, if he held your hand and you held his hand, he could still find ways to defeat you.

Theoretically, the cards break even over the long run, although that is not necessarily true in tournaments because of their limited time span. As I mentioned earlier, all tournament winners have more than their share of luck during the tourney. But it is often the way they play the marginal hands and turn them into profitable ventures, especially in tournaments where there are so many more factors to consider than there are in ring games, that makes the difference between success and failure.

Levels of Thinking

Advanced poker players think at several different levels of thought. The most basic level is whether you think you hold the best hand. One step up the ladder is what you think your opponent holds. A level above that is what you think your opponent thinks you have. The highest plateau of poker thought processes is what you think your opponent thinks you have, and the way you think he expects you to play your hand if you have what he thinks you have, and then how you think he will play his hand if he has what you think he has.

The reason I often have difficulty playing in low buy-in tournaments as opposed to the higher buy-in tourneys I usually play is because I am up against a different mind set. Many of the lower-limit tournament players I have battled simply play their hands and gamble the way they see fit, rather than using the more advanced game strategy and higher level of logic I am accustomed to defensing against in major tournaments. Sometimes, less experienced players don't know where they are in a hand, so how can you put them on the correct hand and make an optimal response? It is easier to understand the play of a veteran high-limit tournament player whom you know is thinking in logical terms.

If you are thinking at a higher level of play, you must adjust your thinking to the thought processes of opponents who are working at a lower level. Don't always try to outthink them. I honestly believe that one reason higher level players sometimes do not fare well against less sophisticated opponents is because they are outthinking themselves. They fall prey to "FPS," the fancy play syndrome that Mike Caro describes. Fancy plays might have a good long-term result against sophisticated opponents, but may fall flat against less advanced opponents who are oblivious to the maneuvers of advanced players. What good is it to make creative plays against players who cannot appreciate them?

A lot of top players seem to fall in love with their tricky plays, the ones they like to use against talented, high calibre opponents. But when they use these same plays against confused opponents, they just get called. Instead, they should probably value bet their good hands and continue putting pressure on their opponents when they think they have the best of them. This is not to say that you should never make a deceptive move against lesser opposition, but you definitely should not overdo it.

Of course, the positive side is that when an opponent who does not operate at a higher level of thinking occasionally enters the upper stratosphere of tournament play where he must oppose world-class opposition, he often becomes confused and lost. The tactics he used at the lower limits to defeat opponents of equal skill become transparent to higher calibre opposition and he loses.

Making Reflexive Plays

Certain plays may be "automatic" in side games, but they are not automatic in tournaments. Suppose, for example, you are playing in a side game and an opponent raises on the river. You hold a medium-strength hand or aces-up and make a quick, reflexive call even though you know he probably has either a straight or a flush. Even though he is not likely to be raising with anything your aces-up can beat, you call him anyway.

You must constantly be on guard against making these reflexive plays in tourneys, particularly against loose blind defenders or liberal opponents who are likely to call your bet or raise. Against these types of players, you have to base your play on hand-value rather than making an automatic bet on a steal or semi-steal, for example. Think about every bet you make before you throw in your chips in tournament play, and how you will play against each opponent, because you cannot replace your chips once you lose them.

Be Aware of the Total Number of Chips in Play

The number of chips in play is easy to calculate. In a World Series event, you receive a stack of chips equal to your buy-in. When you are playing a $1,500 event with 204 players in the tournament, you know there are $306,000 worth of chips in play. That amount will vary somewhat because the odd chips are raced off at the ends of certain betting rounds, but the total will usually remain fairly close to the original amount.

You should always know how many chips you need to make the last table, the average chip count at the last table. If nine players are at the final table, divide 9 into $306,000, which comes to about $34,000 per player. You know that if you collect $34,000, you have enough to play at the last table in average chip position, probably in around fourth or fifth spot, with several players below your and several above you.

You can use the same calculations to find out what the average chip count is at various stages of the tournament. Say the tournament is down to 40 players. With $306,000 chips in play, the average chip count is exactly $7,650 per contestant. Use this method to continually find out where you stand. For instance, if you have $15,000 in chips with 40 players remaining, you know that you are one of the chip leaders and can use your superior chip position as a weapon.

Although this countdown is not as important in the early stages, it becomes increasingly important from the middle stages forward. Sometimes, you may think, "Gee, I don't have enough chips to play at this limit," but you may not be in as bad shape as you think. Suppose you're playing $200-$400 limits and you have $4500 in chips. After some fast mental arithmetic where you divide the total chips in play by the 80 remaining players, you discover the average stack is only $3,700. You have an above-average stack. If you calculate that you are below-average, you may decide to take a few more risks to get your chip count up to par or higher. Conversely, if you have more than the average number of chips, you might want to tighten up a notch to be sure you don't jeopardize your good position by taking too many risks.

During the Benefit Poker Seminar held in 1994 in Las Vegas, Mike Sexton and I shared the stage with Mike Caro. One of the world's finest all-around tournament competitors, Sexton encouraged players to always keep track of their chip position relative to the number of chips in play. It is just one more tournament tool you can use to your advantage. Obviously, it has worked well for Sexton.

The Wall

"Many people know how to reach the wall (the final table). Very few people know how to climb over the wall (win the tournament). I know how," John Bonetti told me several years ago. Bonetti is a classic example of a super-aggressive player who, when he gets to the final table, usually has a superior chip position. A player like Bonetti has far more firsts than he has seconds, and far more seconds than he has any other finish. If a super-aggressive player gets to the final table with a big stack of chips, he is relentlessly aggressive, which causes many of his opponents to fold a lot of hands against him because they don't want to get involved with him.

This intimidating style is very effective when you have a lot of chips at the last table. Of course, it can also cause you to crash and burn earlier than you might have if you had been playing a more conservative game. But sometimes you must take the bitter with the sweet, because you can win a few extra tournaments you may not have won otherwise. Recall that the payoff is usually very top heavy for the top three finishers, and especially so for first place, which is all the more reason why a slashing, intimidating style with a lot of blood on the table can be very effective.

In contrast, Mike Sexton and I have a lot of fourth and fifth finishes. We both try to slide up the payscale one step at a time, similar to a fencer who uses fancy footwork in search of a slight advantage to score points rather than going for the quick kill. Either of these two styles can get you to the winner's circle, but in different fashions.

If I were making a last-longer bet with a super-aggressive player, I would probably have a substantial advantage over him, but if we're talking about either making the final table or winning, he would have the advantage. With his style of play, he won't linger as long as I do with a short stack, especially in the middle stages. Super-aggressives make aggressive plays with marginal hands to give themselves the best chance to win a lot of chips. If his aggressiveness works, he will frequently get there with a big stack; but he also frequently gets eliminated early. I may wind up in the money more often than players like Bonetti because I have numerous second-table finishes, but I may not end up with more prize money because he will have more first places than I do. Decide for yourself which style of play, or combination of styles, is right for you when you get to the wall. ♠

Chapter 18
TOURNAMENT TRENDS: ADJUSTING TO CHANGE

The new millennium has brought a new and expanding horizon to the tournament poker landscape. No longer do tournaments have 20-minute or one-hour rounds—some have 15-minute or 45-minute rounds. Nor does every event double the blinds at the beginning of each new round—many now increase the limits far more gradually. Further, the trend these days is for a flatter payout schedule with more money going to more players and less money being awarded to the top three finishers. What do these changes mean to the average tournament poker player? They call for refining your tournament strategy for special situations and making adjustments to maximize your tournament rewards.

Changes in Tournament Structure:
New Modes Require Adjustments

Since this book first was published in 1995, several innovative new tournament structures have been introduced that call for certain modifications in your tournament strategy.

(1) The TEARS Structure

Without doubt the greatest innovation in tournament structure is Tex Morgan's computer software program, TEARS, which stands for Tournament Evaluation and Rating System. The way it works is that the tournament director tells the computer how long he wants the event to last and how many entries there are in that day's event. The computer then calculates the length of the rounds needed in order to achieve the results. The major feature of the program is that the increments are increased by only 50 percent or less in each round. "Players see more 'play' for their buy-in than they did in the past," Morgan said. "Smaller blind increases, combined with shorter rounds, reduce the luck factor." This type of structure favors the more skilled player because it gives him more time to ply his tournament skills.

(2) Playing the Final Table on Day Two

Most major tournaments now conclude the first day's play when the action gets down to the final table. The typical tournament that used to end in the wee hours of the morning now is shortened during the first day with final-table play resuming mid-afternoon on the second day. The tournaments that are using the TEARS format use the same slower increases at the final table and also add some additional playing time to each round. Playing the final table on day two after a night's rest rather than playing one marathon session definitely favors the more highly skilled tournament players and reduces the luck element even further. The tendency to stage tournaments with slow rises in increments and playing the final table on day two has led to some very strong final tables.

How to Refine your Strategy to Take Advantage of Slower Rises and Playing the Final Table on Day Two

The main thing that you gain when the limits rise more gradually is more maneuverability, even with a shorter stack. Shorter stacks have more time to adjust and more time to wait for premium starting hands. This doesn't mean that you can sit indefinitely; it just means that you can be more selective with the hands that you enter pots with.

The bigger stacks need to be even more patient and not go for the kill too quickly. By gambling too much, they risk doubling up the shorter stacks and reducing their own chances of winning or placing in the top three.

As usual the medium stacks have the most difficult decisions to make. You have to know when to go after the tall stacks, as well as the short stacks, and when to back off from either of them. You're trying to not get crippled by the tall stack and not double up a short stack (thereby becoming one yourself). Knowing when to hold'em and when to fold'em is the challenge of the medium stack.

(3) Huge Increase in the Number of Tournament Entrants

Tournaments with all sizes of buy-ins have experienced enormous increases in entries. It is not at all unusual to have 400-plus entrants in medium buy-in events ($300 to $500). The 2000 WSOP $10,000 championship event attracted more than 500 players for the first time in history with the top prize being elevated to $1.5 million for the first time ever. Continuing its incredible growth, the Big One had more than 800 entries in 2003 and the champion, online satellite winner Chris Moneymaker, took home $2.5 million.

As a result of big-field tournament action, new faces keep emerging, some of whom remain viable as tournament contenders while others are one-shot wonders and then disappear from the pack never to lead it again. The potential profit in these huge tournaments is enormous. It feeds upon itself. The more entrants, the greater the prize money and the greater the prize money, the more people want to play and the more attendance swells.

In huge-field tournaments that still retain the double rises in the blinds and antes at each level, the luck factor increases enormously, but in those events where the rise in increments is kept to 50-percent, skill usually prevails. Nonetheless big-field tournaments are harder to win due to the sheer volume of players.

Further, the skill level of players continues to increase dramatically because of several factors: (a) More legal places to play tournament poker; (b) Online poker tournaments at major Internet gaming sites; (c) Software programs with which people can practice poker; (d) More good, strategically sound poker books for all levels of play.

What does this mean to you? Number one, don't let the numbers overwhelm you. Remember that you only have to beat the field one table at a time, *your* table. You cannot control events going on at other tables, you only have control over your own. Second, you must maintain more patience and discipline than ever before—you cannot try to win the tournament too soon. One of the dangers in a big tournament is that when some players get off to a flying start and accumulate a big stack of chips, they try to run over their opponents too early and end up blowing off a lot of their chips. This is one of the biggest flaws I see in the play of aggressive players who have big stacks early on—they make too many plays with marginal hands too early. Do not fall into this trap. You must protect your chips and continually pace yourself.

(4) Fast Action Tournaments

Events with short time periods still are on the rise because so many casinos now are sponsoring tournaments to stimulate live action games. The advantage of playing these low buy-in, fast-paced tournaments is that they attract many lesser skilled players who don't know proper tournament strategy and therefore make many mistakes that more sophisticated tourney players can capitalize on to accumulate large stacks of chips. The disadvantage is that some of these same (weak) players will make the wrong play at the right time and put a beat on you that cripples you and greatly reduces your chances of winning the event, especially if they draw out on you in the later stages when you don't have enough time to make a comeback.

Play a solid, selectively aggressive game. If you've accumulated chips, you don't need to gamble because the weaker players will be doing that for you. You don't have to force the action because they will be coming to you. Weak players usually are either too passive or too aggressive. If they're too passive, you can be aggressive against them. If they're too aggressive, you can wait in the bushes and pick them off with your stronger hands.

(5) Flattened Payout Schedule

There also is a trend to flatten the payout structure, making the payout less top heavy and paying more tables. Quite often the flatter pay scale results in less deal making at the final table because the percentage of payout differences between first, second and third places is smaller. For example, in the traditional structure first place may pay 40 percent, second place 20 percent and third place 10 percent, whereas flattened structures might award 28 percent for first, 22 percent for second and 16 percent for third.

If I am playing a tournament in which the differences in payouts are smaller and I have a decent amount of chips, I would have a greater tendency to play for it rather than negotiate. If a more traditional payout structure is used, I would have more reason to negotiate a deal, which is why more that 80 percent of tournament finalists have negotiated a modified payout in the past. Many people believe that deal making needs to be eliminated in order to attract corporate sponsorship and they view the flattening of payouts as a way to discourage deals.

Other Trends in Tournament Poker

(1) Increased Interest in No-limit Hold'em Tournaments

Increased tournament activity has resulted in far greater interest in no-limit events. Virtually every championship event at every major tournament is a big buy-in, no-limit hold'em. The increase in attendance at the three no-limit hold'em events at the WSOP has been phenomenal. Why? Because poker has become more available worldwide with increased exposure through the Internet and television. People are fascinated by big league tournament poker. Is there any poker player who doesn't dream of becoming the World Champion one day?

The irony is that no-limit hold'em side action is virtually nonexistent. The inescapable conclusion is that tournament poker has saved no-limit hold'em as a viable poker game. The word "no-limit" intimidates some poker players, making them fearful of playing the game. I like to think that *Championship No-Limit & Pot-Limit Hold'em*, the book that I coauthored with T.J. Cloutier, has helped many people overcome their doubts and fears about competing in no-limit events.

Interest in no-limit hold'em was further stimulated by cable television broadcasts of the tournament sponsored by Ladbrokes Casino on the Isle of Mann in 2000, in which the audience could see the hole cards of the players. The introduction of the nationally televised World Poker Tour in 2002 was another milestone in the growing popularity of no-limit poker. Viewers are able to see the downcards of players and hear the commentary of Mike Sexton and Vince VanPatten at the championship table.

(2) The Growth of Tournament Poker in Southern California and Europe

Southern California has become a veritable tournament mecca, perhaps replacing Las Vegas as the tournament capital of the world. Another major trend in tournament poker has been the growth of tournaments in Europe, in particular the ones at the Aviation Club in Paris, as well as others in the UK, Holland, Austria, Finland and Russia. For the first time ever, it is becoming trendy for top American tournament players to travel abroad for these fine events. This huge increase in international poker also has increased satellite action and has sent many European players to Las Vegas for the World Series.

(3) Nonsmoking Events

The nonsmoking trend definitely is the mode in the United States (although not in Europe). California has been nonsmoking for several years and tournament participation has increased. With the inception of the Sam Boyd Poker Classic in 1999, I coordinated the first nonsmoking tournament in Las Vegas, which played to rave reviews. The World Poker Challenge in Reno followed suit and in 2002 the World Series of Poker also became a nonsmoking tournament. On the East coast Foxwoods in Connecticut and the Taj Mahal in Atlantic City have made their cash games as well as their tournaments nonsmoking.

(4) Cooperative Scheduling by Tournament Venues

For the betterment of everybody, many casinos have entered into cooperative rather than competitive activities. Foxwoods Casino and the Taj Mahal cooperate in the scheduling of their major tournaments each year, while the Gold Strike and Binion's Horseshoe in Tunica, Mississippi, jointly host Jack Binion's World Poker Open. The Reno poker rooms cooperate in scheduling their tournaments and share tournament staffs.

(5) Internet Tournaments and Satellites

The 2003 World Champion of Poker won his $10,000 seat via an online satellite sponsored by PokerStars.com, which sent 37 satellite winners to the World Series of Poker, testament to the astounding growth of Internet poker. PokerPages.com led the way in 2001 by sponsoring a freeroll tournament that placed one player in the $10,000 championship event at the WSOP. ParadisePoker.com began sponsoring one-table $100 buy-in limit hold'em tournaments in 2000. Many other Internet cardrooms, such as UltimateBet.com and PartyPoker.com, followed suit so that people can play poker tournaments and satellites virtually any time from any place.

(6) Tournament Rules Are Becoming More Standardized

European tournament sponsors have made significant strides toward the standardization of tournament rules with most tournament venues cooperating with other. In the United States attempts have been made to do the same with limited success to date. The standardization of tournament rules is good for poker. Having a standard set of rules will help tournament players feel more comfortable and confident that quality floor decision are always made, thus erasing some of the confusion that has been characteristic of some tournament decisions.

(7) Personnel who Specialize in Tournaments Have Become Commonplace

A coterie of floor personnel and dealers travel from state to state to work various tournament venues. When players see familiar faces and recognize the names of tournament personnel from one place to the other, they feel more at home. Many professional tournament personnel learn the names of players and, for example, can call the board for cash games more efficiently and smoothly.

(8) Increased Promotion of Satellites, Even at one Venue or Tournament for the Next one

Many casinos and even small card clubs like to send one or two of their regulars to the poker mecca at the Horseshoe in Las Vegas. Therefore satellites for the World Series of Poker and several other major events are held in cardrooms all over the world. The same thing has become true for many other major tournaments. Some casinos, such as the Bicycle Club in Bell Gardens, California, even sponsor "mini" World Series events in which you can practice your tournament skills using the WSOP structure without having to pay the big buy-ins at the Big One. ♠

Chapter 19

THE BUSINESS OF BIG LEAGUE TOURNAMENT POKER

Playing in the big leagues of the poker tournament world is no small business venture. Just as any businessman must do to realize a profit at the end of each year, a tournament specialist has to keep track of his ROI, his return on investment. He has to weigh his prospects of winning against his potential loss in deciding how many and which tournaments he will enter. He must decide whether to enter into partnerships in any or all of his tournament ventures, and what percentage of shares in his action he is willing to sell in order to optimize his chances of chalking up a profitable year. He also has to keep his own record book, design his own schedule, make airline and room reservations, and learn to deal with the inevitable following of fans and wannabes who will follow him into the spotlight if he is fortunate enough to become a celebrity on the tournament circuit. During my 20-plus years as a poker professional specializing in tournament play, I have experienced both the proverbial thrill of victory and the inevitable agony of defeat. In this chapter, I will share with you some good—and some bad—business practices that all tournament players should be aware of before they embark on the roller coaster ride of the international tournament circuit.

Financing Yourself

With the advent of the World Poker Tour in 2002, several $5,000 to $25,000 tournaments were added to the major tournament schedule and greatly increased the cost of playing the circuit. I estimate that in order to finance yourself on the big league poker tournament circuit—playing virtually all the major tournaments with buy-ins of $500 or more, including the World Series of Poker, the World Poker Tour, and the major "minor" tournaments such as the Orleans Open—costs approximately $300,000 per year for entry fees alone. Obviously, you have to earn a lot of money from your tournament wins to make a good enough return on your investment to justify continuing on the circuit.

If you are a winning tournament player, someone who has won some majors and has placed in the money on many other occasions, you would need to set aside close to $1 million just for tournament play in order to finance yourself and guarantee that you would not go broke. This million would finance you for three years on the circuit and allow you to endure big fluctuations without going broke, pay your travel expenses, and toke appropriately (tokes average 2 to 3 percent in the major tourneys, 5 percent in $100-$300 buy-in tourneys). I am including $5,000 and $10,000 buy-in tournaments (which are mainly seven-card stud, no-limit hold'em and limit hold'em) in these estimates. Of course, you could probably do it for somewhat less, perhaps $200,000 per year, if you skipped certain events and played others only if you won a satellite. But to guarantee not going broke, you would need close to a million dollars.

The reason you would need this much money, assuming that you follow the schedule that players such as T.J. Cloutier and Phil Hellmuth do—which is to play all the majors—is because you must be able to withstand enormous fluctuations. For example, you may run bad in tournaments for one or two years—it has happened to me and to other major tournament players, as well. You may start out with a bang, but then things level out. Very few players can consistently maintain good results, year in and year out, no matter how good they are.

Cards have a lot to do with negative runs, plus your own management skills and your temperament. When you're feeling down and things are going bad, it's a tough job to always snap out of it. When things are going well, you sometimes feel that you're bulletproof and invincible. But poker has a way of humbling you, of making you realize that you're not the only good—indeed, not the only great—player out there.

To make it on the tournament circuit—to offset the buy-ins, the travel expenses, the tokes, and to make a consistent profit—you have to be a truly great player. "Good" doesn't cut it—you have to be great. Good players can win a tournament, but to get consistent results tournament after tournament, year after year, you have to be great. Some good players can develop themselves into great players, advancing to the next level and becoming world-class competitors, but not everybody can make that transition.

The poker tournament circuit is analogous to the Peter Principle, in which people get promoted in bureaucracies until they reach their maximum level of incompetence. They continue to advance up the ladder until they land in a situation they cannot handle with their former level of expertise and that is where they get trapped, at their highest level of incompetence. On the tournament circuit, players can sometimes advance only so far. They can compete with good results at the lower echelons of the big-time tournaments, such as the $100-$500 levels, but once they start to play with the big boys at the $1,000 buy-in level and upward, they have reached their own personal wall. They no longer get good results because there are simply too many highly skilled players in the upper stratosphere. If their skills are far above average, yet not quite in the world-class category, they will have a very difficult time competing successfully against players who have achieved the higher level of excellence.

How do you achieve these high-level skills? Of course, you must read and study, but most importantly, you must play. Each of us has our own special skills and talents; only you are able to determine how far you can go. It is no disgrace, either, when you discover that you don't get good results playing in the top-level tournaments against all the world champions. You can still have good overall success by not playing the bigger buy-in tournaments unless you win a seat via a satellite and can get in cheaply, or acquire a sponsorship that gives you a chance to maintain your personal bankroll without putting it in serious jeopardy.

The players who get staked big-time in the major circuit are all proven champions. It is virtually impossible to find financing from a backer on this large a scale unless you already have a winning record. So unless you have established your credentials, you cannot expect to get staked like perennial winners such as T.J. Cloutier do.

Being Financed by OPM

Other People's Money is one way tournament specialists finance themselves. You might be asking yourself, "Why should I want to get staked if I'm all that good?" I have been backed by several sponsors at different times in my tournament career. Being backed is different from selling pieces of your action. Suppose you enter a $1,000 tournament and decide to sell pieces of your action. You can sell 10 percent of your action for $100; or if it is one of your better events, you may get a premium price of $150 for 10 percent of your pie. Or you might sell 50 percent of yourself for $600. In other words, you try to get a premium for your best events.

Sometimes, however, you may not get a premium. If you are entering the $10,000 WSOP event and have only $4,000 to invest in yourself, you might sell $100 shares, each of which will buy 1 percent of your action. You could go around collecting money from a variety of sources until you have raised enough to make the buy-in. At one time, I sold shares in my WSOP $10,000 buy-in action to 14 different investors, who put up from $100 to $2,500 each.

Being backed by someone is a different story. A backer accepts the entire burden of your tournament expenses. I used to be backed exclusively by Phil Hellmuth, a World Champion himself, and I would play for 50 percent of the net profit at year's end. If I registered a deficit, I would have to carry it over into the next tournament and if I suffered losses, I would need to make them up. Travel expenses would be paid but if I lost, they too would need to be made up eventually.

Not all players receive 50 percent from their backers; they sometimes get less. I have played tournaments for as low as 20 percent on a total freeroll basis. In this type of agreement, I didn't have to make up any money and our arrangement applied to only one or two events, rather than to a long-term commitment. Sometimes these short-term arrangements, in which you may be playing for only 30 or 40 percent of your own action, are the only way you can compete in a tournament. They aren't necessarily bad deals, either, although some players let their pride get in the way of making such arrangements and hold out for a larger percentage than a backer is willing to allow them. Personally, I would rather be playing for even a small percentage than not playing at all. It is better to have 30 percent of something than 50 percent of nothing.

Tournament specialists accept backers for several reasons. Number one is that not everyone has a sufficient bankroll to finance a tournament career in the big leagues and to withstand the inevitable fluctuations. Even if they do have enough money to finance themselves, it still makes sense to share the risks. You guarantee yourself that you will be in action by coming to an agreement with a backer, which gives you more security because you know that you will be in the tournaments, win or lose.

Naturally, you must have a long term positive expectancy or you wouldn't be backed in the first place; but with a backer, you can handle the fluctuations because he is accepting the risk. If you suffer a dry spell and lose, the agreement can always be terminated, but you don't have to reach into your pocket for any makeup money if the agreement is closed. In other words, the investor is taking the downside risk.

Why do investors back big league tournament players if they have to accept 100 percent of the loss and share only 50 percent of the profits? They do it because the player they are backing is a proven winner, a champion, so they can expect a long-term positive return on their money. From my point of view, even if I had $1 million in the bank to finance my tournament ventures, I would still accept backers. I am quite happy with this type of arrangement and would probably still continue with my backers, no matter what my bankroll was.

I feel a great loyalty toward Phil Hellmuth, who stuck with me through thick and thin for several years. Of course, Phil once rebutted me with, "No, Tom, I've stuck with you through thin and thinner!" I got a chuckle out of his retort because he was right—I went for over a year without making any money for either him or myself —but Phil never once lost confidence in me; in fact, he helped restore my former confidence in myself. "If he believes in me, how can I not believe in myself?" I wondered. For a while, I had begun to doubt myself, as any player does when he suffers a long dry spell, but Phil continually encouraged me. His patience began to be rewarded as my self confidence returned and I began making up the deficits and getting in the black once again.

Even if you have a sufficient bankroll to finance your career in the big leagues of tournament play, it seems to me that it still makes sense to accept a backer. Just knowing that you can always remain in action because there is money behind you, or being able to handle the fluctuations without having to worry about losing a substantial part of your bankroll, and not being fearful that you cannot justify playing in a big buy-in tournament because you're in a negative cycle are definite advantages of having a backer.

Of course, there also is a downside to agreements with backers. The disadvantage is that you receive only half of the profit. If you are a winning player with a long-term positive expectancy, you will be giving up one-half (or sometimes, even more) of your earnings.

Backers sometimes enter into arrangements with multiple players on different types of agreements. For example, he may partially back two players and finance a third player 100 percent. The backer also may occasionally give a player a freeroll for one specific event, usually his best game. Or he may freeroll one or more players into a few satellites, in which case he receives a percentage of their earnings if they win the satellite and come into the money in the main event. If they don't win the satellite, the backer simply absorbs the satellite fees and does not pay the player's entry fee into the tournament event. Some players receive freerolls for satellites only, while others receive satellite freerolls plus entries into a few specific events.

Bookkeeping is usually done on a tournament-to-tournament basis. For example, any deficit from a previous tournament is carried over to the next one. Then, if you are in the black at the end of that tournament, you can draw money from the account. If you are not in the black, you go forward to the next tournament until you make a profit. At the end of each tournament, then, if a "horse" is in the black, the horse is entitled to his share of the profit and a fresh line is drawn going into the next race.

The Ethics of Partnerships

Players have asked me, "Isn't there an ethical issue involved when an investor backs several tournament specialists?" Yes, there is an ethical consideration when you are sponsored by a backer who also sponsors some of the players you will be competing against. But tournament players are honorable people, and we hold to the concept that in all competitions of skill, the guidewords are, "It's every man for himself." If my backer has other horses in his stable, there is to be absolutely no collusion between me, the other players that my backer is financing, or between me and my backer, in the event that we both are playing in the same tournament.

As in any poker game, it is always player-against-player, every man for himself. Any collusion such as soft playing among buddies, or partnership plays that involve squeezing a third player out of a pot, is totally unethical and wrong. I am completely against such behavior at the poker table and will have no part of it. When you are dealing with ethical people, neither they nor you want to see or participate in this type of conduct, particularly when it is common knowledge that you are all being sponsored. If anything, I would rather go in the opposite direction, being totally aboveboard and playing my hardest against co-sponsored opponents, to ensure that there is no inference whatsoever regarding possible collusion. If I have to go against a player who is putting me all in, or vice-versa, I simply have to play against him with no hint of favoritism. We all understand that we need to play our best at all times, whether against other players or against each other.

To illustrate this point, let me relate an incident that occurred a few years ago in a no-limit hold'em tournament at the *Queens Classic,* in which T.J. Cloutier and I were both being backed by the same sponsor. In one particular hand, we had to play a huge all-in pot against each other. I had raised before the flop with a pair of queens and he decided to move in on me. Thinking it through, I knew that he had a hand, but not necessarily one that was better than mine. I also knew that he sometimes makes aggressive plays, so I made the call. Sure enough, he had A-K and my two queens held up, allowing me to double through him. After I crippled him, T.J. was eliminated from the tournament much earlier than was normal for him, while I went on to the final table. Our mutual sponsor just laughed about it when we discussed the hand.

These are just the breaks of the game when there is more than one horse in a sponsor's barn. You have to run against the other thoroughbreds just like you would against the rest of the competition. Since I had no vested interest in T.J.'s finish in the tournament, nor he in mine, it would not have put any money in my pocket if he had won, and it wouldn't have put any money in his pocket if I had won the tournament.

Staking Other Players

If you are thinking of staking another player, naturally you must have an adequate bankroll. If you don't have sufficient funds, it can be a highly risky venture. No matter how skilled a player is, he is a definite underdog in any tournament with a large field of over 200 players. The only way that a player can beat those odds is to play a lot of tournaments at a highly-skilled level. So if you are considering staking a tournament player, find someone that you know well and who has a positive long-term winning expectancy in order to make it worth your while. (Occasionally, a player will request anonymity when you stake him and you should respect his desire.)

Corporate Sponsorship

Unlike other individual competitions such as golf and tennis, poker tournaments are not yet sponsored by corporations, although some additional prize money has occasionally been offered. To the best of my knowledge, no players are currently being backed by a corporate sponsor. Since other types of games are being heavily sponsored and endorsed by companies, it seems to me that it is only logical that poker tournaments should also be backed by corporations. It has been suggested that companies are leery of sponsoring poker players on the tournament circuit because if a profit were made, they would have to declare the income, but if a net loss were posted, they could not deduct it because it would be classified as a gaming loss. This may be a good point, as the IRS has both challenged and has been challenged in this venue several times in the past.

If poker tournaments eventually gain corporate sponsorship, it probably will be due in large part to the positive response of the public to the nationally televised World Poker Tour. Because they can see the players' downcards and hear the commentators explain the probably reasons for the players' actions, the television audience can more closely identify with the skill and drama inherent in tournament poker. Along with the huge increase in the number of people playing poker on the Internet, the expansion of Indian reservation gaming, the legalization of casino gambling in most of the United States, and the ongoing growth of poker in Europe and Asia, the WPT is improving the image of the game and thus promoting poker as a far more socially acceptable activity than ever before in history.

Another factor contributing to the social acceptance of poker is the increase in the number of women who play poker at a high level of expertise and enter tournaments in competition against men. As the atmosphere of cardrooms and casinos becomes more acceptable to female players, who are no longer frowned upon for invading an all-male domain (so to speak), the ladies will feel more comfortable in the competitive poker environment, which can only improve the future of poker for everybody. Several female trailblazers already have become national poker stars— Maureen Feduniak, a grandmother, played at the championship table of a televised WPT tournament; Annie Duke, a high-stakes cash game and tournament player who is the mother of four young children , was featured in People magazine in 2003; and Kathy Liebert, a young professional player, became the first woman to win $1 million in a tournament when she won the PartyPoker Million poker tournament on a cruise ship. These women have helped proved that poker is a game for everyone—for all ages, all races, and for both sexes.

Making Deals at the Final Table

I believe that you should make a final-table deal whenever it is to your advantage. Often there is a tremendous spread between first, second and third places, and an even larger spread between fourth place and lower. (First place usually receives 37-40 percent, second gets around 20 percent, and third place receives about 10 percent.)

Most deals are made between the last two or three finalists, and occasionally between four of them. Because of these big percentage gaps between the top payoffs, and particularly when the limits are very high, it often makes sense to make a deal. Also, luck becomes a dominant factor in the final stages, so that even if a player has an edge in skill, that edge often is dwarfed by the size of the antes, blinds and limits. Therefore, a highly skilled player may not have enough time to outplay his opponents, and so he may logically consider making a deal.

Of course, if you have a lot of money and just feel like gambling and playing for it, or if you believe that you have both a superior chip position and a skill advantage on your opponents, by all means go for it. But if the skill level and the chip counts are close between you and your opponents, and if your financial condition is not the greatest, dealing certainly is a worthwhile consideration.

I would venture to guess that in approximately 80 percent or more of the major tournaments with an entry fee of at least $500, some type of deal is made between the final contestants. In small daily tournaments it is not unusual for the finalists to make a settlement among themselves. Even when first place awards $1,000 and fourth place pays only $200, deals are made between the final four in the dailies, so when there are tens of thousands of dollars at stake, as there so often is in the major tournaments, dealing is quite acceptable.

So long as there is no corporate sponsorship, with players posting 100 percent of their buy-ins, I believe it is quite ethical to negotiate settlements at the final table. If the world of tournament poker ever does receive corporate sponsorship, however, a new set of ethics probably would have to be put into effect. In this case, players would need to understand that, because of the additional prize money being offered by the corporate sponsor, they should not jeopardize the integrity of the tournament by making deals on the end.

Determining Your Share

When a deal is made at the final table at the WSOP, the usual method is for the chips of each finalist to be counted to determine how many chips each player has won in relation to the total number of chips in play. For example, say that Player A has 50 percent of the chips, Player B has 30 percent, and Player C has 20 percent, with a prize fund of $40,000 for first, $20,000 for second, and $10,000 for third. First of all, each player is guaranteed at least a third place finish of $10,000, which is subtracted from the total prize fund of $70,000, leaving $40,000 to be distributed. This $40,000 is then divided on a percentage basis.

In this example, Player A would receive $20,000 additional money; Player B would get $12,000; and Player C would receive $8,000. Adding these totals to the guaranteed $10,000 each finalists wins, Player A winds up with a $30,000 payday; Player B with $22,000; and Player C with $18,000. So instead of receiving $40,000 for first, the top finisher receives $30,000; second gets $22,000 instead of $20,000; and third receives $18,000 instead of $10,000. Players generally agree that this type of hedge makes sense.

In reality, other types of arrangements are also made. For instance, the chip leader often gives an extra premium to the shorter stacks. Remember that the fewer chips you have, the more precious they are and the higher their value. The more chips you have, the less valuable they are. So the usual case is that the chip leader makes an additional concession to the shorter stacks, rather than the other way around.

Of course the better your negotiation skills, the more likely you are to get the best of it in working out a deal on the end. Although the most equitable method is a percentage division of the remaining prize money based on a chip count, who says splits must be totally fair? For example, say that you're the player in third place with 20 percent of the chips and you decide that you want $20,000, which is the size of the second-place prize. You believe you still have enough chips to compete, and you know that one hand may drastically change the chip positions of all three finalists. (It is not unusual for the third-place player to win one hand and become the leader while the former leader is reduced to third place.) Combining these factors with the fact that you think you have a skill edge over your opponents, you may try playing a little hardball in negotiating a deal. Or you may be in good financial condition and don't want to take the worst of it, so you decide not to strike a deal at all.

Players sometimes ask me if having a backer affects your authority to strike a deal at the final table. In my case, I have been given the go-ahead to negotiate whenever I believe it is in my (our) best interests. If my sponsor(s) are at the tournament when I arrive at the final table, however, I never make a deal without first discussing it with them. Sometimes they will say, "No, I don't think that's a good arrangement," and I will usually concur with their wishes. But if they are not around, I am fully empowered to use my best judgement and discretion in making settlements.

When I am playing satellites, however, our usual agreement is that I will play to win it without making any deals on the end. Occasionally, I have also been advised not to make any deals with certain players in a particular tournament. If I am asked by my sponsor(s) not to make any deals, I won't negotiate a settlement. But usually, I have a lot of discretion in deal-making because my backers trust my judgment and know that I will try to negotiate the best possible settlement.

Record Keeping

You have to sign a W-2G form at the major tournaments for the amount of money you collect. The offsets to your win are your receipts for your buy-in and other tournament expenses (travel, room and board, etc.), so be sure that you keep a record of everything. I record them daily so I always know what the buy-ins are and how much I have cashed out, which gives me a figure for my net profit.

Since gaming involves such a wide spectrum of activities, I also maintain a daily record of all my gaming wins and losses. This way, I always know where I stand and have a ready record for my IRS return. Many players also have sources of gaming income other than tournament wins, which they do not record. Not reporting this income is illegal, but in fact many gamblers do not report it.

The IRS will usually accept daily diaries of your gaming wins and losses. For example, suppose you come to Las Vegas to play a big tournament and you have a high-money finish. You can deduct all of your trip-related expenses from your win, plus any other gaming losses such as losing sports betting tickets and slot losses which have been monitored through your slot club membership. Of course, you don't always get receipts for all your gaming losses, such as a loss you might suffer at the crap table, so you have to record them in your daily journal. Keeping a piece of paper in your wallet at all times and recording your wins/losses is easy to do on a daily basis, or at least every other day.

Tipping

The amount that most players toke the tournament dealers is about 5 percent for first place in smaller tournaments with $100 or less buy-in, and around 2 or 3 percent in tournaments with buy-ins of $500 or more. I also toke any "worthy notables" such as special dealers or floor personnel who are especially good at their jobs.

The modern trend is for casinos to reserve 3 percent of the total prize fund for the tournament staff. If that is the procedure in the tournament that I'm playing, I scale back on the amount of the additional tip, if any, that I leave for the staff.

Dealing with Your Fans

If you are not a famous player, dealing with a "fan club" will not be one of your problems, although even hometown heroes who compete in only the local tournaments often develop a following of fans. Once you attain a high level of tournament expertise and recognition via your winning record, whether on the local circuit or the international tour, fan clubs can become a distraction.

Because I have reached a certain plateau of fame, and because I also am a teacher and author, I am often surrounded by both railbirds and students who want to talk with me during the tournament. I try to give my students as many helpful suggestions as I can during the event, but sometimes I become distracted from my tournament play and spread myself a bit too thin trying to accommodate everyone's requests. During the dinner break, I may spend time discussing strategy Other times, however, I may feel the need for some personal quiet time, make my excuses, and disappear during the dinner break to either meditate or to review my play and decide on my best strategy for the rest of the tourney.

Even though I may see a lot of well wishers on the rail during a tournament, I can tune out most distractions and maintain a clear focus on the job at hand (which is one of my fortes). But having too many rooters can affect your concentration and your results, so you have to guard against that. It is similar to "having too much of a good thing," and consequently you may try too hard and make mistakes because you are distracted. I have seen players win a big pot and then try to tame the cheers of enthusiastic rooters by giving them the high sign to tone it down a bit.

The Occupational Hazards of Tournament Specialists

Poker is not a nine-to-five occupation. Erratic schedules are the rule rather than the exception, although I do know some ring players who show up in the cardroom at 11 a.m. and play until 8 p.m. everyday. The "stuck factor" is also a consideration in setting up a playing schedule or in planning mealtimes. It is difficult to leave a good poker game just to eat dinner or attend a movie, particularly when you are losing — or when tourists are throwing off their money to you. You simply have to stick with the game to maximize your win against the players who are throwing the party. When these things happen, you simply have to change your plans. It has been my experience that a spouse doesn't like it when you frequently change plans on them.

It seems to me that it takes a very special person to tolerate this topsy-turviness, to accept it as an occupational hazard, and to deal with it in a way that doesn't prove detrimental to the happiness and emotional well-being of the poker player in the family.

Therefore, whether they are tournament specialists or not, divorce seems to be an occupational hazard for professional poker players. It takes a *truly* understanding spouse to handle the up-and-down fluctuations of the typical professional tournament player, especially one who travels extensively on the tournament circuit. Sometimes I am on the road for a month or two at a time because as soon as I finish one tournament, another one begins two days later. It is a rare breed who can successfully mix marriage with tournament poker, although I have seen some solid married couples who do it quite well.

Most professional poker players are night owls; I have always been one myself. Although I don't like playing graveyard because it makes me feel like a zombie or a vampire who only comes out at night, I am typically awake until 3 a.m. and ordinarily get up at 10:00 a.m. Since most poker tournaments begin between noon and 1 p.m., playing a late-night poker session would cut into my sleep time and need for rest. I prefer sticking to what I call "tournament time" all of the time, because I play in tournaments most of the year. In 2000, for example, I entered 190 satellites and tournaments.

When I was in the world of business where people begin working at 8 a.m., I had a very difficult time. Poker players don't usually start their day until noon and generally lead an erratic life-style, so I did not adapt very well to the nine-to-five routine of business because I am not a morning person. Part of the beauty of the poker business is that we can tailor our hours to suit our needs.

Most professional poker players continually exercise their brains, but sometimes allow their bodies to turn to mush. Many of them smoke and are overweight; they do not lead a very healthy lifestyle. Even we nonsmokers are continually subjected to detrimental secondhand smoke, so some type of daily exercise program is essential for all poker players to maintain their stamina. It is far too easy to fall into the rut of getting up, immediately starting to play poker, and eating big meals at the free buffets during tournaments. Putting on extra pounds and becoming lazy about getting exercise is an easy path to follow, one which I have been guilty of myself. But I have tried to avoid these pitfalls by taking walks and by seldom putting my car in valet parking, because sometimes just walking to and from the parking lot is all the exercise I will get in one day (although I don't recommend not taking valet parking to everyone, as valet is a much safer way to park your car).

Watching what I eat is also part of my personal fitness regime. I used to try to assuage my depression over getting knocked out of a tournament by eating two or three entrees and several desserts (which I love) at the players' buffet. If you ever read the cartoon *Cathy*, you will recognize her as a rather erratic character who has a lot of neurotic hang-ups. One of her classic comments is, "The worse things get, the better we eat."

Maintaining Emotional Stability

All poker players who are on a downslide have difficulty in handling depression. I have seen some of the most highly skilled of my colleagues, world class players who usually maintain a positive attitude, act totally befuddled and stressed-out when they are on a losing streak. Bouts of depression have victimized me, too, although I have recovered from them. I suffered a bad streak on the tournament circuit not too long ago, and my self-confidence began to waiver. I began to wonder if I had ever been that good, that talented.

Poker is a great test of a player's character. In my opinion, the truest test of a poker player's character is not how he behaves when he is winning, but how he reacts when he is losing. You can fairly accurately judge how a person runs his own life, what his inner character is like, by observing his actions at the poker table—who are the risk takers, who are the more Joe-conservatives, who are the flamboyant personalities, who are the devious types. I love trying to typecast them.

One of the things I most admire about my writing partner T.J. Cloutier is that no matter how bad things get, he has the ability to shrug them off and continue to play his A-game, remaining undaunted and positive. With just a few words of advice and a positive attitude, he has helped me maintain an even emotional level. Following his example, I have tried to cultivate that attitude within myself.

I also think that it is wise to take time off while the tournament is still going on. During a three-week tournament, I usually try to take a day or two off. It is the only way I can stay reasonably fresh. If you try to play every tournament, plus satellites and some side-action games, you will spread yourself too thin. I know players who put in 14-to-16 hours a day, everyday, when a tournament is going on. How can they expect to get good results on that type of schedule?

Tournament play drains you emotionally and physically to a far greater extent than side action. There are so many more factors to consider during tournaments that your concentration has to be at its peak. After four or five hours of tournament play, I am usually tired and pass any side-action games. Of course, I do play side action when tournaments are not in progress. For example, if I have a week off, I will play three or four days for about five hours a day, usually about 20 hours for the week.

These days most of my side-game play is done in the comfort of my home on the Internet. I play on several different online sites and jump in and out of games frequently, as time permits. I find that having a life outside of the poker arena is very important to me.

Monetary Pressure

Playing poker professionally is similar to being a salesman who works on commission. When you make sales, you get a commission and your lifestyle can roll on at a nice clip. If you don't make sales, you don't receive commissions and your lifestyle suffers because the bills go on whether or not you're making any money to pay them.

Poker players have an even tougher row to hoe. If you are a salesman, at least you don't lose any money when you lose a sale, but a poker player puts his bankroll on the line every time he sits down at the table. In fact, he could actually have a negative income through losing, which can be very stressful. More poker players go broke *not* because of their losses, but because they cannot make enough money at poker to maintain an adequate lifestyle. For example suppose that you are a player who makes $10,000 per year at $5-$10 or $10-$20 limit poker. You are a winning player, yes, but try to live on that!

What happens to many poker players is that they are broke all the time because they cannot make enough money to pay their living expenses and maintain a decent playing bankroll. They lose some of the money they need to live on, and then have to find sources of credit, so a lot of borrowing goes on in the world of poker. Without an outside source of income, then, many poker players live at only the subsistence level.

Performance Pressures

We can become the implements of our own self-destruction if we put too much pressure on ourselves to perform. Personally, I do put a lot of pressure on myself to succeed and because I expect a lot from myself, I sometimes become my own worst enemy. Being in a partnership with sponsors who bend over backward to reduce the stress, however, is a great balm.

Putting unrealistic demands upon yourself as a professional poker player can cause you to go into a monumental funk when you don't meet your expectations. One way to avoid this pitfall is to guard against setting your hopes too high. I sometimes go into a tournament saying to myself, "I am never going to book another win at the tournament table. I am not counting on any income whatsoever from poker." Then when I win and make a profit, it's like a bonus. This sort of counter-positive thinking seems to work for me by relieving my psyche from the pressure of needing to win.

When a poker player comes back from a big loss in a game after getting off to a bad start and sticking it out by playing many hours longer than he intended—when he bails out and escapes the losing trap—it is almost like cheating death. You have dug yourself a deep grave through a combination of either bad or unlucky play. But then you resurrect yourself and rise from the dead.

Unfortunately, not all top level players dig themselves out from unhealthy gambling habits. I cannot count the number of world-class poker players who win tournaments consistently, but who are broke all the time because they cannot control their gambling in other areas where they don't have the skill edge they have in poker—craps, sports betting, even roulette. Poker has enough skill to it that superior players will consistently win the money, so why leak any of it into games of chance (although they may be okay for occasional entertainment). It would seem that the same gambling spirit which makes some of the best poker players so formidable at the table is the very character trait that causes their demise in gaming arenas where they are less skillful. Too often, they wind up self-destructing. ♠

Chapter 20
QUESTIONS PLAYERS ASK ABOUT TOURNAMENTS

Players frequently approach me to ask questions about tournament strategy. Here is a list of questions and answers that I hope will help you win the next tournament you enter— just as long as you're not playing against me, okay?

Is there a success formula for winning tournaments?

Yes, but there is no *magic* formula. Playing a very solid game and being selectively aggressive are two important ingredients of the formula, plus picking your spots well, gambling when it is warranted (such as in multiway pots that are not prohibitively expensive when you need to draw to suited connectors), and using good judgment.

Above all, learning how to *survive* long enough to give yourself a chance to get lucky is the key. Anybody who has ever won a tournament has gotten lucky! But to maximize your opportunity to get lucky, you must know survival skills because you can't get that great rush of cards in the later stages of the tournament unless you're still around.

The success formula, then, is developing your *tournament* skills so that you can maximize your poker playing skills and your good judgment in order to give yourself a chance to get lucky and take home the trophy (and the money, of course.)

Should the length of the betting rounds affect my strategy?

Yes. In one-table satellites, for example, where the betting limits escalate every 15 minutes to 20 minutes, you will often have to gamble with less than premium hands because you simply don't have enough time to wait for premium cards when the limits are rising so rapidly.

You hope to get some premium hands early that hold up and give you a good chip lead so you can win it, but there is no guarantee that even your best hands won't get outdrawn. This happens because, with the short betting rounds, a lot of players are gambling with lesser hands so that many of the pots become multi-way—and, of course, the bigger starting hands go down in value in multi-way action.

You must be keenly aware of when the blinds and the limits are about to rise and adjust your play accordingly. Sometimes, if you have accumulated a lot of chips early, you can play somewhat more conservatively, but overall you will be playing faster than you would if the rounds were longer.

How does the size of my stack affect the way that I play a hand?

It makes an enormous difference in your strategy. If you are short-stacked, almost all-in, you may have to defend your blind with a weak hand simply because you have no more chips left. Or if you have a large stack, you will often play a hand against a short stack that you would not play against another big stack or against another good player.

Actually, you use your stack as a weapon throughout the tournament. The bigger your stack, the more artillery in your arsenal. The smaller your stack, the fewer bullets in your gun.

Another important concept is that the more chips you have, the less value they have. The fewer chips you have, the more value each one has. Therefore with a short to medium stack, you must play tighter than a bigger stack and wait for your best opportunity so that you can get your money's worth with a higher quality hand. With a bigger stack, you can be more willing to gamble and play a few more marginal hands that could develop into big hands and break the short stacks. The size of your stack, then, influences your decisions throughout the tournament.

How do I play a short stack late in the tournament? A big stack?

When you have a short stack, you will frequently have to take a stand with less than a premium hand. The shorter your stack, the more important it is to use extremely good judgment about when to jeopardize it. This is especially true when you have only one or two bets left, because you know that you will be called by at least the big blind, if not by one of the bigger stacks. So you have to wait for your best shot, which requires good judgment. This doesn't mean you necessarily have to wait for A-K, but on the other hand, you don't want to jeopardize your chips by going all-in with a hand such as 10-9 or K-7 if you can wait for a few more hands to be dealt before you are forced to take a stand.

The times I have taken a stand with hands like A-6 offsuit and gotten busted out of the tournament are too painful to list. You will sometimes be forced to play ace-rag hands, but I would rather go all-in with a hand such as K-Q or Q-J suited than ace-rag, because I seem to get better short-term results with these types of hands.

Of course, with a big stack, you should "do your job:" attack the short stacks whenever you can. The more chips you have, the more options you have. Although you can play a few more hands than you could with an average or short stack, you still have to use good judgment, especially against other big stacks. You have to be selectively aggressive and wait for premium hands before you attack one of the other big boys at the table.

You can also capitalize on the tight play of your opponents by betting more aggressively against them when they have only an average or short stack. Even though they may suspect that you may be raising with less than a premium hand, there isn't much they can do about it if they only have a medium-strength hand. Big stacks are weapons—use them.

Should my tournament strategy be affected by my opponents?

Absolutely yes. You are playing your opponents—and their stacks—just as much as you are playing your cards. You should be evaluating them constantly: which ones are tight, which ones are loose, who switches back and forth based on the size of their stack. Sometimes, a player with a lot of chips will play aggressively and will enter a lot of pots, but if he loses a few hands, he will change his strategy and tighten up. Your opponents' seat positions and chip positions in relation to you is always important.

How can I defend against a maniac?

If I am playing in a rebuy tournament, I usually will be willing to gamble with a maniac when I have any kind of decent hand, and certainly when I have a premium hand, especially if I plan to rebuy. But in freezeout tourneys, maniacs can pose quite a problem. They can be extremely difficult to play against because you can't replace those precious chips if you lose them. The maniac not only jeopardizes his own chips, he also jeopardizes yours, so you simply have to play tighter against him. Unfortunately, there is no defense against a maniac putting a big beat on you when he draws out against you. I have suffered some of my worst drawouts from maniacs when I misjudged the strength of their hands and gave them too much action. Players tend to give a lot of action to maniacs who are very aggressive raisers, and they deserve more action than tighter, more conservative players do. But you still have to use excellent judgment because maniacs are hard to read.

Because it's hard to put them on a hand, you may find yourself putting in more action than you should when a raggedy flop like Q-4-3 comes off. You think it is a great flop for your pocket kings, only to find that the maniac has raised with Q-4 suited and beats you with two pair. But even a maniac won't jeopardize his whole stack with a totally useless hand, so if he continues to raise you, slow down. Remember that your best tournament strategy is not to get "full value" from every hand in every situation: it is to survive. If a maniac puts you in jeopardy by making you put in too many bets with either your medium-strength or premium hands, be careful. Even pocket aces are not invincible. Tend to do more check-calling against them.

One of the biggest dangers of maniacs is that they may herd you right into the nuts: you put in an aggressive raise against the maniac, and you have him beaten, but you get picked off from the rear from someone who has an even better hand. For example, maybe you played a K-Q against the maniac's early raise and the flop comes K-7-5 unsuited. The maniac fires in a bet and you immediately raise him. The opponent who cold-called the raise behind you before the flop then puts in a third bet. Kiss your K-Q good-by—it just can't be any good. When you're caught in a whipsaw between the maniac and a solid player sitting behind you who has also called the pre-flop raise, you must be very cautious. Too often, the maniac puts you on the defensive and you will simply have to give up a lot of medium-strength hands rather than risk your unreplaceable chips.

The good news is that sooner or later, the maniac will usually self-destruct as the result of his overly aggressive tactics. But sometimes, that doesn't happen. On more than one occasion, I have seen a maniac win the tournament either because he didn't get picked off often enough, or because he kept getting lucky flops. So sometimes, a player wins the tournament that you would usually build a side game around. This is one of the strange attractions of tournament play: occasionally, an unusual style or strategy will disrupt the normal flow of the tournament and give a new face his moment in the limelight. But in the long run, a maniacal style of play will usually lead to early self-destruction.

What guidelines should I use in playing the blinds?

When you're competing in a tournament, especially one that doesn't allow rebuys, you have to play more conservatively from the blinds. Some of the hands you would defend in a ring game against a middle position raiser are clear passes in tourneys. Your opponents are usually playing more conservatively in tournaments so you have to give even a middle position raiser a lot more credibility than you would in a ring game. You probably would not defend ace-rag against a raise from a solid player, for example, which you might defend in a side game against a late position raiser. If you have small pairs in the big blind and the pot is not going to be played multi-way, you should probably pass, whereas you may have called in a rebuy tournament or a in a ring game.

Those half-price blind hands can become some of the most expensive hands you play. You're out of position on each betting round, and although you might flop something, your pairs are often outkicked because you're playing a weaker hand that you would normally play if you were not in the blind. So be very selective about what hands you defend from the blind and who you defend them against. Be more reluctant, for instance, to defend against loose players who could be holding almost anything and will be constantly putting pressure on you. You could be forced to jeopardize a lot of bets, so be cautious and use good judgment to keep yourself out of big trouble.

How much should I expect to increase my chip position in each round?

Naturally, if you can double-up, you have done an outstanding job. But in the first round when you begin with $500 in chips and the limits are $15-$30, for example, if you can increase your chip count to around $750 or $800, you should be very happy. Even increasing it a modest 20 percent to $600 is very helpful, because some players will lose half their stacks or more, and a few will even go broke during the first round. In general, if you continue to increase your stack by about 50 percent during each round (100 percent is even better), you will find yourself at the final table in good chip position. Even an increase of 25 percent per round will put you in good enough status to go all the way.

On what factors should I base my rebuy and add-on decisions?

The bigger the field and the more money up for grabs, the more inclined you should be to rebuy. Also, the earlier the stage of the tournament, the better the time to rebuy because it will make a bigger difference in your chip strength. Sometimes, you can rebuy for three or four rounds, but by the time the third round is almost over, several players will usually have built their stacks up to $1,500-$2,500 (and in pot-limit tournaments, sometimes even higher). Continuing to rebuy for $500 when you are up against players with five or six times that amount is probably not a correct decision at that point.

A prominent poker author has suggested that it usually is correct to rebuy when you go broke in a fixed payout rebuy tournament. Yet I have seen players rebuy so often in these tournaments, that even if they had come in second, they would have lost money; and if they had won, they would have barely come out in the black. To me, it is absurd to think that you would have to win the tournament just to come out even.

Generally speaking, it is correct to rebuy. In the typical Orleans type of tournament, for example, I am always prepared to rebuy and make the two-for-one add-on. I am even more inclined to rebuy when bad players hold the most chips, players who I know will gamble a lot and jeopardize their chips with less than premium hands. Other factors to consider are how many chips the rebuys and add-ons will give you in relation to your opponents; whether the strongest players have all the chips; and the overall size of the tournament.

Sometimes, I will enter with the idea that I will never rebuy, particularly in big buy-in tourneys like the WSOP Omaha events that offer rebuys for $1,500 or $2,500. I just take my best shot with my original buy-in because I don't want to invest $4500 to $6000 (or even more in the $2,500 event). In my opinion, that's too much for a tournament that pays only nine places, and will sometimes only give you your money back even if you have a final table finish of around eighth or ninth place. So if the field isn't large enough for the prize money to guarantee me some kind of profit if I make it to the final table, I will decide not to rebuy before I enter the tournament. Common sense and good judgment must prevail.

Should the number of payout slots affect how I play at the last two tables?

Yes. When the action gets down to three short-handed tables in a tournament that pays two tables, for example, the short and medium stacks play very tight poker. Even the larger stacks tighten up to guarantee themselves a money finish. This is when the best tournament players make the most headway by playing aggressively against overly-tight opponents. This strategy sometimes backfires when you get picked off by a player who wasn't playing as conservatively as you thought he was, or when you run into a better hand. Although you can crash and burn, if you can successfully capitalize on tight play at the last tables, you can greatly enhance your chip position.

Your strategy also may be affected by your attitude: Are you just shooting for a payoff shot, or are you aiming to win the tournament? Some players are content to slide into the money and then worry about winning later, while others are willing to go all-out to accumulate as many chips as they can to take to the final table with them. These players don't care if they finish one or two spots out of the money; their main concern is maximizing their chip position. Either style is OK; it depends on your goals.

In general, however, the number of payoff slots greatly influences how you play, especially at the final table when the prize money begins to seriously escalate. When there is not a big difference in money between 9th-8th-7th places, it is usually correct not to worry about sliding up just a few hundred, or even a few thousand, more dollars when the top spot pays thousands of dollars more.

But that doesn't mean that just sliding up the pay scale is not a viable goal. It all depends on what you want to achieve: a maximum chance for surviving a little longer, or a maximum opportunity to win the most chips possible and increase your chance to win the tournament. So always keep the big picture in mind. The big picture, naturally, is giving yourself a chance to win the whole enchilada.

How important is bluffing in limit tournaments? In no-limit tournaments?

I believe that people bluff far too often in limit poker, whether they are playing a cash game or a tournament. In all forms of poker, you have to be able to size up the situation fairly accurately before you decide to try a bluff. But there are times when bluffing is definitely correct in tourneys. In the latter stages when players are reluctant to call a raise with a marginal hand, tight players can often be manipulated and maneuvered (especially when they are in the blinds) with a bluff or a semi-bluff.

In limit poker, it costs only one or two extra bets to call a raise. Because of the relatively inexpensive cost of calling a suspected bluff, you have to use excellent timing when you do decide to bluff. But in no-limit, the big bluff is often king.

You have a far greater chance to be successful with a bluff or semi-bluff because of the big-bet aspect of no-limit poker. Players frequently cannot continue playing past the flop with big drawing hands because it is too expensive to draw to a straight or flush. So if you have correctly put an opponent on a draw, you can often pick up the pot by firing in a bet. Bluffing is also very important in no-limit tournaments when the play becomes shorthanded. You must raise more often and try to steal more blinds, because it is very difficult for players to defend blinds or call raises with mediocre hands such as Q-J suited, K-J, or A-10. Even if they suspect you are bluffing, your opponents may be afraid to call because they don't want to jeopardize their chips by taking the chance that you have a weaker hand than what you are representing.

Should you usually play the button aggressively in hold'em?

In my opinion, most players are a bit too aggressive on the button, although there are times when you can raise with a substandard hand on the button. One is when you are up against very conservative players who are more willing to give up their blinds. Another time occurs during a tournament when your opponent has a mediocre or inferior chip position and would therefore be reluctant to get involved with average strength hands he might have called with in a ring game.

Aggressive play on the button has a greater chance for success in the later stages of a tournament against shorter-stacked opponents than it would have in the early stages, or in ring games in general. Remember that in limit poker, you will have to show down a hand most of the time. This is far less frequent in no-limit where big bets can force opponents to fold marginal hands. In limit games, many players are suspicious of button raises when they are in the blind, and rightfully so. Therefore, if you are playing against loose, aggressive blind defenders, an overly-aggressive posture on the button can get you into a lot of trouble. You will need a better-quality hand to attack liberal blind defenders.

This doesn't mean that you necessarily need big pairs or ace-king, but you should be reluctant to attack the blinds with hands like 10-9 against loose, aggressive players who are not only capable of calling but will also frequently reraise with marginal hands such K-Q, K-J (which might be better than the one you are raising with). So always use your best judgment about whom you decide to attack.

How do you cope with playing against intimidating opponents, such as past champions?

First of all, try not to feel intimidated by anyone, but also look for reasons *not* to get involved against world-class opponents with less than premium hands. If you always enter the pot with a solid hand, it is very difficult for even a champion player to outplay you. Avoid marginal hands and tricky situations that require a lot of judgment. Be less likely to get involved with suited connectors against a champion level opponent on your left side.

In fact, if you have a super sharp player on your left side, you will have to go through him on every hand you play. This forces you to play better because you are aware that you have a very tough opponent on your left. Naturally, you would rather have him on your right in order to have position over him, but you cannot select your seat position in a tournament.

Being afraid of a world-class opponent is a mistake—being cautious is a better option. No matter how good he is, if you begin with superior starting hands against him, there isn't much he can do to outplay you if he has a slightly inferior holding or even one that is equal to yours.

When should you go all in?

I prefer going all-in when I can be the aggressor rather than just the caller of someone else's bet that puts me all-in. But it actually depends to a great degree on your chip position, your opponent's chip status, the quality of your hand, and whether you are on the defense or the offense. Where did the raise come from? Usually, the earlier the raise, the higher the quality of the hand; the later the raise, the more marginal the hand (especially in shorthanded play). Super aggressive opponents are capable of raising with any two cards against shorter stacks to try to get them all in. This is why I prefer going all-in when I can be the aggressor, thus giving myself a better chance of winning the pot with a raise (especially before the flop).

In the rebuy events I play, the betting goes to no-limit when it's down to around seven players. What guidelines do you suggest for novice no-limit players?

Whether or not you realize it, you are actually playing no-limit before the term "no-limit" is actually in effect. This happens because, when the limits are very high and you cannot play a full hand to the river without going all-in, you are in effect already playing no-limit poker since you are only one hand away from elimination. For example, say you are in the later stages of the tournament (even before the final table) with $1,600 in chips. The limits are $500-$1,000 with 12 players remaining. As soon as you put in a raise, you will have most of your chips in the pot. If you then follow with a $500 bet on the flop, you will have only $100 left. Virtually any player who has already put $1,500 into the pot will call you for $100 more on the turn. In effect, then, you are playing no-limit poker.

"No-limit" seems to have an intimidating effect on some players, but it shouldn't have. Any time you have fewer chips than it takes to play one hand through to the river, you are playing no-limit, so don't be so worried about it at the final table because you probably have more experience at no-limit poker than you think you do. When the game officially goes to no-limit, many of your decisions will be based on the size of your stack. If you have a good starting hand but you don't have enough chips to bet it all the way to the river, you may as well be aggressive with it early and try to get in as many chips as possible. By committing early, you may be able to eliminate players with marginal hands who might otherwise call if you hadn't put on the heat with a raise or a reraise.

What are the major differences between tournament strategy and cash-game play?

Many hands that are playable in a ring game are not playable in a tournament. When you know that you cannot replace chips when you lose them, you are more reluctant to become involved with small pairs or suited connectors when the pot is not being played multi-way. But the biggest difference between tournament play and ring games is that you have only a fixed amount of chips to wager with in a tournament; if you lose them, you cannot replace them. So you have to be more selective about your starting hands and about when you enter a pot in tournament play. You need to play more conservatively than you do in your everyday ring games. Your chip count and that of your opponents often guide your decisions, so that some hands you would play in a ring game cannot be played at all when you have short chips in a tournament. You are not concerned whether a player will be all-in in a ring game, but in a tournament you must always be cognizant of this factor.

Is it ever correct to slow-play a monster hand during a tournament?

Yes, slow-playing a big hand is often correct. If you're up against opponents who are less likely to continue playing a hand because they think you might have the deck crippled, they will be on the timid side. Suppose you flop quads, for example: you hold pocket sevens and the flop comes 7-7-8. When you flop quads in hold'em, the deck becomes fairly crippled, so you try to induce a bluff from an opponent. What you hope to accomplish by slow-playing your cinch hand is that someone will catch up a little by pairing his big card, or by making a straight or a flush, and give you some action.

The same holds true in seven-card stud, especially when you hold high rolled-up pairs such as three aces or kings. You know that if you raise or reraise early, your opponents will give you credit for a big hand and will be less likely to get involved. But if you just limp in, they won't give you credit for trips because they think that if you had a big pair, you would have raised. They are more likely to believe that you have three to a straight or three to a flush.

You only slow-play with very big starting hands. For example, you decide to limp in with pocket aces from early position in a shorthanded hold'em game, hoping to get some action behind you. Slow-playing happens a lot more often in pot-limit and no-limit hold'em than it does in limit play. This is true because the slow-playing player hopes someone behind him will bet so that he can raise the pot and trap them for a big bet.

If your monster hand is likely to get beaten, the story is a little different. Suppose you have limped in with pocket aces and make top set on the flop, but it also comes with suited connectors. Now you have less reason to slow-play because your opponents could have more possibilities for drawing out against you.

When you get high-carded to another table, what is your best strategy just after you sit down?

If I am not familiar with some of the players at the table, I like to just sit and observe for a hand or two, unless I get a very big starting hand. Players often expect me to play selectively aggressive, so they tend to test the waters with a raise here and there. So if I start off by raising, they are more likely to look me up just to see what I'm raising with. Therefore, when I first sit down at a new table, I prefer showing them a pretty decent starting hand in the first pot I enter . . . then I may take a few more liberties later on. The major idea is that you should not just jump into the action right away unless you have a strong starting hand. It is better to take a slightly more conservative approach until you can get a fix on the other types of players at the table.

What are the biggest mistakes that tournament players make?

Players make several major mistakes, one of which is not drawing to the nuts for either one end of the pot or the other in split games such as Omaha high-low. Another one is trying to win the tournament too early. They gamble, amass a large stack, get to the fourth table, and try to win it right then. It simply cannot be done. Playing too many hands and gambling too much, rather than changing gears and slowing down, is the biggest reason why big stacks crash and burn far sooner than they should.

Many players are also too liberal in defending their blind hands. Remember that most blind hands are substandard and if you call, you will be playing a hand you would not normally have entered the pot with voluntarily. Getting tied on to these "cheap" hands can become a costly mistake.

Playing too tight in the later stages is another mistake players make. They desperately try to hang on for some kind of money finish and end up jeopardizing their chance to reach the final table in decent chip status. Even players with big stacks will sometimes play far too tight, especially shorthanded when the blinds and antes come around much faster than in a full game. A tall stack sometimes will play so tight that the blinds erode his chip position unnecessarily. In *Poker Tournament Tips From The Pros,* Smith includes a list of 26 mistakes players often make in tournaments. I suggest you read that chapter for further insight.

Today's tournaments have fairly short rounds, especially those with small buy-ins. Should this affect my strategy?

If rebuys are allowed, you can gamble more knowing that if it doesn't work, you can always rebuy and keep firing away with your better hands. You hope to hit a few flops in hold'em, or you might gamble more than you ordinarily would with drawing hands in seven-card stud. Once the rebuy option is over, you have to be selectively aggressive. You cannot continue to wait for those big starting hands.

You will also have to play some of your medium-strength hands somewhat faster, especially if you can get multi-way action on them. For example, you might even call a raise with 8-7 suited in hold'em when you are in good position. If you're getting a good enough price, it may be worth it to see if you can hit that one magic flop with five or six-way action. You have to play solid and aggressive poker in the 20-minute betting rounds that are typical of this type of tournament. Maybe "intelligently aggressive" is a better term for the correct approach to short-round tourneys.

Are there any types of tournaments that you should not enter?

Two of the factors you should consider when you decide to enter a tournament are the number of entrants and the calibre of your opposition compared to your own expertise as a tournament player. In some cases, the field is short with a world-class lineup, which means that you don't have much positive expectancy because you don't have a skill edge. Also, when the field is short, the payout is smaller so you have to judge whether the projected size of the prize fund is big enough to justify the size of the buy-in.

If the field is exceedingly short *and* exceeding tough, you may be well-advised to pass that particular event and save your buy-in for a more favorable situation. Or you could just play a satellite for it, going in with the idea that if you win it, you'll play in the tournament, but if you don't win you won't pony up the buy-in for that tournament event.

In your 1985 book, you talked about slow, medium, and fast action tournaments. Has anything changed in today's tourneys?

Yes. At the time I wrote the book, slow action tournaments were those which took two or more days to complete and had two-hour betting rounds. Bak then, all the World Series of Poker events were two-day tournaments with two-hour time frames, with the exception of the main event which lasted for four days. Today, the only tournaments that have two-hour betting rounds are the $10,000 buy-in no-limit Texas hold'em championship event at the WSOP and some of the World Poker Tour championship events.

I described medium-action tournaments as having one-hour time frames. Today, almost every major tournament has a one-hour time frame, and many of them are in the 40 to 45-minute range, which was virtually unheard of in 1985 when my first book was printed. Most tournaments are now what I used to call medium action, with 40-minute to one-hour rounds. Events with rounds that last 30 minutes or less—and all satellites, which usually have 15 or 20 minute rounds—are what I call fast action tournaments.

In general, tournaments have become faster, with more players and with better players, so you have to use a speedier approach to your tournament strategy than you did in the past. Solid, selectively aggressive players who are not afraid to bluff, who know when to move the chips, and who can detect the situations where they can most likely get away with picking up the blinds and antes—these are the players with the best chance of succeeding in today's tournament environment.

How important is the luck factor in winning a tournament?

I don't care who you are or how good you are, when you won a tournament, you were very lucky. The cards had to break right for you and your timing had to be impeccable. In other words, you had to catch good cards that were better than someone else's good cards, and especially at the higher limits. In all stages, you had to continue catching more than your fair share of cards.

Naturally, the higher your skill level in tournament play, the luckier you are likely to become. Part of your game play should be developing great survival skills so you can last long enough to find an opportunity to get lucky with a good rush of cards. The luck factor is extremely important, yes, but if you don't have the skill to go with it, you cannot get lucky often enough to make tournaments profitable.

How does the ante and/or blind structure affect your game strategy?

Naturally, the fewer the chips you have in relation to the opening blinds and antes, the more you will have to gamble with medium strength hands to win your fair share of chips. An excessively tight approach isn't going to work. A good example is the WSOP when you begin at the $50-$100 limit and have only $1,500 in chips to start with. A conservative, tight approach won't work because, with the limits rising every hour, if you only break even during the first round, you will then have to enter the second round with that same $1,500 in chips when the limits are $100-$200. This means that you are already in an inferior chip position even though you have broken even. The fewer chips you have, of course, the more seriously you are in jeopardy.

The more chips you have in relation to the opening limits, the less reason you have to gamble with marginal starting hands. A typical example is a big no-limit tournament where you might start with $10,000 in chips with blinds of $25 and $50. If you start making it $1,000 to go when the blinds and antes are so small, the only time you will get any action is when somebody has you beaten. Therefore, you have less reason to overbet your hand and gamble too much because what you can win is still relatively small compared to what you can lose or jeopardize.

Occasionally, you will have a big hand and be challenged by someone who doesn't give you enough credit and comes in with a worse hand than yours. But most often, you will simply win a small pot uncontested in these opening rounds.

The general idea is that when you have a lot of chips in relation to the starting limits, a more conservative, solid, selectively aggressive approach is best. Or with a relatively small stack in the same situation, the more willing you should be to jeopardize yourself with less than a premium hand, while still using good judgment.

When is it appropriate to slow-play and when is it dangerous?

In limit hold'em games, the earlier your position the less reason you have to slow-play, particularly at a full table. It may be appropriate to slow-play when there are only two tables remaining with five or six players at each table and it is almost time to consolidate to the final table; or at the final table when only four or five players are left. In these circumstances, you may decide to just limp in with a pair of aces or kings, which are the only two hands you should slow play.

Slow-playing is particularly effective if you are against loose, aggressive opponents with big stacks whose hands have been holding up, because you may be able to suck them into the pot. I don't recommend slow-playing with a pair of queens, because you are more vulnerable. If you do slow play queens, a player holding either K-X or A-X may enter the unraised pot and beat you if an ace or king comes on the flop.

No-limit hold'em is a different story. Many players will limp in with aces or kings from early position hoping that an opponent sitting behind them will enter the pot with a raise and give them an opportunity to reraise. Sometimes it is appropriate to continue the slow-play after a very aggressive opponent has made a big raise behind you. In this case, you can smooth-call him and then try to trap him on the flop. At other times you may reraise him before the flop, depending on the size of your stack and his stack. If you believe that a reraise which will put him all in is the correct play, because your opponent has made a substantial commitment of chips and cannot get loose from his hand, go ahead and reraise before the flop. But if you both have a lot of chips, you may wait and try to trap him on the flop in order to win a very big pot.

If you are short-stacked, be more inclined to reraise and go all in if you think you will be called; if you are not called, it's no big loss because you win anyway. The most judgement is required when both you and your opponent have medium to large stacks, and there is no substantial pre-flop commitment of chips. This is when you should be more willing to slow-play.

It is dangerous to slow-play from the flop onward when several opponents are in the pot and the flop comes with suited connectors, for example, which make draws possible. In this scenario, you should bet and try to win the pot immediately, especially in either pot-limit or no-limit games. It is when the flop comes raggedy and there are fewer players in the pot that it is more advantageous to slow-play. The more players in the pot the less reason to slow-play from the flop on.

If a player is all-in and you have a big hand, should you raise before the flop or should you just call?

Specifically, should you just call to encourage other players to enter the pot and have a better chance to knock him out, or should you raise to try to beat him heads-up with the best hand? The answer depends partly on the nature of your hand. If you hold a hand such as A-K or A-Q, it is probably OK to just call. Then if someone who has come in behind you bets on the flop, you can fold if you flop nothing. It also depends on the stage of the tournament. There is a huge difference between playing at the last table against a short stack who could slide up the pay scale, and playing when two or three tables are left, when knocking out an opponent is not quite as meaningful on the payscale.

With a big pair, I may just call although I would be more inclined to raise. I don't care if everybody else folds because I will be playing heads-up with the probable best hand and have a chance to both break my opponent and pick up the blinds. With less than a big pair, I would be more inclined to just call. Sometimes, too, the side pot may be just as valuable (or even more valuable) than the main pot. In this case, if breaking an opponent will not have as much impact on the payscale, you might just call. The bigger your hand, the more inclined you should be to raise. The smaller your hand, the more often you should just call and not give the all-in player protection.

Why is changing gears so important?

It is extremely important to change gears from tight to loose, and from loose to tight, to confuse your opponents (depending on your chip count, of course). If you play just one way all the time, an intelligent opponent will typecast you and know exactly where you're at most of the time. If you only enter the pot with A-K or better in a hold'em tournament in the first two or three positions, for example, they know you have a big hand and won't give you much action unless they have an even bigger hand or a comparable hand.

Also, if they know you are extremely tight and conservative, they will take more liberties against you. They will bluff you more often, and try to steal your blinds more frequently. So one of the primary reasons to switch gears often is to keep your opponents off their guard so that they never know quite what to expect from you. This way, you won't fall into predictable patterns and be easy for them to defense against.

How can I can prepare for a tournament?

There are plenty of ways to prepare. One of them is to read the best literature available on the game. Another is to keep notes on various tournament players, and to review your notes when you are likely to be facing them the next day. Getting a good night's sleep is important so that you come in fresh, prepared, with a positive mental attitude. You also need the ability to shrug off bad beats in the final stages of the tournament; this is where your positive mental attitude will help. Don't let anything faze you or deter you from your goal of playing mistake-free poker, maximizing your strong starting cards and getting maximum value out of your best hands.

How do you handle income tax?

If I had to give a succinct answer, I would say, "Pay your taxes, of course," but it isn't quite that simple. Tournament wins are subject to taxes, which is one reason why some players have discontinued playing tourneys and are now playing only in side games. They don't have to sign the W-2 G forms that tournament winners must sign. However, the thrill and allure of tournaments overshadows the fact that you have to pay taxes on your earnings. Having to sign tax statements may have temporarily slowed the growth of tournaments, but overall attendance has rebounded very strongly.

You should save every tournament-related receipt, including your travel expenses, so that you have legitimate write-offs against your winnings. It also helps to keep a diary, a record of your wins and losses on a daily basis. The IRS usually accepts your daily record book as verification of your tax statement. Your records should include not only your tournament statistics, but also any of your other gaming wins and losses. You can often deduct losses from other types of gaming, such as losing sports betting tickets, if you can document them. You can even deduct slot losses, if you belong to a slot club which monitors your win-loss record.

Of course, the reality is that many players conveniently forget to record some of their side-game wins, which are difficult to verify. If they have an income outside of poker, such as a salary or a self-owned business, they see no need to record all of their gaming income. Some poker players who rely solely on their wins for income prefer to be "invisible;" that is, they never file income tax returns. I believe they are making a mistake. Even if I have had a zero-income year, I file a tax return. I carefully document my gaming wins and losses and back them up with receipts to prove the validity of my claim.

Who are some of the toughest opponents you have played against?

Extremely aggressive players who always know where they're at in a hand and who are unpredictable in their starting hands are tough to play against. These players are selectively aggressive and almost never enter a pot without putting in a raise, especially when they are first to act. They raise on such a wide variety of hands that it is difficult to determine when they have a big hand and when they don't.

Two-time World Poker Tour champion Gus Hansen and World Series of Poker bracelet winner John Bonetti, who constantly put pressure on their opponents, are good examples of people who play this style of tournament poker. They are great "big-stack" players. That is, when they amass big stacks of chips, they are relentless and try to eat you alive at the table. They are extremely hard to play against. Bonetti and other seasoned tournament players prove that there are no age barriers in the world of poker. Bonetti didn't begin terrorizing the tournament world until he was almost 60 years old and hasn't let up since.

Another type of very tough opponent is a player like Mike Sexton. He is very solid, selectively aggressive, and has just enough gamble and play in him that you never know when he is shooting a bluff your way. Most of the time, he starts with a good hand, and he knows just when to slow-play. He has a great sense of exactly where he's at and what to do, and he is good at trapping opponents.

Naturally, some of the big names in poker such as Chip Reese are hard to play against because they're difficult to read and capable of making a lot of moves. Two of the toughest stud players I've ever faced are Danny Robison and David Hayden. They both have a great sense of when to move with marginal hands and they have a great sense of timing. They are also capable of making big laydowns so that, a lot of times, you don't get paid off if you make a hand against them.

Certain players are more dangerous in certain games than in others. Phil Hellmuth, 1989 World Champion of Poker and author of *Play Poker Like the Pros*, is one of the best no-limit hold'em players on the tournament circuit today, in my opinion. And he has great all-around hold'em skills. Johnny Chan is still one of the greatest no-limit players on the circuit. In the late 1980s, he totally dominated the big Horseshoe tournaments, making tremendous calls and great reads on his opponents.

T.J. Cloutier, my esteemed writing partner and co-author of our Championship Series of poker books, has been the most successful no-limit hold'em tournament player in the world the past few years. Not only can T.J. play a large stack with power, aggression and good judgement, but I've also seen him make many comebacks with a short stack. Some players can play a large stack very well, but they're not as good on a short stack. T.J. is more than good—he's great with a short stack. His instinct with a short stack is keen and he knows when to move. He'll get a tough hand beaten, leaving him short-stacked, but he will still be utterly fearless. And he is truly awesome with a big stack because he has good judgement and uncanny timing.

Hans "Tuna" Lund also is an extremely dangerous no-limit player, always capable of making a move at the right time. Another player who impresses me is Mansour Matloubi. He plays a solid all-around game and has good instincts, too. He always knows where he's at, plays a short stack extremely well, and has a great feel for poker.

Brad Daugherty, co-author of *Championship Satellite Strategy* and 1991 World Champion of Poker, is an all-around great player. He has a terrific sense of timing, is very solid, and yet is capable of bluffing and moving his chips when necessary. Daugherty plays all games very well and has solid discipline. I've never seen him go on tilt, which adds to my respect for him.

Another great tournament player is Vince Burgio. In 1994, he won a World Series of Poker bracelet for seven-card stud high-low split. Previously, he had taken second in draw lowball. Vince was Best All Around Player at the 1992 *Queens Classic,* and won the $5,000 no-limit hold'em event at the 1994 *Diamond Jim Brady* tournament, the same year he finished fourth in the World Series title event. Obviously, he has tremendous all-around tournament skills.

I also give former World Series of Poker champion Berry Johnston my utmost respect. He is a fantastic talent and one of the best Omaha players alive. Erik Seidel is another great tournament player with many top-three finishes in big buy-in no-limit and limit events. Among the younger players under 40 years old are Ted Forrest, winner of three World Series titles in 1993; Huck Seed, who won the championship event in 1996; and Todd Brunson, son of the legendary Doyle, which proves that younger players with great instincts can carve a niche for themselves sooner rather than later in their poker careers.

What was one of your worst beats?

I have had numerous terrible beats put on me, as has any poker player who has been in the arena for as many years as I have. But the worst one I have ever taken in tournament play happened during a Bicycle Club tournament a few years ago. There were eight players at the final table when the limits reached about $2,000-$4,000. Three of us were tied for the lead with about $30,000 apiece in chips, which added up to slightly more than half the chips left in the tournament. Everyone else had either a medium stack or a short one, so we three were the clear-cut leaders.

Right in front of the big blind, I am dealt pocket aces and raise with them. One of the medium stacks reraises. I raise him again. He raises me back. I raise once again and put him all-in. He has pocket queens against my rockets in the hole. Boom! Off comes a queen on the flop and he beats me. On the very next hand, I am in the big blind and *again* I have pocket aces. A very aggressive player, one of the other co-leaders with $30,000 in chips, brings in the pot for a raise from middle position. I immediately reraise, he raises me again, I raise him back, and he puts in *another* raise. I raise again. By now, I am short-stacked. The flop comes K-K-X. I bet and he raises me.

I don't like my hand anymore, but I have only enough chips for one more bet, so I put in my last bet—and I hate doing it because I suspect he has a king, but the pot is very large. Sure enough, he shows me A-K. He wins the pot, I go broke. So in just two hands, I go from being one of the chip leaders with more than twice as many chips as fourth through eighth spots in the tournament to bombing out in eighth place. And instead of winning $40,000 for first, I drag my weary body home with $2,000.

I was *sick,* you know? I've never heard of anyone losing two consecutive hands with pocket aces at the final table of a tournament. And yet it happened to me, the worst eighth-place finish I've ever had. The player who put the final beat on me with the A-K evidently misjudged me: He thought that I was on tilt from having my aces cracked by queens on the previous hand, so he gave way too much action with his A-K before the flop, putting in the two extra raises which eventually trapped me. I was not a happy camper.

Aside from winning the WSOP title in 1983, what do you consider to be your greatest victory?

I've won three other World Series events, including the limit hold'em event against 234 players the same year I won the championship. Winning the limit title, which at that time I thought would be the ultimate victory in my poker career, might have been my next biggest thrill. But it's a close call with my victory in 1992 against Berry Johnston in the finals of the limit Omaha tournament at the WSOP, which was the first time that two former winners of the main event had played head-to-head at the final table of another event. The lead seesawed back and forth all night. We played two-and-a-half hours head to head. At one point, he had me outchipped by 9-1, but I came back to win. Since Berry is considered to be one of the finest Omaha players in the world, I consider that victory—along with my 1983 limit hold'em win—to be my two greatest triumphs next to winning the 1983 championship. ♠

Chapter 21
INTERVIEW WITH A CHAMP
by Linda Johnson
(from Card Player magazine, 1994)

Neighborhood parents used to call to complain that, "The McEvoy boys took our son's allowance in a poker game." Tom McEvoy, 1983 World Champion of Poker and his two younger brothers and one younger sister learned to play poker at a young age. "If they were silly enough to play with us in the first place, they got what they deserved," he responded. Regardless of the complaints, he continued to enjoy poker, playing as often as possible through his college years. After earning his B.S. degree, McEvoy became an accountant, but retained a strong urge to make poker his ultimate profession.

Linda Johnson: What made you decide to make the change from being an accountant to becoming a professional poker player?

Tom McEvoy: I had pretty much had it with my life as an accountant. I worked for 12 years in a variety of accounting jobs with different companies, commuting 40 miles to work each way. That doesn't sound like much when you live in L.A., but 40 miles each way through all kinds of horrible Michigan weather, blizzards, and everything else is not very pleasant. I was tired of working for other people and was willing to do something totally drastic. The possibility of taking a shot at poker in Las Vegas intrigued me.

I was a very avid table tennis player for years, and was an officer in the national table tennis organization. I developed my competitive instincts in table tennis and attended the national championship at Caesars Palace in Las Vegas in 1977, so I thought, "Why not play some poker and see what will happen?" I didn't realize it at the time, but I got hit with the deck and won about $1,000 in six days at Caesars Palace playing $10 limit seven-card stud.

Then I started thinking—I had won $1,000 in Las Vegas in a week, which equates to $52,000 a year, much better than the $18,000 I was making as an accountant. My last day in the corporate world was May 14, 1978. I received some severance pay, which I returned to Las Vegas. I flew back and forth for a year testing the waters, and realized I would never be happy with my life until I took a crack at poker. But I couldn't continue paying living expenses in Michigan for my family plus my expenses to fly back and forth to Vegas. It was either move or go back to work. Everyone thought I was crazy and that I would come back like a whipped dog within six months. I was absolutely determined to prove them wrong—and I did.

LJ: How did your wife and children feel about the move?

TM: They were reluctant to make the move at first, but were finally convinced to try it. We sold our house and moved when the school year was over. We packed up a trailer with a sign on the back of it that announced "Vegas or Bust!" In July 1979, we arrived with about $5,000 in cash. I had to play on that and support the family, but fortunately, I was successful and never had to find a "day" job.

I had heard of Texas hold'em but had never played a hand of it. I made up to mind to learn how to play the game and to master all forms of poker. I knew about the World Series of Poker, but I wasn't even aware that it was going on. One day during the Series, I walked into Binion's just as Bobby Baldwin was playing heads up against Crandall Addington. I stayed around and watched the finals. My jaw kinda dropped open in awe and I vowed to myself then and there that I was going to play in the World Series of Poker someday.

LJ: What helped you the most with your poker education?

TM: I was one of the first people to purchase Doyle Brunson's book, now titled *Super/System*. Back then, it was called *How I Won a Million Dollars Playing Poker*. I looked up the address of the publishing company that Doyle Brunson had founded, and I went down there and asked for a copy of it. I saw Doyle sitting there behind a desk, and said, "Wow, that's him!" I acted like a total country hick, I'm sure. He autographed the book and I told him that someday I would be playing poker with him. He just smiled that big ol' grin of his. That was in December of 1978.

LJ: How did you get started playing tournaments?

TM: The very first tournament I ever played was at the Golden Nugget, before I moved to Las Vegas. It was a $110 freezeout. I would up in second place and was hooked for life. After that I started playing tournaments all over town.

LJ: Your life changed in 1983. Tell us about it.

TM: I had sold shares of myself to get into two of the World Series of Poker $1,000 buy-in hold'em events. I had enough money to play one event, but not two, so I sold shares so that I could play in both of them. Lo and behold, I won the limit hold'em tournament. It paid $117,000 and I ended up with about $65,000 of it after paying my backers.

One of my backers, Frank Hunter, begged me to try a one-table satellite to get into the $10,000 event. I had played very little no-limit hold'em, but I had been playing a lot of tournaments so it didn't take much urging to get me to take a crack at it. At no point was I willing to put up $10,000 of my hard-earned $65,000. It got down to three players in the satellite: Jimmy Doman, David Sklansky, and me. Sklansky had the lead; I was kind of a distant second.

At that point, Johnny Chan came over to the table and asked if I would like to sell 20 percent of my action for $1,000. I had not even won the satellite yet, so it sounded like a good deal to me. If I lost the satellite, the $1,000 would give me enough money for another satellite shot at no further risk. So I said sure. Frank also agreed. After trading percentages with some friends, I wound up with 33 percent of myself in the big event.

LJ: What was your game plan as you entered the tournament?

Interview with a Champ

TM: I was determined to win before the tournament started. None of the big names were going to intimidate me, I vowed, and I was not going to be bullied around by them. I can't tell you the number of times I put my stack all-in. At the end of the first day of the tournament, I had a little over $11,000.

For those unfamiliar with the World Series of Poker, approximately 45 percent of the field is eliminated the first day. The second day, the casualties mount at a higher rate. In fact, they have a fixed formula now, where on the second day, they play down to 27; the third day they play down to six; and on the final day, the last six play. Back then, it didn't work that way. They played a fixed number of hours on the first and second days. Whoever survived played the third day. On the third day, they played down to the final nine.

LJ: What was the chip position on the final day?

TM: Rod Peate had the chip lead with $100,000 more than Doyle Brunson. Doyle had about $265,000 and I was third with $117,000. The oddsmakers had me as an 8-to-1 shot even though I was third in chips and there were only nine players left, which I thought was rather insulting.

Rod and Doyle eliminated players fairly quickly, and we were soon down to three-handed play. We played three-handed for only about 20 minutes. I had beaten Doyle out of a big pot—over $120,000— then Rod's hand held up and Doyle was eliminated. Within three hours, we were playing heads up on the final day, which was exceptionally fast.

They asked us to take a break, a three-hour recess, which had never been done before, because they wanted us to make the late news telecast. The previous year, heads-up play had ended very quickly, but I told them it would take much longer this year. Even though Rod was in the lead by $200,000, I still had a lot of chips in relation to the blinds. Sure enough, that's the way it happened, a long, drawn-out siege. We played until 1:45 a.m. We were playing such a tight game that not much happened for hours. I didn't care how long it took, I just wanted to win. Some of the media people were suggesting that we were deliberately making it last longer for the publicity.

LJ: What was the final hand?

TM: I had pocket queens. Rod had the K-J of diamonds. What it was over, I jumped straight up in the air and landed on my chair. My picture was snapped and made the front page of the *Review-Journal.* Because it lasted so long, a lot of the media missed their deadlines. I was written up in virtually every newspaper in the country, and I appeared on *Good Morning America.*

LJ: How did it feel to win the world championship?

TM: I was absolutely on cloud nine. I've never used drugs, but I had a natural high that was superior to anything that anyone could have used. My dream had come true and I was on top of the world. I realized that my whole life had changed virtually overnight.

LJ: Prior to your victory, you were playing in the $10-$20 games. What changes did you make in your poker life after the World Series?

TM: Basically, I continued to play $10-$20, then decided to take some selected shots in bigger limits. I kept good records and held my own overall.

Interview with a Champ

LJ: I understand that you ran into some bad fortune after your big win. What happened?

TM: A funny thing happened on my way to fame, fortune, and wealth—I lost all my money. I made the mistake of assuming that fame equated fortune, but I found out that it doesn't. I thought I would automatically get rich. Instead, the opposite happened. A whole series of disasters struck. A lot of it was my own fault for being far too trusting. Coming from a Midwestern background, I was used to people giving me their word of honor and keeping it. It was a shock to find out that people would make promises to me with no intention of ever keeping them.

I fell into the trap of "helping" people. I can't tell you the number of deadbeats I loaned money to. It got so bad that I would average at least two requests a day, minimum. I got so overwhelmed with this and saw so much desperation in people's faces, that many times I would give them money just so they would go away and stop bothering me. Trying to help people by giving them money virtually destroyed my life, and certainly destroyed my financial stability.

LJ: What kind of investments did you make?

TM: I was always a collector of U.S. stamps and had a fairly impressive collection. The World Series win enabled me to complete huge sections of my collection. I made the mistake of running into some crooked stamp dealers who were perpetrating a scam on a lot of investors of rare U.S. Stamps. They had a laboratory in the hills of Sunland, California, where they were expertly doctoring stamps. An inside man issued fraudulent certificates on these items. Several people were involved, including some auctioneers with whom I dealt.

Unfortunately, when I had the money to invest in those rare stamps, it was at the precise time that these guys were operating their scam. Several of them ended up gong to jail. I got partial restitution from some of my disastrous investments, but they pretty well destroyed me financially. I estimate that I lost close to $100,000 as a result of this and, ultimately, was forced to sell my collection because of financial pressures.

LJ: What kind of effect did the financial pressure have on your family life?

TM: At first, my victory in the World Series in 1983 revitalized things. But over time the pressures tore my family life apart, and after 23 years of marriage, my wife and I wound up getting divorced in 1990.

LJ: Phil Hellmuth used to stake you in tournaments. How did that professional relationship get started?

TM: I had just come off the 1992 World Series of Poker with my fourth title. I was being backed at the beginning of that tournament, but the man who backed me ran into a temporary cash-flow problem and wanted to put a halt to our arrangement. I had made quite a bit of money for him with my first and second-place finishes. Shortly after that, I got a call from Phil and we made a verbal agreement that he would start backing me.

LJ: How did your agreement work?

TM: Our arrangement was that I would get 50 percent of any net profit, but I would have to make up any tournament losses. If I lost in one tournament, I would have to carry it over to the next.

The agreement could be terminated by either party, but Phil stuck with me through thick and thin.

LJ: You said you've won four World Series events. What has happened to the four bracelets you won?

TM: After the 1983 World Series, I went to Hawaii with Johnny Chan on a little five-day jaunt. I made the mistake of bringing both my World Series bracelets with me. I accidentally left one of them in a public place and when I went back, the bracelet was gone. In 1986, I won my third bracelet in the razz event. I got a feminine version of the bracelet with my wife's name on it and gave it to her. In 1989, my remaining bracelet mysteriously disappeared from my hotel room. Even though I had won three bracelets, I had possession of none of them. In 1992, I won my fourth bracelet, which I have taken great steps to guard. I keep it locked up in a safe-deposit box most of the time, but during big tournaments, I dust it off and wear it. It's also a positive reinforcement, because no matter how bad things have been at times, you can't buy a World Series bracelet, you have to earn it.

LJ: What poker goals remain for you?

TM: Although I've had tremendous success as a tournament specialist (I've played more than 3,200 tournaments and have won about 14 percent of them), I want to win the world championship at least one more time. Another of my goals is to be the first tournament specialist to be voted into the Poker Hall of Fame.

LJ: There are a lot of characteristics and traits that are important for tournament players to possess, but if you had to narrow it down to one, what would that be?

TM: One requirement, above all, is to never give up. I can't tell you how many times I have been in a seemingly hopeless chip position and have come back to win. You must have heart and *never* give up.

POKER JARGON

One of the distinguishing characteristics of any profession is its language, that unique set of words which its practitioners use in describing the functions they perform. Physicians, for example, do not say, "I removed Mr. Smith's gallbladder." They say, "I performed a cholecystectomy on Mr. Smith," which is a type of code they employ to transmit data among themselves.

Poker professionals also have a unique dictionary of terms they use to communicate with each other. They don't say, "I made three cards of the same rank when the dealer spread the first three common cards." They say, "I flopped trips." Nor do they complain about "having my four aces topped by a straight flush on the last card." To them, it is "suffering a bad beat on the river."

The following is a list of expressions which Tom McEvoy uses in this book, the poker jargon you will hear in cardrooms around the world.

An ace working. You have an ace in your hand. "If you are called, you might be holding the best hand, especially if you have *an ace working*."

Blank. See **Rag**.

Bully. Play aggressively (particularly in hold'em) in an attempt to get your opponents to fold what may be the best hand. "My opponents weren't going to be easily *bullied*, so I didn't want to do a lot of aggressive raising."

Case chips. Your last chips. "It took my *case chips* to call Sexton's raise on the river."

Change gears. Change your style of play from aggressive to passive, from tight to loose, from fast to slow, etc. "I had to *change gears* to survive the late stage of the WSOP."

Cold call. Call a raise without having already put the initial bet into the pot. "Bonetti *cold called* after Tuna raised the big blind's forced bet."

Come over the top of. Raise or reraise an opponent's bet. "Are your opponents more liberal and therefore more likely to *come over the top* of you with a raise?"

Commit fully. Put in as many chips as necessary to play your hand to the river, even if they are your case chips. "If I think the odds are in my favor, I will *commit fully*."

Counterfeit. The board pairs your key low card in Omaha high-low, demoting the value of your hand. "My A-2-6-Q got *counterfeited* when the board came 2-4-J."

Double through. Going all-in against an opponent in order to double your stack if you win the hand. "I was so low on chips, I knew I had to *double through* somebody to build up my stack."

Flat call. Call an opponent's bet rather than raising. "Playing somewhat less aggressively than I perhaps should have, I just *flat called* the raise."

Get away from your hand. Fold, usually what appeared to be a premium hand until an unfavorable flop negated its potential. "It's easy *to get away from* a high hand in Omaha high-low when the flop comes will all low cards."

Get the right price. The pot odds are favorable enough for you to justify calling a bet or a raise with a drawing hand. "You can generally defend the big blind with any pocket pair because you will usually be getting *the right price*."

Get full value. Betting, raising and reraising in order to manipulate the size of the pot so that you will be getting maximum pot odds if you win the hand. "After raising on every round, I was able to *get full value* when my hand held up on the river."

Get there. Make your hand. "What happens when you don't *get there,* when you miss your hand? You cry a little."

Give action. Betting, calling, raising or reraising. "Be cautious about *giving too much action* if your kicker is weak."

Give up your hand. Fold. "I *gave up my hand* when he raised."

Gypsy in. The same as limping in, but used exclusively in lowball. "Hellmuth just *gypsied in* with a smooth 8."

Home run hitter. A player who likes to make big plays which require maximum risk. "Some players have a *home run* attitude in the late rounds—they are willing to risk a strike-out to make the final table. Bonetti is one of them."

Jammed pot. The pot has been raised the maximum number of times, and may also be multi-way. "You should usually pass with a weak hand if the pot has been *jammed* before it gets to you."

Keep honest. Call an opponent on the river, although you believe he has a better hand than you do. "You'll always know what your opponent holds, but you'll also lose a lot of money if you always try to *keep them honest* by calling."

Key Card. The one card that will make your hand. "I knew I needed to catch a deuce, the *key card* I needed to win."

Key Hand. The hand in a tournament that proves to be a turning point, for better or worse. "There is usually one *key hand* which, if you make it, will win the tournament for you. Unfortunately, it also goes the other way."

Lay down your hand. Fold. "Sometimes you have to *lay down* your hand because it gets too expensive to play it."

Lead. You are the first one to enter the pot after the blind's forced bet. "T. J. *led out* with his A-Q."

Limp in. Enter the pot by calling, rather than raising, another player's bet. "You might decide to just *limp in* with a pair of jacks and see the flop cheaply."

Limper. A player who enters a pot for the minimum bet. "With two *limpers* in the pot, a pair of jacks should be your minimum raising hand."

Glossary: Poker Jargon

Live cards. Cards which you need to improve your hand in seven-card stud, and which have not appeared in your opponent's boards. "Since my flush draw was *live*, I bet it."

Make a move. Try to bluff. "When Phil *made a move* at the pot, Huck called him down."

Maniac. A very aggressive player who sometimes plays hands his more sensible or conservative opponents would not consider. "*Maniacs* sometimes crash and burn earlier than they should in tournament play."

Nit. Bide your time patiently waiting until you receive a playable hand. A *nit* is a very tight player. "I *nitted* through most of the first round."

Nuts. The best possible hand. "Dana won the pot when the A♣ fell on the river, giving her the *nut* flush."

Pay off. You call an opponent's bet on the river, even though you think he has the best hand. "I decided to *pay him off* when he bet the paired board on the river."

Play back. Responding to an opponent's bet by either raising or reraising. "If a tight opponent *plays back* at you, you know he probably holds the nuts."

Play fast. Aggressively betting a drawing hand to get full value for it if you make it. "Many players play fast in the early rounds of rebuy tournaments to try to build their stacks."

Play with. Staying in the hand by betting, calling, raising, or reraising. "I wasn't sure exactly where he was at, so I decided to *play with* him on the turn."

Putting on the heat. Pressuring your opponents with aggressive betting strategies to get the most value from your hand. "You might consider *putting on the heat* when your opponent is slightly conservative, or when he has a short stack against your tall stack."

Rag (or blank). A card that doesn't help you. "The next card was a 4♠, a total *blank*."

Rag off. You get a card on the river that doesn't help you. "Even though the flop *ragged off*, my pair still held up."

Ragged(y) flop. The cards in the flop are ones that do not appear to be able to help anyone's hand; i.e., there are no straight, flush, face card, or pairs on board. "In last position with just one or two opponents, your correct play is to try to pick up the pot with a bet when the flop is *raggedy.*"

Read. When you can determine exactly what your opponent is holding, or the significance of his betting strategy. "His play was so erratic, it was hard to *get a read* on him."

Ring game. Not a tournament game. "The side action *ring games* during tournaments can be quite lucrative."

Rock. A very conservative player who always waits for premium cards before he plays a hand. "Smith was playing like a *rock*, so when she bet into me, I knew she had me beat."

Run over. Playing aggressively in an attempt to control the other players. "If they're not trying to stop you from being a bully, then keep *running over* them until they do."

Glossary: Poker Jargon

Smooth-call. You call rather than raise an opponent's bet. "Herb *smooth-called* me on the flop, but raised on the turn with his trip jacks."

Splash around. Playing more loosely or more hands than you probably should. "If you start *splashing around* too much when you have a big chip lead, you'll often lose it fast."

Take off a card. Calling a single bet in order to see one more card. "Milt decided to *take off a card* to see if he could hit his inside-straight draw."

Take off the gloves. Using aggressive betting strategies to either get full value from your hand, or to bully your opponents. "Phyllis decided it was time to *take off the gloves* and so she threw in a reraise."

Throwing a party. Several loose or amateur players are making significant monetary contributions to the game. "You have to stay in the game when they're *throwing a party.*"

Wake up with a hand. You are dealt a hand with winning potential. "It looked to me like Daugherty *woke up with a hand* in the small blind."

Where you're at. You know the value of your hand compared to your opponent's hand. "Hamid may have raised just to find out *where he was at.*"

World's fair. A big hand. "Suppose the flop comes 8-8-4 in different suits: you know you're up against either nothing or *the world's fair.*"

COMMANDMENTS OF CONDUCT FOR TOURNAMENT PLAYERS

- ☞ Thou shalt not soft play a friend
- ☞ Thou shalt not throw off chips to a partner
- ☞ Thou shalt not bet out of turn
- ☞ Nor make any movement designed to either induce or inhibit the actions of an opponent
- ☞ Thou shalt not abuse the dealer
- ☞ Nor defile or condemn the play of your opponents
- ☞ Thou shalt not remove chips from the table for use in a subsequent tournament
- ☞ Thou shalt not trade assigned seats with anyone when a designated table change occurs
- ☞ Thou shalt take your new seat hastily
- ☞ Thou shalt not alter the playing cards in any way
- ☞ Nor splash your chips into the pot

- ☝ Thou shalt not give any verbal or nonverbal communication to others regarding your hand

- ☝ Thou shalt request and rely upon tournament floor personnel to solve procedural disputes in the play of a hand

- ☝ Thou shalt not use inappropriate language at the table

- ☝ Thou shalt dress neatly yet comfortably

- ☝ Thou shalt not slow roll the winning hand

- ☝ Nor ask to see the losing hand

- ☝ Neither shalt thou show your cards to another player

- ☝ Thou shalt not announce another player's hand before he shows it down

- ☝ Thou shalt not intentionally distract your opponents

- ☝ Nor shalt thou talk to someone while he is playing a hand

- ☝ Thou shalt be a considerate smoker

- ☝ Thou shalt not play table captain as that is the dealer's job

- ☝ Thou shalt always act in a professional manner that enhances the image of poker

CARDOZA SCHOOL OF BLACKJACK
- Home Instruction Course - $200 OFF! -

At last, after years of secrecy, the **previously unreleased** lesson plans, strategies and playing tactics formerly available only to members of the Cardoza School of Blackjack are now available to the general public - and at substantial savings. **Now**, you can **learn at home,** and at your own convenience. Like the full course given at the school, the home instruction course goes **step-by-step** over the winning concepts. We'll take you from layman to **pro.**

MASTER BLACKJACK - Learn what it takes to be a **master player**. Be a **powerhouse**, play with confidence, impunity, and **with the odds** on your side. Learn to be a **big winner** at blackjack.

MAXIMIZE WINNING SESSIONS - You'll **learn how** to take a good winning session and make a **blockbuster** out of it, but just as important, you'll learn to cut your losses. Learn exactly when to end a session. We cover everything from the psychological and emotional aspects of play to altered playing conditions (through the **eye of profitability**) to protection of big wins. The advice here could be worth **hundreds (or thousands) of dollars** in one session alone. Take our guidelines seriously.

ADVANCED STRATEGIES - You'll learn the latest in advanced winning strategies. Learn about the **ten-factor**, the **ace-factor**, the effects of rules variations, how to protect against dealer blackjacks, the winning strategies for single and multiple deck games and how each affects you, the **true count**, the multiple deck true count variations, and much more. And, of course, you'll receive the full Cardoza Base Count Strategy package.

$200 OFF - LIMITED OFFER - The Cardoza School of Blackjack home instruction course, retailed at $295 (or $895 if taken at the school) is available here for just $95.

DOUBLE BONUS! - **Rush** your order in **now**, for we're also including, **absolutely free**, the 1,000 and 1,500 word essays, "How to Disguise the Fact that You're an Expert", and "How Not to Get Barred". Among other **inside information** contained here, you'll learn about the psychology of the pit bosses, how they spot counters, how to project a losing image, role playing, and other skills to maximize your profit potential.

To order, send $95 (plus postage and handling) by check or money order to:
Cardoza Publishing, P.O. Box 1500, Cooper Station, New York, NY 10276

POWERFUL POKER SIMULATIONS
A MUST FOR SERIOUS PLAYERS WITH A COMPUTER!
IBM compatibles CD ROM Windows 3.1, 95, and 98, ME & XP - Full Color Graphics

Play interactive poker against these **incredible** full color poker simulation programs - they're the absolute **best** method to improve game. Computer players act like real players. All games let you set the limits and rake, have fully programmable players, adjustable lineup, stat tracking, and Hand Analyzer for starting hands. MIke Caro, the world's foremost poker theoretician says, "Amazing...A steal for under $500." Includes free telephone support. **New Feature!** - "Smart advisor" gives expert advice for every play in every game!

1. TURBO TEXAS HOLD'EM FOR WINDOWS - $89.95 - Choose which players, how many, 2-10, you want to play, create loose/tight game, control check-raising, bluffing, position, sensitivity to pot odds, more! Also, instant replay, pop-up odds, Professional Advisor, keeps track of play statistics. Free bonus: Hold'em Hand Analyzer analyzes all 169 pocket hands in detail, their win rates under any conditions you set. Caro says this "hold'em software is the most powerful ever created." Great product!

2. TURBO SEVEN-CARD STUD FOR WINDOWS - $89.95 - Create any conditions of play; choose number of players (2-8), bet amounts, fixed or spread limit, bring-in method, tight/loose conditions, position, reaction to board, number of dead cards, stack deck to create special conditions, instant replay. Terrific stat reporting includes analysis of starting cards, 3-D bar charts, graphs. Play interactively, run high speed simulation to test strategies. Hand Analyzer analyzes starting hands in detail. Wow!

3. TURBO OMAHA HIGH-LOW SPLIT FOR WINDOWS - $89.95 -Specify any playing conditions; betting limits, number of raises, blind structures, button position, aggressiveness/passiveness of opponents, number of players (2-10), types of hands dealt, blinds, position, board reaction, specify flop, turn, river cards! Choose opponents, use provided point count or create your own. Statistical reporting, instant replay, pop-up odds, high speed simulation to test strategies, amazing Hand Analyzer, much more!

4. TURBO OMAHA HIGH FOR WINDOWS - $89.95 - Same features as above, but tailored for the Omaha High-only game. Caro says program is "an electrifying research tool...it can clearly be worth thousands of dollars to any serious player. A must for Omaha High players.

5. TURBO 7 STUD 8 OR BETTER - $89.95 - Brand new with all the features you expect from the Wilson Turbo products: the latest artificial intelligence, instant advice and exact odds, play versus 2-7 opponents, enhanced data charts that can be exported or printed, the ability to fold out of turn and immediately go to the next hand, ability to peek at opponents hand, optional warning mode that warns you if a play disagrees with the advisor, and automatic testing mode that can run up to 50 tests unattended. Challenge tough computer players who vary their styles for a truly great poker game.

---

6. TOURNAMENT TEXAS HOLD'EM - $59.95
Set-up for tournament practice and play, this realistic simulation pits you against celebrity look-alikes. Tons of options let you control tournament size with 10 to 300 entrants, select limits, ante, rake, blind structures, freezeouts, number of rebuys and competition level of opponents - average, tough, or toughest. Pop-up status report shows how you're doing vs. the competition. Save tournaments in progress to play again later. Additional feature allows you to quickly finish a folded hand and go on to the next.

GREAT POKER BOOKS
ADD THESE TO YOUR LIBRARY - ORDER NOW!

OMAHA HI-LO POKER by Shane Smith - Learn essential winning strategies for beating Omaha high-low; the best starting hands, how to play the flop, turn, and river, how to read the board for both high and low, dangerous draws, and how to win low-limit tournaments. Smith shows the differences between Omaha high-low and hold'em strategies. Includes odds charts, glossary, low-limit tips, strategic ideas. 84 pages, 8 x 11, spiral bound, $17.95.

7-CARD STUD (THE COMPLETE COURSE IN WINNING AT MEDIUM & LOWER LIMITS) by Roy West - Learn the latest strategies for winning at $1-$4 spread-limit up to $10-$20 fixed-limit games. Covers starting hands, 3rd-7th street strategy for playing most hands, overcards, selective aggressiveness, reading hands, secrets of the pros, psychology, more - in a 42 "lesson" informal format. Includes bonus chapter on 7-stud tournament strategy by World Champion Tom McEvoy. 160 pages, paperback, $24.95.

POKER TOURNAMENT TIPS FROM THE PROS by Shane Smith - Essential advice from poker theorists, authors, and tournament winners on the best strategies for winning the big prizes at low-limit re-buy tournaments. Learn the best strategies for each of the four stages of play—opening, middle, late and final—how to avoid 26 potential traps, advice on re-buys, aggressive play, clock-watching, inside moves, top 20 tips for winning tournaments, more. Advice from McEvoy, Caro, Malmuth, Ciaffone, others. 160 pages, $19.95.

WINNING LOW LIMIT HOLD'EM by Lee Jones - This essential book on playing 1-4, 3-6, and 1-4-8-8 low limit hold'em is packed with insights on winning: pre-flop positional play; playing the flop in all positions with a pair, two pair, trips, overcards, draws, made and nothing hands; turn and river play; how to read the board; avoiding trash hands; using the check-raise; bluffing, stereotypes, much more. Includes quizzes with answers. Terrific book. 176 pages, 5 1/2 x 8 1/2, paperback, $24.95.

WINNING POKER FOR THE SERIOUS PLAYER by Edwin Silberstang - New edition! More than 100 actual examples provide tons of advice on beating 7 Card Stud, Texas Hold 'Em, Draw Poker, Loball, High-Low and more than 10 other variations. Silberstang analyzes the essentials of being a great player; reading tells, analyzing tables, playing position, mastering the art of deception, creating fear at the table. Also, psychological tactics, when to play aggressive or slow play, or fold, expert plays, more. Colorful glossary included. 288 pages, 6 x 9, perfect bound, $16.95.

WINNER'S GUIDE TO TEXAS HOLD 'EM POKER by Ken Warren - This comprehensive book on beating hold 'em shows serious players how to play every hand from every position with every type of flop. Learn the 14 categories of starting hands, the 10 most common hold 'em tells, how to evaluate a game for profit, and more! Over 50,000 copies in print. 256 pages, 5 1/2 x 8 1/2, paperback, $14.95.

KEN WARREN TEACHES TEXAS HOLD 'EM by Ken Warren - In 33 comprehensive yet easy-to-read chapters, you'll learn absolutely everything about the great game of Texas hold 'em poker. You'll learn to play from every position, at every stage of a hand. You'll master a simple but thorough system for keeping records and understanding odds. And you'll gain expert advice on raising, stealing blinds, avoiding tells, playing for jackpots, bluffing, tournament play, and much more. 416 pages, 6 x 9, $24.95.

VIDEOS BY MIKE CARO
THE MAD GENIUS OF POKER

CARO'S PRO POKER TELLS

The long-awaited two-video set is a powerful scientific course on how to use your opponents' gestures, words and body language to read their hands and win all their money. These carefully guarded poker secrets, filmed with 63 poker notables, will revolutionize your game. It reveals when opponents are bluffing, when they aren't, and why. Knowing what your opponent's gestures mean, and protecting them from knowing yours, gives you a huge winning edge. An absolute must buy! $59.95.

CARO'S MAJOR POKER SEMINAR

The legendary "Mad Genius" is at it again, giving poker advice in VHS format. This new tape is based on the inaugural class at Mike Caro University of Poker, Gaming and Life strategy. The material given on this tape is based on many fundamentals introduced in Caro's books, papers, and articles and is prepared in such a way that reinforces concepts old and new. Caro's style is easy-going but intense with key concepts stressed and repeated. This tape will improve your play. 60 Minutes. $24.95.

CARO'S POWER POKER SEMINAR

This powerful video shows you how to win big money using the little-known concepts of world champion players. This advice will be worth thousands of dollars to you every year, even more if you're a big money player! After 15 years of refusing to allow his seminars to be filmed, Caro presents entertaining but serious coverage of his long-guarded secrets. Contains the most profitable poker advice ever put on video. 62 Minutes! $39.95.

Order Toll-Free 1-800-577-WINS or use order form on page 429

CARDOZA PUBLISHING ONLINE

For the latest in poker, gambling, chess, backgammon, and games
by the world's top authorities and writers

www.cardozapub.com

To find out about our latest publications and products, to order books and software from third parties, or simply to keep aware of our latest activities in the world or poker, gambling, and other games of chance and skill:

1. Go online: www.cardozapub.com
2. Use E-Mail: cardozapub@aol.com
3. Call toll free: 800-577-WINS (800-577-9467)

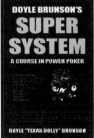